Nine Lives and Counting

Mereo Books

2nd Floor, 6-8 Dyer Street, Cirencester, Gloucestershire, GL7 2PF
An imprint of Memoirs Books. www.mereobooks.com
and www.memoirsbooks.co.uk

Nine Lives and Counting
ISBN: 978-1-86151-665-7

First published in Great Britain in 2025
by Mereo Books, an imprint of Memoirs Books.

Copyright ©2025

Randalph Bland has asserted his right under the Copyright Designs
and Patents Act 1988 to be identified as the author of this work.

A CIP catalogue record for this book is available from the British Library.
This book is sold subject to the condition that it shall not by way of trade or otherwise be
lent, resold, hired out or otherwise circulated without the publisher's prior consent in any
form of binding or cover, other than that in which it is published and without a similar
condition, including this condition being imposed on the subsequent purchaser.

The address for Memoirs Books can be
found at www.mereobooks.com

Mereo Books Ltd. Reg. No. 12157152

Typeset in 12/18pt Plantin MT Pro
by Wiltshire Associates.
Printed and bound in Great Britain

Randalph Bland
NINE LIVES & COUNTING

Life on the edge – a true story

CONTENTS

About the Author
Preface
Acknowledgments
Introduction

PART 1:
Anything for a laugh: tall tales from a misspelt youth

CHAPTER 1 - War Zone 3
CHAPTER 2 - Scotland the brave 8
CHAPTER 3 - Rheinland summers 55
CHAPTER 4 - Bicycle Race 76
CHAPTER 5 - As thick as thieves 88
CHAPTER 6 - No Money, No Life... 114

PART 2:
Out of the nest
The great escape from home

CHAPTER 7 - 1975 AD 129
CHAPTER 8 - Student days in Glasgow 134
CHAPTER 9 - Jai Jai Nepal... 206

PART 3:
The fun's over
Close calls in the big bad world

CHAPTER 10 - UN Passport... 267
CHAPTER 11 - Boat People 271
CHAPTER 12 - Beirut.. 296
CHAPTER 13 - Sabra and Shatila 317
CHAPTER 14 - No man's land 329
CHAPTER 15 - Goodbye Sudan 336
CHAPTER 16 - French in, English out.................................... 363
CHAPTER 17 - Calcutta 369
CHAPTER 18 - Nepal revisited.. 395
CHAPTER 19 - Wedding bells.. 399
CHAPTER 20 - Too close for comfort 403

ABOUT THE AUTHOR

Born in Scotland in 1957, Randalph Bland is now retired and lives with his Lebanese wife in Greece, where he settled after working for forty-plus years in twenty different countries for twenty different employers.

After a lowly start and periods with near-empty pockets, towards the end of his working life Randalph had the occasional privileges of shaking the hands of royalty, writing speeches for ambassadors and letters for a president, and drinking morning coffee with high-ranking government officials. Nevertheless, he never lost sight of the rest of humanity and remained connected with and trusted by the man in the street wherever life took him.

Randalph worked as a construction worker, landscape gardener, civil engineer, project manager, operations manager, business consultant, head-hunter, translator, editor, copywriter, business owner, management trainer, management coach, humanitarian worker, regional advisor in refugee contexts, and finally as a diplomat entrusted with a handsome budget to look after humanitarian interventions for the Swiss Federal Department of Foreign Affairs.

Outside work, he has seen the Himalayas from the top, coral reefs from the bottom, an Asian jungle from inside, the raging North Sea in winter, and the valleys and summits of the Vosges mountains in France upside down from the open cockpit of a WW1 French Stampe biplane. He has been married, divorced, remarried, supported a family of three lovely kids, renovated an old farmstead in rural Switzerland and done his best to keep smiling, no matter what.

As this book went to press it was autumn 2024. In the coming months he is planning to travel with his wife to work as a volunteer with kids in support of a grass-roots environmental project on a tropical island in Indonesia. He keeps telling himself that someday he'll slow down, but doesn't believe a word of it. After all, who says we only have nine lives?

PREFACE

The inspiration for writing this book came early in the morning of Tuesday, January 2nd, 2024, when I was admitted to the cardiac ward of Chania Regional Hospital on the island of Crete, where I was told I needed urgent open-heart surgery. Not wanting to believe the doctors, I shrugged their verdict off. After all, so far I had convinced myself that I was bullet proof. But when I did the maths, I realized that my nine lives were used up and that nobody was talking about a tenth.

The next day, I asked my wife Bertie to bring me my laptop and started writing. I was convinced that my life wasn't worth recording, especially since I wasn't a writer, and because in any case there were already so many brilliantly-written books lining the shelves of the world's bookshops. Nevertheless, as the spectre of my operation approached, I started sketching a structure for a book and began filling it with the ideas and recollections that surfaced in my mind.

A week later, just before I passed out on the operating table, I saw in a flash countless images of my younger days, the faces of the people that were important to me at the time, memories of the pranks we got up to as kids, and wanted to tell the world about them and the moments, good and bad, we shared together. When I woke up twenty-six hours later, all I wanted to do was write. I needed to leave a trace about what life was like back in the days before mobile phones, email, Google, cameras and political correctness, and before today's urban madness stripped away spontaneity, the fun of life, humour, and the feeling of freedom we had back then. I wanted to document those days of considerably fewer rules and regulations, less compliance and far less interference from above, as an observation reflecting on the increasingly controlled and monitored direction life on earth is taking.

In particular, regarding the first and last five years of my working life, when I was deployed in humanitarian emergencies in Asia, Africa and the Middle East – as well as during the decade in my fifties when I worked inside the walls of corporate big business as a consultant, trainer and management coach – I wanted to cry out about the way in which the hands-on, can-do attitude of only a few decades ago is being replaced by complex procedures and processes inside which people shy away from responsibilities and taking decisions, frequently ignoring common sense as they bow down to the god of compliance.

The result is Nine Lives, which I hope will give you a hearty laugh at some of the fun this kid revelled in back in industrial Scotland in the 1960s and 1970s and the desperately precarious situations he got himself into once outside the nest. I also hope that my many biased opinions, outbursts and condemnations of how society is governed will provide some food for thought as we collectively totter on the edge of a planet on the brink of digital delirium.

Instead of writing my story from the 'I' perspective (I did this, I did that), I chose to write it in the third person (he did this, he did that), thus creating a distance from which I feel I can be more objective when it comes to writing about myself and my experiences.

I hope you enjoy it.

Sincerely,
Randalph Bland

ACKNOWLEDGMENTS

On my bumpy road through life, hopping from one job to another and from country to country, I've been loved, befriended, encouraged, helped, challenged, tormented, threatened and tested by many, occasionally coming face-to-face with death, but somehow always finding a foothold to avoid it.

This book is dedicated to those who stood by me along the way, who let me into their hearts, picked me up when I was down, kicked my butt when it needed kicking, told me the truths I didn't want to hear, and remained loyal friends, no matter what.

In particular, I'd like to extend hearty thanks to my good friends Heinz and Michael in Switzerland, who nagged at me for years to write my memoirs, and to my more recent friends Rob, on Crete, who joined them in their nagging, prodding me at every encounter or call to write my story, and Annemarie and Dr Cliff Saunders for their unceasing encouragement to publish this 'yarn' about my younger years.

Special thanks go to my brother Jack, who corrected dates and facts and straightened out some bends in my stories where I had fallen prone to exaggeration or imagination, as well as to Chris Newton of Mereo books for his expert editing and professional help in getting the book published.

Not least of all, thanks go to my wife, Bertie, who encouraged and looked after me during the long hours at the computer screen.

Lastly, thanks go to you, the reader who will hopefully enjoy my rant and have a few laughs on the side. I sincerely hope you get as much pleasure out of reading this collection of tales, observations, reflections and outbursts from my distant past as I did writing about them.

INTRODUCTION

Nine Lives and Counting tells the story of Randalph Bland's early years up to the age of 27. By that time young Randalph had already worked in ten different countries, found himself in the middle of two civil wars and rubbed shoulders with near death on nine separate occasions.

The story begins in Beirut in summer 1982 with Randalph being shot at from the cannon of a US warship as he drives along Beirut's Corniche at night, braving the strictly-imposed shoot-on-sight curfew, just for the hell of it. It ends in late 1984 with Randalph in war-torn Angola on the tarmac of Huambo airport in the early light of dawn, gazing in horror at the burning wreckage of the plane he missed by only a few minutes that morning as it gets hit by a ground-to-air missile and erupts in a ball of fire, hurtling to the ground with his three comrades on board only a few miles from where he was standing.

The book is written in three parts. The first part, 'Anything for a Laugh - tales from a misspelt youth', focuses on Randalph's childhood in a working-class, mixed-ethnic family in Ayrshire, Scotland in the 1960s and early 1970s. 'Anything for a laugh' relates the impact his parents and environment had on him, the many borderline pranks he and his cronies got up to as kids to escape from them, and how the passion for travel got hold of him.

The second part, 'Out of the Nest - the great escape from home', is about Randalph's student days in Glasgow in the late 1970s and the pains and pleasures of this naive young man stumbling to find his way in life far from home. It follows him in the summer jobs he gets hired for in his hometown, in Sweden, Germany, England and on a remote Scottish island, and highlights some of the raucous pranks he gets up to for a laugh along the way. 'Out of the Nest' ends with Randalph fulfilling his determination not to give his life up to a career in engineering in Scotland as he steps out into the big wide world at the age of twenty-two and finds himself in rural Nepal, a million miles away from the familiarity of the culture he grew up in.

The third part, 'The fun's over - close calls in the big bad world', follows young Randalph to South-East Asia, Africa and the Middle East during the first half of the 1980s, where he gets a first-hand taste of humanitarian disasters and the collective madness of war, and what it feels like to come uncomfortably close to death. In The fun's over, the carefree fun and laughter of his youth are silenced firstly by the debilitating weakness of a life-threatening disease, then by the harsh conditions of working in a refugee camp, the heart-stopping horror of cleaning up a massacre, the panic of fleeing from a military invasion, the helpless feeling of being abducted, the terror of armed robbery, and near-death experiences in an uncanny series of aviation incidents.

The stories and anecdotes related in the book are based on actual events, and the various people appearing in the text all existed. While some have passed on to whatever comes next after life on earth, many are still around today. To protect the integrity of everyone still here or departed, the author has changed most of the names and some of the locations and dates and has adapted the stories of some potentially sensitive events.

Throughout the book, every now and again Randalph is prone to slipping unbridled comments and outbursts into the text about the bullies, the ruling classes and the heartless warmongers that run the show. He hopes that you, the reader, will be able to receive these in their context and use them to reflect on whatever it is inside us that drives us collectively into the abyss of violence and destruction that sadly is the norm in too many places around the world today.

PART 1

Anything for a laugh: tall tales from a misspelt youth

CHAPTER 1

War Zone

West Beirut, 1982. La Corniche. It's dark. Ominously silent. The city's under military curfew. Only two or three lamps light up the deserted, bombed-out streets. Rubble is lying everywhere. To the south, the rumble of war is groaning in the distance. Every now and then a sharp crimson explosion lights up the sky.

Randalph is by himself, cruising along the sea front of Ras Beirut on low beam in second gear in his employer's metallic-silver 1980 Peugeot 505. He's alert like a stalking cat and tingling with adrenaline in the knowledge that he shouldn't be doing this. He's been warned a hundred times about the dangers and potential diplomatic consequences of being caught out at night during the curfew. But Randalph needs excitement. He needs thrills. He's a junky for the spice of life. He needs the buzz of doing something 'wrong' that he can get away with.

Deep down, Randalph's a rebel at heart who hates

authority and hierarchy and has a reckless disregard for rules and regulations. His biggest fear is being caught at doing something he shouldn't be doing and he'll invent any story to escape the shame and discomfort of being proven or suspected of being the culprit, like driving around in a war zone for the hell of it under a military curfew.

Randalph's also one of those guys who daydreams about being a hero, imagining himself eternally triumphant and fearless, righting the wrongs of the world and blowing away the bad guys. He invents scenarios in his mind where he comes out on top, celebrated as the street king, the big guy, and a deadly force to be feared and reconned with. Meanwhile in the real world, he's just plain Randalph – an ordinary guy who's got a knack for getting himself caught up in extraordinary events.

Only a couple more bends around the sea front and he'll be back safely in Hamra, with the car parked neatly along the kerb. No one will ever know what he was doing.

But maybe this time they will: behind him, a loud explosion lights up the sky. Randalph glances in the mirror and sees smoke and flames. What the hell was that, he wonders, aware that whatever it was he mustn't get involved? To his left he sees the bright flash of a shell being fired in the distance. A few seconds later there's a second explosion, this time closer behind him. He tries to estimate the distance. Thirty metres? Twenty?

Time speeds up and Randalph's daydreaming is shattered like a pane of glass hit with a hammer as he realises in a gush of adrenaline-fuelled panic that he's the target. Suddenly he feels dangerously exposed, soaking in the cold sweat of fear moistening his hands and running down his back as he remembers in a flash the sinister grey outline of the warship he could see by day patrolling the Lebanese coast. Was the shot coming from the ship? Were they really aiming at him? Jesus Christ…

Foot down. Third gear. Fourth. Overdrive. At the lighthouse he takes the corner wide and fast. With a wild tug he wrenches the screeching Peugeot sharp right and up the hill to Bayard Dodge. He has to get to Bliss Street and then Mahoul Street, where he'll be safe, and he has to get there fast. As the car sways, squealing and bumping over what's left of the road surface, he hits the red and white striped bullet-pierced oil drum marking the remains of the blown-out checkpoint at the entrance to Hamra.

Once in Mahoul, Randalph slows down as he enters the familiar built-up streets whose high buildings shield him from the warship's guns. He's terrified – not so much of being hit but of how to explain the destroyed wing, bumper and remains of the left headlamp. His mind races as he thinks of a plausible story to invent…

WELCOME TO LEBANON

After graduating from Strathclyde University as a Civil Engineer in 1979, Randalph had volunteered to go to Nepal to escape from what his restless soul was convinced would be a career of drudgery. After botching his studies, he held the secret belief that he would in any case be a useless engineer and didn't want to take the risk of people pointing this out to him. Rather than running the gauntlet of discovery, disgrace and boredom, he opted for running away and saving the world.

After a year and a half in Nepal with the job of helping the local authorities develop water supply systems in remote rural areas, Randalph registered his availability for humanitarian and disaster relief on the roster of a newly established non-profit organisation in London that was recruiting engineers for the UN and other agencies and sending them to faraway places. Randalph's faraway place was an island refugee camp for Vietnamese Boat People in the South China Sea, where he toiled for six months on an assignment that ended in near disaster, with Randalph arrested and sentenced to death.

At home again, having escaped with the help of a robust diplomatic intervention, it was only a matter of days before he got a call from the same organisation, who this time asked if he was available for an assignment to Lebanon. Totally oblivious to what was happening elsewhere in the world, in particular in the Middle East, Randalph agreed.

Looking back, at the time Randalph wasn't even sure where Lebanon was. It didn't matter. He blindly accepted. He was not the kind of person that invests time in thinking about things before doing them. The day after the call he took the night train to London, where he got a short briefing, contact names, flight tickets, a pep talk, and a clap on the back.

By the time the briefing was over, rush hour had begun and the London Underground was packed. Although he moved as fast as he could through the crowds to catch up on lost time, jumping from train to train as if the devil was chasing him, he arrived late at the check-in gate.

In those days, aid workers still benefited from public admiration and to his amazement, the public address system at Heathrow was speaking his name. Randalph for once followed instructions and stopped at the nearest info desk, from which he was escorted to his gate, where the plane was waiting for him. Someone at the organisation with the sort of connections that can delay a scheduled passenger flight had put a call through to the airline, explaining who young Randalph was and where he was going.

As he stepped onto the plane, sweat pouring down his face, sheepishly thanking the crew for waiting and expecting to see angry passengers pointing at their watches, to his amazement he was greeted by smiles and applause. For a brief moment Randalph was a star – the blue-eyed, all smiles, red-bearded saviour of humanity for whom even passenger planes wait.

Randalph's stardom followed him all the way to Lebanon where the events he got caught up in propelled him onto the evening news at the BBC and in articles in *The Observer* and Scotland's *Daily Record*. The same events, however, haunted him for the rest of his life. To this day he still freezes when he smells the stench of rotting flesh and looks for cover when he hears the scary howl of fighter jets in the sky...

CHAPTER 2

Scotland the brave

Back in his school days, Randolph was a softie, too sensitive for the rough world of the streets he grew up in. He was afraid of fights. Not having the courage to speak out or defend himself had plagued him throughout his younger life. Under the swift sanctioning hand of his father and punishments and bullying at school, he learned young that speaking out was dangerous. Unless you were up for a fight, if you opened your mouth in south-west Scotland in the 1960s and 70s, somebody would close it for you.

Randolph wanted to be one of the lads, but never became one. Once he scored a goal in the primary school playground and for the duration of an entire afternoon felt the warm glow of feeling accepted by his classmates and the other boys chasing the ball. The pleasure was short-lived, lasting only until the next time he was called names on the road home from school. The other boys called him 'Bubbles', because he would spontaneously burst into tears when teased or bullied. Later in life, he consoled himself that it was precisely his soft heart that endeared him to the ladies, but also opened his eyes to the harsh realities of the world and the suffering of others.

Randalph, back row second from the right, and his classmates at Kilmaurs primary school in the late 1960s.

On one summer's evening, licking the wounds of humiliation inflicted by some bully or other at school, Randalph had his first taste of revenge. Walking home alone from the local Boy Scouts Cubs group, when he was sure no one was watching and in a fit of rage against the world that seemed like it was out to get him, he smashed all the window panes on the primary school's ground floor corridor window with a salvo of pebbles picked up from the playground. All nine panes of glass flew in splinters. He would have smashed every window in the school if he had had the guts. Hell would break out the next morning, but no one would ever know who did it. That'll teach them, grinned Randalph to himself.

Randalph became an outsider, keeping himself to himself, constantly wary that somebody would betray him or jeer at him. He didn't fit in. He had not yet realised that when he grew up his disdain for the crowd and the heartless ignorance of society would turn him into a loner, doing things his way, choosing his road to go down, operating out of sight of others, out of reach of being found out. The loner in him would become his path to freedom.

ANYTHING FOR A LAUGH

Randalph was born in Ayrshire in south-west Scotland at the end of the 1950s, at a time when many still walked or cycled and when double-decker buses had a leather blind that dropped down behind the driver's cabin at night. It was a time when kids could play pranks and get away with just about anything. Getting caught meant a kick in the arse by whichever adult caught you, and later a beating by your angry father. The police were never involved. There was no need. Kids' mischief was dealt with swiftly on the spot by the community.

In spite of being easily bullied at school, Randalph was never miserable. He enjoyed having fun and had a particular skill in having fun at the price of others. This was inspired by his father, Jimmy. Jimmy was the third eldest child of a family of eight brothers and six sisters, raised in Kilmarnock town centre in a two-bedroom flat, where the boys slept in one room, the girls in another, and the parents in the living room.

Randalph remembers as if it was yesterday the day when his dad took him into the woods near their village, where a ragged old man lived in a tin shack. A thin column of wood smoke was rising gracefully in ethereal strands of blue light from the shack's makeshift chimney pipe, which had been secured to the wooden sides of the shack with lengths of rusty wire. Jimmy put his finger to his mouth, signalling to Randalph to be quiet, pointed to a nearby tree where Randalph should hide, and approached the shack holding an empty jute coal sack in his hand.

Jimmy was a smallish, stocky man, but tall enough with outstretched arms to reach the top of the chimney, where he delicately placed the sack and tiptoed back over to the tree where Randalph was hiding. A few moments later the shack's rusty door swung open with a noisy grating sound of unoiled hinges and an angry old man with a stubble beard and ragged jacket stumbled out. "Is that you again Jimmy fucking B?", he shouted. "Ya useless fuckin piece o' shit. Come back here again and I'll cut ye up and stuff ye in the oven". By then, Jimmy and very young Randalph were already outside hearing range, laughing their heads off as they charged through the forest. Jimmy was a rascal, and Randalph followed suit.

On several other occasions, Jimmy used to play his favourite trick on the neighbours. On New Year's Day or at some other highlight of the year, he would tell Randalph and his brother to go upstairs and stay in their shared bedroom, which was on the back side of the house. He would then sneak out of the back door, pile tin dustbins up against a neighbour's back door, knock the door vigorously, run back to his own kitchen door, close it gently, run up the stairs to the boys' bedroom, hold his finger to his mouth threateningly in a sign of 'silence' and, glancing out of the window at the outraged neighbours, would shake with supressed laughter, trying in vain to keep it in by covering his mouth with his hand. Jimmy delighted in watching the neighbours who had burst out of their kitchen in a cacophony of rolling dustbins and were looking right and left, shouting, swearing, and threating to kill the culprit.

To convince the neighbours in the block of houses they lived in that it wasn't him who played that particular trick, Jimmy even piled up the dustbins against his own back door, sneaked around the gable end of the block to his front door, went through the house from front to back, then charged out of the back door, through the bins, threatening to skin alive the bastard who did this, shouting loud enough for the whole neighbourhood and beyond to hear. Remarkably, he was never caught in the act.

Years later, once Randalph had settled and founded his own family in French-speaking Switzerland, he enjoyed telling his kids about how he and his street mates used to tie door handles together on the upper floor of a two-storey block of flats opposite the old primary school near the village centre, then ring the bells, knock loudly on each door, hurl abuse at the tenants when they tried to open them, and run for their lives. Back then, 'anything for a laugh' was a way of life.

On Tuesday nights, walking home in the dark from the

weekly village Cub Scouts meeting and later from the Boy Scouts groups, Randalph and his pals would take bigger risks, ringing bells, knocking on doors, and getting chased by some furious tenant who they invariably outrun. It was impossible for a tired working man to catch a lively kid with his adrenaline level off the scale and the ability to jump fences, the agility to scale walls, and the sheer determination of the hunted never to be caught.

Unlike some places in the world, letters in the UK are mainly delivered through the 'letterbox', or 'mail slot' in American and Canadian usage, which is a slot, usually horizontal but sometimes vertical, about 30 cm by 5 cm (12 inches by 2 inches), cut through the middle or lower half of the front door of houses and apartments. To Randalph and his gang of cronies, letterboxes were a source of wicked amusement. They loved to ring a random doorbell or knock on the door, wait for the tenant to approach the door, then, as soon as they were within firing range, squirt a powerful jet of sticky orange juice prepared in a 'Fairy Liquid' bottle through the letterbox at them and run for their lives. The gang would then split up and run like lightning in different directions. The dispersion trick gave them that millisecond advantage over the tenant who had to make up his mind about who to chase. It worked every time.

By the time he had reached puberty, Randalph had carried out several dozen successful raids and pissed off a lot of people in the village. By day, he and his cronies would have to be careful not to go near the scene of the latest hit, in case somebody recognised them. Grievances, thankfully, were short lived, and while the mischievous boys were definitely guilty of making a mess of someone's pullover and floor carpet, if they were caught they would be savagely dealt with, otherwise soon forgotten. In those post-war years of crippling strikes and industrial action, grown-ups had many more serious social issues to deal with.

THE RAILINGS

However, the gods who had been keeping a tally on young Randalph's serial mischief and were lying in waiting to punish him got their revenge on the opening night of the new Boy Scouts group hut on the main street of his village, Kilmaurs. While the villagers were gathering inside for the opening ceremony, Randalph and his mates were fooling around on the wall outside the hut. With their backs to the hut and the railings, their game that day was to stand on the wall, their arms wrapped around the protruding spikes at the top of the railings, and hang on while the other boys tried to push their feet from the wall. When Randalph's feet were pushed, his arm slipped and one of the spikes he was clinging to ripped through his left bicep, coming out at his elbow. There was blood everywhere. The scene looked like the inside of a butcher's shop. The white shirt of his classmate, Gordon, who helped to lift him off the railings, and the shirts of the handful of other boys who were helping him were covered in it.

Randalph recalls that no one was screaming. There was no time for crying, although someone had vomited on the path leading to the hut. Worried nonetheless that there would be no blood left in him by the time an ambulance arrived, he was bundled into someone else's car and rushed to the emergency ward of Kilmarnock Infirmary, where he was stitched up and kept for a week. Randalph remembers vividly the soft look in his father's eyes when the anaesthetic wore off and he woke up, and the chiding he got from his mother for being such a stupid boy. She was probably right. It took six months before he could begin to bend his arm and two full years before it would fully stretch.

NO FOOTBALL PLEASE

Randalph hated sport. Any sport. On more Saturday afternoons than he cares to recall, he was dragged along by Jimmy to the local football ground. Randalph hated going and felt vulnerable and scared in the crowds of drunken men hurling abuse at the players and regularly hurling empty beer cans into the crowd. At every match there was violence of some kind. Jimmy, who had spent four years in uniform in the army of the Rhein during WWII and another five thereafter during the occupation, was a bit of a hard nut. He hated the violence of the day as much as Randalph did. The difference between the two was that while Randalph cowered, hoping not to be hit by flying beer cans, Jimmy would tear into the gangs of hooligans with some other ex-army comrades of his and come back with his knuckles bleeding.

After the match, Randalph would be marched off to a local pub where the men would meet up and go over their fight with the hooligans. At the time, Randalph was thirteen or fourteen. The legal age for entry to a pub was eighteen. Jimmy would introduce Randalph to the landlord or bartender as "He's wi' me. Is that gonna be a problem?" Randalph cringed as he listened to the grizzly men angrily banging their fists on the table, swearing loudly, and agreeing unanimously that someday soon they'd have to either kill the hooligan bastards or put them in hospital for the rest of their days.

DIRTY BOOKS

Like in almost all villages in industrial Scotland, except for the doctor, the dentist, the banker, the ministers, and some other professionals, the vast majority of the population were tenants of state-owned 'council houses'. People worked in mines, iron works, or factories making carpets, textiles, railway locomotives, tractors, shoes, water valves, machine tools, and other items of the time. In most families, both the father and the mother worked. By the time the mother got home from the factory, the kids were back from school and got their 'tea', equivalent to the English 'dinner'. 'Supper' was a snack for later, before bedtime, by which time the fathers would be back from the pub, many of them with a temper and the urge to kick the shit out of their wives or kids.

These were times of rife social injustice and repression, where you got your kicks when and where you could. As long as you weren't being beat up, bullied or degraded at school or at home, your sole focus was on enjoying yourself. They were also times of strict moral repression, where pissing against a tree could get you booked for indecent exposure and where anything to do with sex was on the one hand unspoken, but on the other the punchline of just about every joke. Scottish society had huge taboos about anything to do with the body. While women at large hugged and kissed each other, men stood rigidly, hands in their pockets, nodding a courteous 'hello' to each other when they met.

This was also the early days of porn, when hungry guys would wank themselves off in their car parked by a hedge or in a car park and throw the 'dirty book' out the window, where it would inevitably be found and 'recycled' by other hungry guys, like Randalph and his best friend Donald, who used to scour the countryside on weekends on their bicycles on the lookout for 'nudy' books. On most trips they would find sticky discarded copies of *Mayfair* or *Playboy* full of curvy tits and bums, while on a good day they would find a copy of *Hustler*, or some other harder porn mag with photos of the ladies taken from the front. It was an unspoken pastime that many indulged in but nobody would ever admit to.

Often the magazines they found were sodden with rain, usually with some pages stuck together with sperm, but always giving a glimpse of the fair sex and firing the appetite and imagination for contact with them. Randalph and Donald had a favourite secret, dry place under the bridge of a disused railway line, accessible only from the fields, where they could hide their booty and come back to drool over it on their next sortie. The two boys probably knew of more disused railway line embankments, undersides of bridges, farmers' huts, roadside shacks, easily accessible dense hedges, and disused barns than a map maker. It took Randalph until his early sixties to rid himself of his enjoyment of porn.

CAREFREE DAYS

On weekends and holidays, when Randalph was not scouring the countryside looking for glossy magazines with juicy curves in to drool over, he could probably be found walking with his brother Jack or his friend Donald in the country lanes or by the rivers outside their village. One of the walks led south out along the road to the village of Crosshouse, past the village creamery (cheese factory), over the railway bridge, then left half a mile later down a field path along a big hedge to 'the viaduct' and the big pipe crossing the river. From there, where they often stopped for a few hours to muck around on the banks of the river, they would cross the footbridge and walk from the other side of the river towards the village cemetery, where Randalph's parents were later buried alongside their neighbours and local friends.

On his last visit to Scotland, Randalph noted sadly that all of his family's old neighbours and friends from the village had moved to the cemetery, almost recreating the community he was familiar with as a kid. Walking around the lines of gravestones with so many familiar names engraved on them was like walking along the streets of his childhood neighbourhood.

At the other side of the lane, opposite the cemetery, Randalph, and whoever he was out walking with, would often stop by Saint Maurs Parish church – one of the three churches in his village – where they would walk around the ancient graveyard with its centuries-old tombstones and Celtic crosses and tell each other scary stories, especially if it was by then the evening and light was fading from the sky.

Sometimes in winter, when the wind was howling, trees were bending and groaning, the ground was crisp, and dark foreboding clouds were charging in from the sea, he and some cronies used to meet there to see who had the courage to crawl behind the oldest of the bent-over tombstones or put their hands under the limestone slabs engraved with skulls and crossbones that covered the ancient graves, all the while scaring each other with stories of witches, warlocks, unexplained disappearances and black magic.

On the same walk, if it was still early in the day and he was out and about with his brother Jack, Randalph would cross over the main road by the church and head down Mill Avenue alongside Morton Park, where the village Gala Day celebrations were held each year in June. From there they would head along the burn (a little river called Carmel Water that ran through the village) to drop in on their 'auntie' Jessica, 'uncle' Adamo and Donald, and either play yet another game of Monopoly with Donald in his tiny bedroom overlooking the fields or fool around with Doug, their lovely playful big black labrador. Doug, pronounced 'Doog', was as much the brothers' dog as he was his owners and often ran away from home to the other side of the village to end up at Randalph's and Jack's, who then had to walk him back down to Donald's.

Doug the labrador with Randalph, 14, and his brother Jack, 12, in their back yard.

At the bottom end of the road where Donald lived was the main road bearing left to the village of Fenwick, heading east along the B751. The road to Fenwick, which was named Kilmaurs Road, and which for a short stretch wound through dense forest on either side, passed by the gatehouse of the Rowallan Castle Estate and the tree-lined driveway inside the grounds leading to the Old Rowallan Castle – the ancestral home of the Muirs and Campbells, where Randalph and the lads used to walk around and poke their noses into the old structure which, at the time, was empty.

Curious about the history of the castle and the estate, Randalph later discovered with the generous help of Google that the earliest part of the castle structure was built in the 13th century, with the main part added around two centuries later, and it had roots going back even further to the 9th century with a castle house built on a bridge over Carmel Water.

Further into the estate lay the 'New' Rowallan Castle – a masterpiece of late Victorian Arts & Crafts, so they say, which today is available for posh weddings, special occasions, or passing the day on the castle's exclusive golf course, for those who can afford it. It was over fifty years since Randalph had rummaged around the estate as a young teenager in ragged trousers and with dirty hands, enjoying being among the trees in that ancient place and happy to just play around with sticks and stones – there was nothing posh or exclusive about the place then.

Before reaching the Rowallan estate, a path led through the fields to an old broken dam and on to the Water Meetings, where the Carmel Water met the Shaw Burn, which then lived happily together all their way down to the sea. The dam was one of Randalph's favourite haunts, where he would spend entire afternoons with Donald and Jack building small dams across the river with sticks, stones and mud, oblivious to passing time, guided only by growing hunger pains as the day went on, signalling that it was time to head for home. This was thirty years before mobile phones destroyed the feeling of carefree days perhaps forever. Parents knew you were out and that you would be back – in those days, that was enough.

To save bus fares, and if the weather was not too bad, Randalph and Jack often walked to Kilmarnock, enjoying the countryside until they reached the perimeter of the town, after which they were mindful of their surroundings and on the lookout for possible trouble as they walked along the main road separating the relatively safe housing 'scheme' (estate) on the right from the notoriously unpredictable and dangerous Onthank and Knockinlaw housing schemes on the left, which were showcased in 'The Scheme', a BBC Scotland award winning documentary series which followed the lives of six families living there.

The sudden change in atmosphere from lush green dairy farmland to boarded-up gangland, while a little scary by day, could be seriously frightening at night. The boys, however, knew the estate fairly well, having regularly visited one of father Jimmy's sisters who lived there with her husband and four kids, and in the end nothing ever happened to them. Besides, it was not the worst area in town.

On other days, when they were heading in the direction of Kilmarnock for a walk only, they would turn left just before the outskirts of the town onto the Old Stewarton Road, walk past the Cunningham Head estate, then take another left back to their village along the Fenwick road. At the top of the hill just before the descent into the village was a farm from where they invariably stopped to admire the idealistic panoramic view across the rolling Ayrshire countryside all the way to the sea and the Isle of Arran beyond. Having reached the village, they would also just as invariably turn right up Donald's road to see what was going on. Days at Donald's were happy days.

Further along the Fenwick Road past the Rowallan estate and the right turn towards Kilmarnock along the Old Stewarton Road, the same Old Stewarton Road continued after a left turn, this time heading straight for the town of Stewarton. This would be a longer walk for the brothers and merited a break along the way at Christine and Karl's, a couple of German-speaking friends of their parents who lived in one of the town's old gatehouses. Once recovered, up to date with the latest chit-chat and replenished with biscuits and sweets, they would head off down the B769 to Cunningham Head, taking a final left towards Kilmaurs, hoping not to be interrogated upon arrival by their mother who always wanted to know where they'd been. Thank God she didn't have a phone, thought Randalph years later.

Once a year in spring their village staged a 'cattle show' in the wooded parkland behind a long brick wall running along the left-hand side of the main road that the boys walked past every time they walked to 'the toon' (Kilmarnock). The main road had a pavement joining their village to 'the toon', encouraging people to walk, and making it easy for misers like Randalph to save on bus fares.

Randalph knew the place well, as father Jimmy's eldest sister had married Uncle Frank, a well-to-do international salesman of high-precision devices from Switzerland who lived on the other side of the wall in a sizeable country house at the entrance to the estate. On one occasion, Uncle Frank threw a dinner-and-drinks party for Jimmy's family of eight brothers, six sisters and their spouses and kids. Staggered at how much the guests ate and drank, Randalph imagined that this one-off invitation had been enough for Uncle Frank forever.

The cattle show brought together local farmers and those villagers who liked the country-life atmosphere, with its cattle, horses, Highland dancing and lots of beer. Randalph loved it there, often thinking that he would have liked to have been a farmer.

The area to the north-west of the village was particularly rich in country lanes, passing between high hedges and offering lovely views of the countryside all around and several possibilities for walks. The walk the boys preferred led west along Irvine Road past Howie's farm to the right just after the bridge over the Garrier Burn, then on to Cunningham Head and straight over the crossroads down to Annick Water, where they could play around by the stream. On their way home they could turn left at the same crossroads, heading north-east towards Stewarton for a few hundred yards, and then first right onto the hedge-lined narrow country road leading to High Langmuir Farm and back to Kilmaurs along what was called 'the farm road'.

Wherever they walked, time stood still. Holding sticks in their hands, with pockets bulging with an apple or full of sweets or biscuits 'stollen' from the kitchen at home, the fresh air, the fleeting clouds, the fields, the crows, the smells of wild rosebuds and ripening rye and barley in summer, and the peace and quiet of the country lanes, provided the boys with an environment where they had everything they needed to enjoy themselves.

In any case, except for building something with Lego or Meccano, playing Scrabble or Monopoly, occasionally playing cards and some board games with mother Helma when there was peace in the house, or just farting about in the hut beside the back door or the garage at the end of the garden making something with bits of metal or wood, home was boring.

Home was also dangerous, especially when Helma was in action mode and on the lookout for chores for the boys to either do by themselves or help her with. She had an uncanny knack of knowing when the boys were enjoying themselves and spoiling the fun, just like her mother from Germany – Oma Schmitz – who spent every second summer with the family until her death, when Randalph was in his early teens, terrorizing the boys with discipline and getting on Jimmy's nerves. What sort of a life had those two ladies had to be so pro-work and against enjoyment, thought Randalph many years later?

BEACH BOYS

Whenever the weather permitted, which was not every day along south-west Scotland's wind-swept cold and rainy Atlantic coast, Randalph would head to the seashore with some cronies on their bicycles, taking the same road west along Irvine Road to the crossroads at Cunningham Head as on his walks, but turning south-west through Perceton and Girdle Toll towards Irvine harbour and the beach beyond. Leaving the bikes at the harbour, he and the lads would then spend the day running around in the sand dunes or daring each other to jump in for a swim.

Randalph loved being in the water and would spend hours running in and out jumping the waves, oblivious, like most teenagers, to the bracing chill of the sea. According to the many facts and figures available today on the Internet, in Irvine and on the other beaches along the Ayrshire coast the average water temperature in winter is around 8.2°C, reaching 8.5°C in spring, rising in summer to 14.3°C, then falling in autumn down to 12.6°C. With no way of knowing the temperature at the time, everybody just called it 'fuckin' freezing'.

Occasionally, after two or three sunny days in succession at the height of summer, the sea temperature would rise to 18°C, which some locals maintained was too hot for swimming. On these days, if the sun shone brightly in the morning, and if these rare days fell on a weekend or public holiday, father Jimmy would bundle the family into the car and head off to the seaside at Troon, Barassie, Saltcoats or Irvine, spending the whole day on the beach under the summer sunshine, sheltered from the wind by a makeshift plastic screen held up with thin tubular steel poles that would blow over when the wind came in gusts, leaving Jimmy cursing and swearing as he tried to salvage the wreckage.

The boys, who were still young at the time, would get burnt red like lobsters, screaming in pain in the back seat of the car when they eventually drove home, where they were dipped in a bath of cold water and smothered in Nivea cream. Later in life, after both parents had died and the brothers were analysing their childhood, they concluded that the trauma of their sunburn explained why, until they became young adults, they hated being outside when the sun was strong, opting for the theory that the body never forgets.

Randalph, who years later spent as much time as he

could in shorts only under the baking sun, feeling best when he was tanned brownish red, replaced that theory with the theory that vitamin D is good for you. He liked being under the sun so much that when he eventually retired and settled in Greece in his mid-sixties, he would spend entire afternoons under the scorching Mediterranean sunshine, sweating litres of water as he pottered around in his garden, digging holes, planting trees, chopping wood, lining flower beds with rocks carried from the beach, sawing branches, pruning twigs or watering, wearing only swimming trunks and a pair of sturdy shoes to stop the needles from citrus tree twigs piercing his feet. On hindsight, even Randalph, who doesn't easily admit to mistakes, had to accept that exposing himself like this to midday Mediterranean sunshine in summer probably contributed to his first heart attack in September 2023. and definitely triggered the second just after Christmas of the same year.

As well as trips to the nearby beaches, once or twice a year father Jimmy drove the family to the 'Heads of Ayr', a steep rocky headland where the boys could scramble up cliffs, catch crabs in the rocky pools and race them along the sand. On a few occasions, they drove even further, to Girvan to the south or Largs to the north, where there were slot machines along the sea front enticing passers-by to try their luck at winning a teddy bear, some sticky sweets, shiny bangles or other items of random crap. On one occasion, the family drove all the way down to spend the day in Wigtownshire, where Jimmy's big brother John had a caravan by the Solway Firth at the Isle of Whithorn.

Wigtownshire is where Jimmy's mother's family came

from. According to documents that Randalph dug up at the district registry office in Newton Mearns decades later on one of his trips back home to Scotland, his great grandfather – the father of Sarah, Jimmy's mother – had been the harbour master in Wigton, where he drowned at sea. Randalph, of course, never met him but liked the idea that among his ancestors was a man of the sea.

He was equally proud of his grandfather, Jimmy's father Grandad John, who, they say, stood 6'4" (190 cm) tall and was station master at Kilmarnock Railway Station. Although he died when Randalph was only a few years old, he had a vivid memory of him towering above him, smoking a pipe and wearing a flat cap and a dark grey waistcoat with a pocket watch chain hanging from it. Randalph clearly remembers Grandpa John taking him by the hand to walk along the platform beside a massive steam locomotive, with steam belching out from the driving valves and smoke billowing from the chimney, as it chugged noisily out of the station, dragging its following of red carriages with wooden doors to wherever they were headed.'

Apart from that precise memory, and one of being washed in the kitchen sink at his Grandma Sarah's flat in Kilmarnock by his Aunt Kathy, Jimmy's elder sister, who wore spectacles with leaf-shaped lenses that pointed upwards at the edges, Randalph had only very vague memories of his grandparents on his father's side.

On his mother's side, he remembered his German grandfather, who had a barber shop somewhere close to where they lived near Bonn, mainly from pictures of him. However, he would never forget his German gran, Oma

Randalph's Grandpa John and Grandma Sarah – a stalwart, upright couple from a bygone age who raised a family of 14 children of which his father, Jimmy, born in 1924, was the third eldest.

Schmitz, who terrorized him and his little brother Jack every time she either stayed with the family during summer or they were staying at her house during their early summer holidays in Germany. Randalph remembers feeling relieved when she passed away when he was a young teenager.

STIFF UPPER LIP

Every now and then, two or more of father Jimmy's comrades in arms would turn up at their house. Randalph never knew why or for what, but always remembered that the discussions were heated and serious. Randalph and his young brother imagined that they were plotting a revolution or an attack on the hooligans. From the corridor behind the living room door, Randalph and young Jack would listen as best they could to the stories, inventing their own version of what these heroes were up to.

Jimmy was above all a humanist, but also a fighter with grit and guts who was not afraid to stand up and speak out for what he believed in. He was the man in the street who knew deep down, as most men do, that war was the luxury of the privileged, the game of the powerful and the indulgence of the greedy. He knew that the real and only enemy was the men at the top – the heartless bastards on both sides who could send millions of eighteen-year-olds to their death for 'King and Country' or the 'Fatherland', while they gathered in the immense spoils of war. He bitterly and vociferously despised them.

Before Jimmy's premature death at the young age of fifty-two, Randalph and brother Jack often listened to him talking with their mother's sister's husband, their Uncle Theodor, who had been a German soldier during the war and spent many abominable years in Russian captivity. He was riddled with bullet holes, cursed with bad health, and as bitter as Jimmy was towards the senselessness of war.

During their summer holidays in Germany, or on the rare

occasions when mother Helma's family came to visit her in Scotland, father Jimmy and Uncle Theo regularly went out for a drink together. Both men talked about the open friendship and total lack of animosity they encountered in the pubs in Scotland as well as in the Wirtshaüser (pubs) in Germany where they drank, and where the customers were just ordinary men like themselves who had been caught up in the vile machinery of power politics and war.

It was clear to Randalph, that unless you were a psychopath, you needed distance to kill. Physical distance. Emotional distance. Philosophical distance. Randalph observed that the 'stiff upper lip' approach provided just that. By not allowing soldiers to have contact with an occupied community – the enemy – they would not build human attachment, and would readily follow orders to kill, if and when ordered to. On the other hand, if soldiers started to play football with the locals or buy from them at the local market, they would soon realise that 'the enemy' is made up of everyday people with the same fears, joys, emotions and challenges as themselves. Pulling the trigger then becomes much more difficult.

Apart from when they were beating each other up, Randalph often wondered at the shyness among British men about physical contact, while across much of Europe, and indeed in most of the world outside British influence, men shook hands, hugged each other, kissed each other on the cheeks, and generally showed physical recognition to their fellow men.

Perhaps because of the stories told by and about his dad, Randalph had a theory that this behaviour was the hallmark and invention of Elizabethan and Victorian England, whose insatiable appetite to conquer and enslave the world and render it British required enforcing distance in order to divide and rule. To Randalph, the stiff upper lip was the weapon of Empire that severed the tie between men's acts and their hearts, allowing them to kill, maim and destroy in the name of the Crown or of obedience to orders from above.

One day, when he was about nine or ten years old and his parents were not at home, Randalph had gone upstairs to sniff around in their bedroom. Tucked away at the bottom of one of Jimmy's dressing table drawers he found three medals and decorative ribbons hidden in a small carton box, which he spread out in wonder and admiration on his bed in the boys' bedroom next door. Surprised by the sound of the front door suddenly opening and his parents returning home, Randalph ran back to their bedroom to put the medals back in their place. In his panic he forgot the box, which, by this time Jimmy had discovered when he climbed the stairs to greet the boys.

As storm clouds blot out the sun and send people running for cover, Jimmy's expression foretold an imminent downpour of retribution and correction. His chin was sticking out like a snarling bulldog getting ready to bite. He was growling as if he was about to pounce, his false teeth pointing upwards to his nose and forehead. He stuffed the medals into his pocket, grabbed Randalph by the scruff of the neck, stormed out of the boys' bedroom, marched him down the stairs, through the living room and kitchen and past his mother, who had heard the commotion and was pleading with Jimmy not to hurt Randalph.

With one hand still holding the struggling, frightened Randalph, Jimmy opened the kitchen door and marched him onto the lawn, where he took the medals from his pocket and thrust them in Randalph's face. "See these, son?" he said in a surprisingly mild voice, then burst into a political speech with "This is nothing to be proud of son; only to be ashamed of. There's nothing in this hand that's worth celebrating. The people who made these medals are the ones who send you to your death. They're the ones who're born into privilege and tell you lies about who your friends are and who your enemies are. They tell you what to do. They tell you who to kill. They make your life, my life and everybody's life miserable. Never, ever kneel to them. Never show them respect. Never believe them."

He went on and on, furiously cursing the establishment and the makers of war, then threw the medals into the garden, warning Randalph never to go near them, never to look for them, never to want them. It was many years later as Randalph witnessed the aftermath of massacre, helicopters vomiting flames on rural villages, gunned-down lifeless corpses piled up on street corners, bodies raped and mutilated on beautiful tropical beaches, and even kids blowing themselves up to stop approaching tanks, that his father's words sank in. By then it was blatantly clear to Randalph that the powerful and the greedy are the ones who rape, pillage and defile the very soul of mother earth.

OUTINGS

While Randalph was still at primary school in the village, once a year in early summer an outing was organised for the kids by the school, usually to somewhere along the Ayrshire coast. He remembers well the feeling of excitement as the massive steam locomotive pulled in alongside the platform and he and the other kids scrambled for a compartment where they could sit together with their friends. These were the last days of steam, which ended in 1968, with the steam locomotive stock across the country severely reduced from over 20,000 locomotives at the time the railway companies were nationalised as British Railways in 1948 to fewer than 370.

In Ayrshire, as well as everywhere else in the country, unlike in Europe, many British Rail carriages had smallish individual compartments which did not connect with each other via a corridor or central aisle and could only be accessed by wooden-framed doors opening directly onto the platforms. Already then, Randalph was impressed at how quaint this design was compared to the roomy, solidly built carriages he was used to travelling in on the other side of the Channel on his summer holiday trips to Germany.

At that time, Kilmaurs railway station was still in use, with trains heading either north towards Glasgow, south towards Kilmarnock, or west to the Ayrshire coast. This was before the infamous Beeching cuts in the 1960s when one third of the country's network and over half of all stations were permanently closed in an effort to reduce rail subsidies. What a tragedy, lamented Randalph for decades to come.

According to Randalph's skimpy understanding of economics and society, if Beeching, and especially the government of the day, had taken a look at how professionally many railway networks are run in Europe, where modernisation has never ceased, with many examples of government-sponsored passenger-friendly initiatives, he would have understood that by investing in a modern, efficient service and network and by expanding its outreach rather than reducing it, the population would probably have travelled by train more frequently, making the service more profitable in the long run.

Beeching or the government would also have noticed that a railway network is a public service that in every country is heavily subsidised. The belief at the time that it had to make a profit was not and is not realistic. But that would have required Beeching and the boys to look beyond the high cliffs of Dover to see how other countries function, and Brits, Randalph often lamented, don't readily do that.

Other favourite outings of Randalph and his school mates were the daytrips by steamer from Ardrossan pier or Glasgow to the Isle of Arran on the wonderful old paddle steamer PS *Waverley*, or along the River Clyde estuary to Millport on Great Cumbrae, or around the Isle of Bute, stopping at Rothesay for a walk around and some tea and biscuits.

Sailing on the *Waverley* was like being in heaven for Randalph and his mates, who could never get enough of the thrill of being on deck on the open sea. Although it was still relatively new, having been built in 1946, even back then in the late 1960s, it was the last seagoing passenger-carrying paddle steamer in the world.

When Randalph later lived on the shores of Lake Geneva in Switzerland his love of old ships was generously rewarded by seeing most days on the lake one or more majestic, elegant, belle-époque paddle steamers belonging to the Compagnie Générale de Navigation sur le Lac Léman or 'Lake Geneva General Navigation Company (CGN)' sail past in style. He lost count of how many times he sailed the lake on them, for some years even walking very early in the morning to one of the neighbouring piers along the shore from where he lived to catch the first boat of the day back to the pier beside his apartment for morning coffee on board, before starting work.

As well as outings organised by Randalph's school, his father's employer, Massey Ferguson, who built tractors and combine harvesters at a big factory near Kilmarnock, also organised annual trips to a pantomime for the employees' kids, either in Glasgow or in Ayr. On those trips, Randalph would be between about eight and eleven years old. He was packed into a bus with sixty other kids from Kilmarnock and the villages around and entrusted into the good hands of the factory volunteers, who looked after them for the evening. His only vivid memory of those trips was sitting in the wings of the Gaiety Theatre in Ayr when he answered a question put by whoever was on stage and got into a tit-for-tat barter with him, with everyone around peeing themselves with laughter.

Jimmy had worked at Massey Ferguson since he was demobilised after WWII and five years in uniform during the 'occupation'. Until Randalph was about ten years old, Jimmy cycled to and from the factory, come rain, come shine, on his heavy old Raleigh pushbike. Wearing always the same tweed jacket, summer and winter, he would head off either in the early morning just before the boys had breakfast, in the afternoon when they were at school, or in the evening just after tea (dinner), depending on whether he was on day shift, back shift or night shift.

Randalph remembers the heavy atmosphere in the house when Jimmy was on night shift and he and his brother had to keep quiet during the day while he was sleeping. It was like being in a curfew. Randalph always had a lump in his throat and an uneasy feeling when his mother told him to go up and wake dad at around 6 pm. It was time for Jimmy to wake up and get ready for work. He never once jumped out of bed bright and sprightly looking forward to spending

Jimmy with Randalph and brother Jack on a family outing to the River Clyde coast.

the night at the factory. When he died of a heart attack at only 52, many said it was because of the changes in rhythm every two weeks between shifts. Whether it was or not no one could say with certitude, but what was sure was that these relentless changes also put a strain on Helma, who cursed the days when Jimmy pedalled off into the night.

AUNTS AND UNCLES

In the 1960s and early 1970s, kids referred to adults close to their family as their aunty or uncle. Randalph's immediate neighbours were his Aunt Helen and Uncle Stan, and in the next block his Aunty Jean and another Uncle Stan. The old lady in the gable end of the next block was his Nana McNaught. Across the road and further along their block, adults became Mr and Mrs such and such.

The many friends of the family were also all called aunts and uncles, as were Jimmy's seven brothers and six sisters. Randalph was amused many years later while working in India, Nepal and Bangladesh to observe that the habit of calling seniors aunty and uncle extended well beyond childhood into adulthood, with the appellation used for just about anyone older in their vast extended families.

Among all the many couples of aunts and uncles surrounding him, Randalph found two especially endearing. One couple was his Uncle Adamo and Aunt Jessica, the parents of Donald, his best friend since their infant years, who lived in their village. Adamo, a tall, square-built north Italian with massive hands, striking Roman features and a shock of thick wavy hair, had stayed in Scotland after the war and was married to Jessica, an outspoken Glasgow lass, akin to Shakespeare's Shrew.

Adamo drove a delivery truck for the local creamery, grew potatoes in his garden, and had a greenhouse full of tomatoes. Their home was Randalph's home, and the door was always open. On weekends and on long summer evenings, Randalph could turn up at any time of the day and just walk in, sit down in the living room on the couch in front of the open fire and enjoy the cosy warmth of being part of the family, or go straight up to Donald's room to play Monopoly. Over the years, the boys had played for hundreds of hours, perhaps thousands, lost in their world of property sales, keeping score of debts on games that would sometimes drag out for weeks. They were inseparable, as happy as Larry in each other's company.

Aunty Jessica never made a fuss about manners and house rules, and more often than not would fry up a pan of chips (fries) for the men and bring them to them in individual plates, to eat on their laps as they watched the wrestling or some comedy programme on the TV. Jessica's chips were exquisite, as she came from a family who owned a fish and chip shop somewhere in Glasgow's Shawlands district.

Frequently, after an afternoon or evening at Aunty Jessica's, Randalph got into trouble with his own mother, who always wanted to know where he was, what he had done, and who he was with. To spark off a battle of words with her all Randalph had to do was mention that he had been at Aunty Jessica's, whose chips were better than hers. If he then added that he liked life better at Jessica's than at home, his mother would wind herself up into a tantrum, take an aspirin bought as 'Askit' powder, go upstairs to her bedroom, then tell Jimmy when he came home from his work that the boys had been bad to her again. Poor Jimmy, torn between loyalties, would then lash out at Randalph and young Jack as soon as he had taken his jacket off, but would soon calm down and apologise. Domestic storms between father and sons never lasted more than a few minutes. Jimmy was not the type who beat up anyone who was weaker than himself.

The other couple were Randalph's Aunt Eileen and Uncle Ronnie. Eileen had befriended Helma when she first arrived in Scotland and was working as a cleaner in the local hospital. Eileen and Ronnie were cultivated, always abreast of what was happening in town, fervent followers of the local amateur opera and drama societies, choirs, and orchestras, and forever the most welcoming hosts. Randalph had spent countless evenings with them, always happy to be in their company, and always sad when the time came for them to leave or for Randalph to go home.

The two families would spend Christmas Eve together at one house, Christmas Day at the other, Boxing Day at someone else's, and the run up to New Year at yet another's, almost always together, forever happy to be in each other's company. Long after Randalph had left Scotland, the first thing he would do when he came back for a visit was to go and see them. Life was good when he was in their company. Years later, when his dear Uncle Ronnie died, and later his Aunty Eileen, it was as if his last safe space on planet

Earth had been violated, swept away, trampled under by the relentless injustice of death.

While the two loved the theatre, ballet and opera, it would be insulting to call them 'culture vultures', as their love of the stage and live performances came from deep within and was never used as a social lever to impress others.

Randalph, although rebellious in his teens when dragged along trailing his feet to watch amateur performances of *South Pacific*, *Fiddler on the Roof*, *Westside Story* and many

Randalph's 'Aunt' Eileen and 'Uncle' Ronnie with their two daughters back in the 1960s – the loveliest people in Randalph's younger years, and still today as he remembers them in his heart.

other musicals he had never heard of, and having to sit through symphonies by Sibelius, Mahler, Wagner, Grieg, Prokofiev and the more popular Beethoven and Mozart pieces, as well as having to endure ballets like *Swan Lake, Sleeping Beauty, The Nutcracker, Spartacus* and *Romeo and Juliet*, he realised later that without Eileen and Ronnie leading the way and hauling Randalph's family with them, he would never have discovered the world of classical live performance. Randalph's debt to those two lovely human beings was immense. To this day he misses them dearly.

FRESH EGGS FOR SALE

There are some things you do only once in a lifetime and the memory stays with you forever. The day that Randalph's family drove up to Tighnabruaich on the eastern shores of the Kyles of Bute to join Aunt Eileen and Uncle Ronnie and their younger daughter there for a cosy weekend in a rented cottage in the Highlands was one of them.

To get there, they had to drive north into Glasgow city centre, then west along Clydebank and through Old Kilpatrick to Dumbarton (this was before the Erskine Bridge was built over the River Clyde). From Dumbarton, they then headed north-west to Alexandria at the southern tip of Loch Lomond, following the loch to Tarbert and across to Arrochar, heading northwest over the 'Rest-and-be-thankful', the highest point on the A83 that divides Glen Kinglas from Glen Croe. The boys were excited. They were in Argyll, the land of legends – the ancient kingdom of Dal Riata, as 'Uncle' Ronnie had pointed out to them before he set off. This was Randalph's first glimpse of Scotland's famous highlands.

Later, on some rainy day when Randalph was browsing over bits and pieces of his country's history, he discovered that from the viewpoint of this famous beauty spot you can see the old valley road, engineered by General Wade during the subjection of Scotland following the Jacobite rebellion and completed in 1750. From there, heading due west until the road forked at Cairndow, the intrepid family drove south along the western shore of Loch Fyne to Strachur, then more or less south, all the way to Tighnabruaich, passing by Ardacheranmor, Ardacheranbeg, Ballochandrain and other places with exotic names the boys tried to pronounce as they drove past the signs at the entrances to these and other hamlets dotted along the roadside.

In those days, maps were fairly large sized sheets of paper that folded into smaller, portable-sized pamphlets. The great thing about paper maps was that you had an overview of the area you were in. They also had a social aspect, in the sense that they brought people together to focus on whatever it was they were looking for. Typically, they were laid out on car bonnets, where they became the focal point for the driver and whoever was with him or her to focus on the road ahead. One of the drawbacks was that you had to be able to read a map and, depending where you were, also be able to use a compass.

Jimmy and Helma were not big outdoors types and Helma was definitely not the world's best map reader. However, the two were very good at arguing with each other, and when the boys forced their way into their heated conversations, they were also particularly skilled at getting them to shut up and threatening them with what would happen if they didn't. This, thought Randalph, was really unfair, as he and his brother used to spend hours on end reading and deciphering maps, and knew their way around the contour lines and other useful geographical representations that maps were full of.

As they trundled along, the war, which had been looming for some time in the front seats of the car finally broke out between Helma, the map reader who insisted she was always right and knew what she was doing, and Jimmy, who cursed and swore ever louder whenever they approached a junction and needed directions in advance, not at the last minute. The Battle of the Maps reached its climax at the fork in the road at Cairndow. The two strategic advisors in the back seat, who had studied the route prior to departure and knew what they were talking about, held a diametrically opposed view from Helma about which way to turn. Their advice was to turn to the left, while she insisted on turning to the right. Their argument, added to the ongoing battle of words in the front seats, had all four in the car shouting at each other and getting more and more flustered until, with a squeaking of brakes and a salvo of swear words, Jimmy stopped the car and cried out 'give me the fuckin' map and all shut up'.

When Helma reluctantly handed the map to him, the truth was revealed. She was so good at reading maps that she had been looking at it upside down. The ensuing explosion when Jimmy blew his top probably scared away flocks of sheep for miles around with their shepherds running for cover, and could probably have been measured on the Richter scale. The fallout transformed the Maps War into a cold war that made the US-USSR standoff look like brotherly love. As often happens in war, the heroes in the back seat who knew the answer all along were never thanked.

Fortunately for the sheep, their shepherds and the puzzled technicians picking up seismic anomalies, the trip home was peace in its essence, with Jimmy diligently following Uncle Ronnie all the way back to Kilmarnock. No one was allowed to talk about maps. Overnight, the subject had become a family taboo.

Remembering the Tighnabruaich escapade jolted Randalph's memory of a particularly sombre period in the life of the family when Jimmy was trying to teach Helma how to drive. This reached its dramatic climax one day on the A77 main trunk road from Kilmarnock to Ayr, just before the gigantic roundabout at Monkton, near Prestwick Airport, where the road's various directional options were clearly indicated on a massive road sign, long before the roundabout.

Cruising down the trunk road at an embarrassingly slow speed with even three-wheeler Reliant Robins overtaking them, Helma drove on under the watchful eye of Jimmy, who was concentrating hard to make corrective remarks at almost every breath she took. Having passed the massive green road sign with still enough time to slow down, get into lane, select gear, and negotiate the roundabout without causing a major pileup, Jimmy slipped the innocent question to Helma about what the last road sign was. "Fresh eggs for sale" she replied, equally innocently. If the reader would like to use their imagination about how the rest of the day unfolded, try to picture three passengers in a family car trying to escape from a rabid bulldog in the driver's seat.

Later, when Jimmy had passed away and Helma still hadn't sat her driving test, Randalph inherited the responsibility of teaching her. By this time, PAG 333, the family's trusty old Wolseley 1500 who had survived three return trips to Germany, had long since been traded in for a Vauxhall Viva, which was not Randalph's idea of class. Sometimes, as he was driving around trying not to be recognised in it, Randalph wondered if Jimmy had bought it knowing that his son wouldn't want to be seen dead in it and therefore wouldn't use it. Whatever, this was neither here nor there as the task at hand might better be performed in the Viva, rather than put old PAG at risk.

With Randalph upgraded from eldest son to Helma's driving instructor, teaching her to drive was back on the family agenda. Someone once said of Randalph, "If patience was a disease, he would be the healthiest person alive". Patience was indeed not one of his many virtues, and what little he had of it was stretched to the limit when attempting to pass on his driving skills to Helma.

After two initial lessons on driving in the countryside, one evening in the summer, not so long after Jimmy's death, Randalph took Helma for a lesson to the quiet little village of Knockentiber on the road towards Crosshouse with the idea of teaching her how to drive in a built-up environment.

Having turned right into the village's small council housing estate, Randalph was coaching her through the approach to a left turn into one of the estate's streets, getting her to check her mirror, indicate, slow down, select second gear, slow down more, then begin a gentle turn into the street when Helma suddenly put her foot down on the accelerator instead of the brake, sending the car accelerating into the corner and heading straight for a car parked on the other side of the road.

As well as screaming at her to stop, Randalph grabbed the steering wheel in an attempt to avoid the parked car, turning their car towards the other side of the road, at which point Helma panicked, froze, and kept her foot on the accelerator propelling their car with increasing velocity straight into the metal pole of a street sign, which bent over as the little Viva stalled and stopped.

Randalph was so furious that he pulled the keys out of the ignition, got out the car, and threw them down the road with all his might and anger. In the way that disasters tend to have cumulative effects, the keys flew far to the side of the road landing somewhere in a garden. The scenario was worthy of a TV sketch: The car had a bent pole with a "Slow" sign on it protruding at around 45° from under the front bumper; Helma was accusing Randalph of having crashed the car, and Randalph, livid with rage, was looking among flower beds and bushes twenty yards away for the flying keys, which were never found.

Mother and son were truly fucked. The only way to get the car back on the road was for one of them to walk back to their home in Kilmaurs, pick up the spare key, and walk back with it to Knockintiber. It was obvious who was going to fetch it. "Wait here and don't move", screamed

Randalph at Helma as he stormed off homewards to collect the spare key.

An hour and a half later when Randalph appeared back on the scene, Helma was nowhere to be found. Even more furious now than when he had stormed off, Randalph climbed into the car, gingerly reversed, trying not to hear the scraping noise as the front bumper chose to stay with the pole rather than be part of a damaged car, parked the car along the kerb, and peeped the horn savagely until Helma appeared at the door of a nearby house followed by an elderly lady.

As it transpired, the elderly lady had heard the commotion on the street and invited Helma in for a cup of tea until Randalph got back, giving Helma ample time to complain to the old dear about how roughly her sons treated her and how difficult life was being their mother. Randalph, who would have laid the two ladies down on the street and driven over them, smiled at the old dear and told her that there were always two sides to every story, then bundled Helma into the car as if he was taking her hostage and drove off, making a point of speeding recklessly all the way home as he knew it frightened her.

Randalph hated these moments of mutual incomprehension when he seethed with anger at his mother, and she blamed him for all the wrongs of her life. Their hostilities continued to the end of her life, with only occasional ceasefires but never with any meaningful peace talks. Trying to find his own peace amongst all the fighting, Randalph grew to understand that wars only end when both sides stop shooting at each other. From that angle, he was as guilty as she was.

WHEN IN SCOTLAND, DO AS THE GERMANS DO

When Jimmy turned forty, he was given permission by his mother, Grandma Sarah, to buy his first car, a little green Austin A40 who's number plate was ESD 179. On weekends, Jimmy used to pile Helma and the boys into the tiny car and go on what he called 'mystery tours' through Ayrshire's rolling agricultural countryside. Inevitably, the tours ended with a portion of fish n' chips rolled up in newspaper that the family enjoyed inside the car behind steamed-up windows, looking out west at the Island of Arran, usually through driving rain, somewhere between Girvan and Troon on the Ayrshire coastline.

Helma – who had survived the total destruction of her hometown Cologne during WWII, where she later met and married Scottish soldier Jimmy during the occupation – loved that view. It reminded her of the Siebengebirge, the hilly region west of the River Rhine, and of the Drachenfels peak, which she told the boys on every tour looked like Goat Fell, the highest peak on Arran. When she died, Randalph and younger brother Jack had an image of Arran engraved in white on her slate-black gravestone, reminding them of the countless times they had watched the sun set together as a family over the island skyline.

Jimmy and Helma on their wedding day in 1948 in West Germany, where Jimmy spent five years in uniform during the occupation, on top of the previous four as a soldier in WWII.

Jimmy and Helma some years later, in the mid-1950s.

As well as her stories of the Rheinland, Helma endlessly repeated the story of how, in the early 1950s when she moved to Scotland with soldier Jimmy, they lived in a gas-lit front room rented out from old Mrs Armour on the main street in the village of Kilmaurs, where they shared an outside toilet with the Armour family and neighbours. Randalph understood how much of a shock this must have been for Helma after spending her early childhood in the then thriving modern cultural metropolis of Cologne, before it was obliterated by 262 air raids and the infamous 'Operation millennium' on the night of 30/31 May 1942, when one thousand bombers decimated the city dropping over 3,000 tonnes of bombs.

At the time of the raid, young Helma was only fourteen and living with her parents and her elder brother and sister in a cellar in the inner city. Her obligatory community service during the days following air raids was to gather and stack the dead bodies in her neighbourhood, which were then burned.

The rudimentary conditions Randalph's young parents lived in when they settled in Bonnie Scotland after the war was not young Helma's only shock. Being German was one thing – she was young, only nineteen, and pardonable on a personal level because the war had not been her fault. However, being Catholic was not easy in bible-thumping Protestant Ayrshire where the Presbyterians believed the Bible alone was enough to receive God's grace. The Catholics, like Helma, were brought up to believe that the Church was equally important to scripture.

To avoid theological disputes, where small differences

in belief can create the bloodiest of wars, Helma developed the habit of never speaking her mind. Religion, politics and anything that could be contrived to highlight any sort of cultural difference between her and the whole of the rest of Scotland were as taboo to her as talking about sex was to the churchgoers in the village's three protestant churches, each of which was founded on slightly different interpretations of belief.

To the annoyance of Randalph and brother Jack, Helma voiced no opinion of her own in company, invariably praising all things Scottish. At home, however, far from prying ears she was forever praising her homeland. Until her death, her pro-Scotland public attitude used to drive Randalph and brother Jack crazy. Try as hard as they might, they never got her to speak out about anything to the contrary to anyone, except to themselves. She was a German Catholic in protestant Scotland, where wartime sentiments and religious prejudice ran deep. "Shhh", she would say, "There's nothing to talk about".

The arguments between the boys and their mother were long and bitter, especially after Jimmy died, leaving Helma to cope with two rebellious angry boys who wanted nothing to do with her romantic daydreams of Rhineland Germany which, they accused her, was the reason why they had forever been picked on and bullied at school.

The boys were outsiders, sons of a German mother secretly proud of her homeland, so blinded by her obsession for all things German that she even sent them to primary school wearing traditional Bavarian 'Lederhosen'. What sort of a statement was that, thought Randalph years later after her death? What had life been like for this woman branded by language, culture, religion and nationality as an eternal outsider?

Despite being victims of the traumatising verbal abuse regularly hurled at the brothers at school – Randalph was jeered as Hitler while brother Jack was nick-named Goering – there were also many advantages to having a German mother. The lasting advantage, which influenced Randalph for the rest of his life, was her love and knowledge of gardening and growing fruit and vegetables. Whereas their neighbours – and indeed most of the people in the village and in the council housing estates in the other towns and villages nearby – had a front lawn, sometimes surrounded by roses, with an occasional bush of hydrangeas stuck in a corner, and a back lawn for hanging washing out to dry with possibly a patch of potatoes at the end of the 'garden', Helma had planted and cared for an oasis of vegetable life. She was Frau Greenfingers. Wherever there was space to plant a seed she grew raspberries, strawberries, gooseberries, redcurrants, blackcurrants, rhubarb, spinach, lettuce, radishes, peas, beans, beetroot, carrots, cabbage, turnips, and flowers big and small. She loved her garden, and so did her sons. It was their shared neutral territory, a place of truce for the boys in their endless war of freedom from their maternal influence.

When she was not in the garden or looking after the family, Helma also did her bit for the family budget by taking orders for the 'Empire Stores' catalogue sales, for which neighbours and friends would turn up and browse through the glossy catalogue pages, ordering new stuff for their household. Occasionally – though too often for Randalph's liking – she also held Tupperware parties, which were popular at the time and from which Randalph invariably did his utmost to escape.

The other advantage of having a German mother was the vast network of friends of the family who were either couples like the boys' parents composed of ex-servicemen who had married a German wife, or Austrians, Polish, and even German prisoners of war who had preferred to stay rather than go home after the armistice. The network also included sympathisers, who took Helma under their wing, protecting her from the brunt of rebuke and potential misunderstandings.

At the time, most of the family's friends worked in factories and did not yet have a phone. The pressure of life was much less than now, in 2024, with the result that people had much more time on their hands to socialise. On any day of the week or over the weekend there was a high likelihood that a couple or two from this merry band of foreigners brought together around their common difference – the German language – would turn up unannounced on Randalph's parents' doorstep, bringing with them cheer, songs, stories, jokes and the exotic taste of European life that Randalph learned to love. When Randalph and his family went on summer holidays to Germany, the same gang of family friends used to give him and brother Jack pocket money to enjoy themselves and have a good time. To Randalph, this was his extended family, a shield of supportive individuals who cared for him and accepted him as he was.

CHAPTER 3

Rheinland summers

Being surrounded by the many Europeans in Randalph's parents' social entourage had turned his romanticising imagination towards Europe at an early age. Since they were babies, every second year Helma would bundle up the boys and head off for long summer holidays at her mother's and sister's house near Bonn in Nordrhein Westfalen, which she never failed to remind them was the birthplace of Beethoven.

What she didn't tell them was that the city was the capital of West Germany from 1949 (to 1990), and it was in the city that the country's present constitution, the 'Basic Law', was declared in 1949. She probably neither knew nor cared – politics and things of state meant nothing to her. Besides, this would never come up as a conversational topic back in Scotland.

While she talked to the boys about the importance of having lived close to the birthplace of Beethoven, she repeatedly reminded her sister's family and friends in Germany that over in Scotland she lived near the birthplace of the great Rabbie Burns, whose poetry she neither understood nor could pronounce. It was as if she was trying to impress on everyone that she had left behind the pinnacle of culture in West Germany and found it again in Scotland.

Her mother, Randalph's 'Oma Schmitz', who died when he was a young teenager, made even greater claims, proclaiming that she was a direct descendant of the Hapsburgs. Was this what happened to you when so much of what you hold dear is destroyed in war, wondered Randalph, as he listened to the exaggerated stories of imagined past grandeur.

For Randalph and brother Jack, the summer trips to Germany were mythical. They loved the twenty-four-hour long train and boat adventure, which started on the night sleeper to London, then the boat train to Dover, the channel ferry to Ostend, the 'Wien Express' via Ghent and Brussels to Cologne, and on to Bonn where they changed to the local train for Hennef, getting off at Siegburg, where their German aunt and uncle, 'Tante Mariane' and 'Onkel Theo', were waiting for them with their bicycles, on the saddle of which they loaded the suitcases, making the last part of the journey by foot to their home. Tante Mariane, who, like her husband, never learned to drive, rode her bicycle daily until she was 94 years old, two years before dying peacefully in her bed in 2023.

Randalph's fondest memory of their summer escape route was in the summer of 1973 when he, then only 16, and brother Jack, 14, made the 24-hour journey alone, trusted by their parents to be able to cross London from Euston Station to Victoria Station on their own. Randalph laments the lack of trust today in families, where so many kids can't have a moment to themselves without one of the parents calling them to check on what they're doing. Back then, once you stepped out of the house you were gone, responsible for your own movements, free to do as much as your conscience or upbringing allowed.

Instead of taking the underground as they were instructed, the boys headed off on foot to see the sights they had heard of, passing Russell Square, Holborn, and down to the Thames by King's College, where they turned right, stopping for a look at the river from Waterloo Bridge. From there they followed the north embankment to Westminster, turning inland along St. James' Park to Buckingham Palace and finally on to Victoria Station. They had secretly planned the route for weeks on a fold-out map of central London found in one of the encyclopaedias that sat on a short bookshelf in their living room. On their way back, four or five weeks later, they shortened the walk, crossing St. James's Park Lake, taking in Trafalgar Square and bordering Soho – they just had to see it.

Once on the other side of the Channel, the boys marvelled at the spacious, modern European passenger train wagons with their individual compartments, clean toilets and long corridors where you could hang your head out of the windows for hours, smelling the heavy summer scent of ripening corn, revelling at the modernity of the cities, and feeling the warm Continental wind in your hair. Except for attending the funeral of their dear 'Uncle'

Ronnie four decades later, this was to be the only trip the brothers ever did together, as their paths later followed distinctly different directions, with Randalph travelling the world, leaving brother Jack behind with mother Helma. Remarkably, years later they both settled in Switzerland, Jack, the younger, marrying the elder of two sisters and living in the German-speaking east side of the country, and Randalph, the elder, marrying the younger sister and living in the French-speaking west.

By the time he had reached seventeen, Randalph had travelled to Germany by train and boat at least half a dozen times. Later, during his university years, he made a point of passing through the country, stopping at his aunt's and uncle's on the four consecutive summer trips he made travelling across Europe on the cheap one-month 'Interrail' travel tickets available at the time to young people under twenty-six years of age. Randalph loved travelling by train and boat anytime, anywhere. It was, is, and probably will always be his favourite means of transport.

As well as their epic train journeys to what was then still a far-off place, on three summers while the boys were still young, with Jimmy at the wheel, the family drove to Germany in PAG 333, their second-hand, burgundy-red, classic Wolseley 1500 which the family endearingly called 'Pag'. It had replaced their old Austin after a destructive encounter with a truck in the middle of the road as Jimmy drove through a bridge in their village too narrow for the little Austin and the oncoming truck to squeeze through together.

Randalph's family car, 'PAG', at home in Scotland in the 1960s, with Jimmy and Helma, and Randalph at the wheel for the photo

On all three road trips to Germany, Jimmy drove the family south through Dumfries, then on to Carlisle, crossing over the Pennines to reach the A1 and the road to Hull, where they boarded firstly the *Tor Anglia* night ferry to Amsterdam, then the *Tor Hollandia* on the next two trips to Rotterdam. The boys were ecstatic. They adored being on board the ships and ran amok on deck from one end of the vessel to the other to watch and comment on the docking manoeuvres in what were then Europe's largest and most modern ports.

Once on the Continent and driving on the right, Jimmy had the tendency to follow close behind the massive, shiny Mercedes, MAN or Daimler semi- and fully-articulated freight trucks with chromed hub caps that lined the slow lanes of the highways, telling the family the story that if anything happened they'd all be safe. The boys knew that the story was to hide Jimmy's embarrassment; he felt unsure of himself on the German highways, where fast cars would whizz by on the outside lane with their lights on and horns blaring, some at 200 km/h.

As much as the boys would have dearly wished he would drive faster, in hindsight Randalph remembers the delight of looking out at the rows of tall poplar trees, their elbows leaning on the car's open windows, and marvelling at the quality of the wide four- or six-lane highways. Everything seemed new to them, and indeed it was. From the embers of the war, Germany had rebuilt its infrastructure from scratch, not in the shabby British way they were accustomed to seeing, but with attention to detail and bristling with quality workmanship.

On the homeward trip, Randalph always felt depressed. He would look on with displeasure and revolt as the ferry docked in the dismal grey untidiness of Hull harbour, with its smoke-blackened buildings, lorries draped in oily anthracite tarpaulins and the occasional tea shop serving stodgy beans, eggs and sausages on not-quite-clean plates with chinks around the edges, to be enjoyed with cutlery that could benefit from a good wash, then washed down with over-brewed tea served in cups stained brown from decades of careless washing. He hated the whole scene. This was industrial England, a far cry from the colour, the international feeling and the exciting atmosphere of the cosmopolitan Dutch ports they had left behind the evening before, not to mention the modern lifestyle and go-get-it determination of the Germans as they reinvented their country.

To Randalph, post-war Germany was Eldorado. In the 1960s and through to the early 1970s, British sterling was a strong currency and the few pounds of pocket money given as spending money to him and brother Jack by their neighbours and parents' friends back in Scotland went a long way against the Deutschmark. Randalph felt rich in this country where everything seemed new, where buildings were being painted with bright colours, new roads built in all directions, and bus, tram and train networks being expanded and modernised.

Every summer spent there, Randalph was on the lookout for the latest transport upgrades, checking timetables for more frequent connections, boarding newer buses, enjoying rides in faster and more comfortable trains, and going on trips to Bonn in trams whose doors were closer to the ground and easier to board than on the last holiday, two years previously. Every second summer the urban skyscape had changed, new buildings had appeared and the roads to get to them had been rebuilt. How they did it he wondered even then, asking also why they didn't do the same back home in Britain, where nothing ever seemed to change.

Germany was rising fast from the ashes of the war. People were free of the oppression and terror of the Nazi regime and had a big appetite for celebrating life. To Randalph it seemed there was nothing to hold the country back. He loved the hard-working hands-on attitude of the people, where red tape didn't get in the way of earning a living, where you could have as many jobs as you had energy for.

Many adults had two jobs; one, their regular daytime job, the other 'Schwartzarbeit' – cash-in-hand jobs painting, decorating, renovating, caretaking or whatever. Life in Germany was buzzing. Randalph could even earn extra pocket money there helping his uncle in the evenings when he came home from work to mix cement, gather scrap metal, scrape paint off wooden planks or carry bricks up ladders for him at whichever renovation job he was working on.

Randalph also loved the good-hearted respect Germans had for the Scots. It looked like the kilted Highland regiments with their brave pipers out in front had won their hearts. Wherever he went, he was treated to jokes and songs about what hung low beneath the Scottish skirt. Later, in 1976, the German singer Nico Haak even scored a popular hit across the country with the satirical song *Unter dem Schottenrock ist gar nichts. Da ist nichts und da war nichts...* At any Wirtshaus where Randalph stopped in for a beer, as soon as the word got out that he was Scottish, someone would start singing this song and everyone would join in. Back home in Scotland, Randalph was just another kid. In Nordrhein Westfalen strangers bought him beers, cracked jokes with him and bade him welcome.

Much later, in June 2024 when Randalph just happened to be passing through Cologne at the time of the UEFA football bonanza hosted by Germany, he was overjoyed to see how the Scots were applauded by the Germans as being the best and the friendliest crowd of supporters in the whole tournament. An estimated 200,000 Scots – the "Tartan Army" – had invaded the country with high spirits, open hearts, smiles for everyone, hundreds of bagpipes, and a massive appreciation of German beer. Everywhere they went they made friends, bridging the gap that politics and diplomacy failed to cross, inspiring journalist Gabriel McKay from the *Glasgow Herald* to write: "Scottish fans have difficulties with travel home because a German fan is hanging on each leg".

In an article titled "Why do Germans love Scotland so much?", multimedia journalist Alisdair Ferguson writes of headlines across Germany piling on praise for the Tartan Army who brought a party atmosphere to a more than welcoming host nation. The article quotes lines from the Cologne-based daily paper Kölnische Rundschau saying "Dear Scots: We love you," and adding that even the police thanked fans for creating a "special atmosphere". Next time I go to Germany, thought Randalph, I'll wear a kilt – the ticket to meeting new friends who buy you beers.

By the time he had reached seventeen, Randalph had spent half of his summers in Germany, staying at his Aunt Marianne's und Uncle Theo's house with their children, his three elder cousins. The house was a traditional two-storey building erected between the two world wars at the end of a row of similar houses, with a third storey comprising two bedrooms and a bathroom in the spacious, typically steep-sloped attic where Randalph and brother Jack slept. Underground there was a cellar with a washroom, tool room, central heating, and a basement for the teenage cousins and their friends, with cushions round the walls, a fridge, a record player, a big tape recorder, guitars, posters of rock bands on the walls and a projector where they sometimes watched movies and early-day porno.

Summers there were carefree. As often as not, Randalph's parents and his uncle and aunt would meet old friends or relatives for coffee and cakes at some 'Eis Salon', where the brothers could eat as much cake and as many tarts as there were on display. To Randalph's disgust, on most occasions the price to pay for his sugary indulgence was a boring walk with his parents or, God forbid, with his 'Oma Schmitz' in some historical park or gardens surrounded by statues and buildings that Randalph cared nothing for.

As if on a pilgrimage, once during every summer holiday Jimmy, Helma and his aunt and uncle would take the brothers on a boat trip up and down the River Rhein, stopping at Königswinter, Bad Honnef and Remagen, where the parents had met during the occupation. It was a kind of remembrance expedition to honour the day, back in 1948, when they had got married there.

Jimmy, Grandma Sarah, Aunt Kathy, Helma, and German grandparents Oma and Opa Schmitz flying low over the River Rhein at Königswinter.

Helma and Jimmy both liked dancing. When the boat stopped in Königswinter they would get out, and to the total embarrassment of the brothers would perform an amateur tango in one of the riverside cafes – their favourite spot – where they were cheered on by the other guests. The brothers cringed every time the boat drew near, knowing that Helma would ask them too to get up and dance. Randalph thinks it was here that he developed a sixth sense, a sort of phobia, that steered him clear of being asked up to dance, knowing full well that he had neither the steps to shine on the dancefloor nor the stomach for leaving it with his tail between his legs. It took him until he turned forty to drop the inhibition and feel confident about asking a lass to take his hand for a spin.

The block of houses his aunt and uncle lived in stood at the beginning of a dead-end street running parallel with the 'Autobahn E5 Frankfurt-Köln', which lay at the top of a steep, 4-metre high, wooded embankment at the other side of the narrow lane that ran parallel to the highway at the end of their garden. The Germans called it "Der Rennbahn". Until the end of the 1960s, the already six-lane highway had minimum speed restrictions on the long uphill slopes. Frequently, you could hear the whir of helicopters as they blared out warnings through their Tannoy speakers at cars moving slower than permitted telling them to leave the fast lane, where the minimum speed was 120 km/h. On the road, the elite highway police drove loud, early-model Porsches that you could hear long before you could see them. Along with their cousin Peter, the two brothers loved leaning out over the windowsill of the attic bedroom to watch the traffic and compete with each other to spot the fastest car.

Randalph's cousin Peter and his teenage friends all had mopeds that Randalph and brother Jack could borrow to go for a run on. Peter's older friends had big motor bikes, like 1000cc Kawasakis and 900cc BMWs. There were no laws about speeding or wearing protective clothing. The only thing that seemed to matter to the Germans then was speed. When Randalph was fifteen, having never ridden a motorbike before, Helmut, one of Peter's older friends, invited him to take his R900 BMW for a ride. He showed him how to start it, how to change gears and how to brake.

Wearing only sand shoes (sneakers), shorts and a T-shirt, Randalph climbed onto the bike, had the engine switched on for him by Helmut, the bike owner, cautiously let out the clutch, drove the length of their street to the end, where he tiptoed his way through a U-turn, then drove back to the group of boys standing at the side of the road.

"Alles klar?" asked Helmut, to which Randalph replied "Ja sicher!" Then he drove off to the entrance to the street, turned left onto the busy Siegburg-Hennef main road and gingerly joined the traffic. He had no idea what he was doing. With one twist of the throttle, it seemed he had reached the next town, Hennef, in a single burst of dazzling acceleration. Once at the outskirts of the town, he did as Helmut had instructed, turning right at the lights, then circling left through the town centre back on to the main road.

Once on the main road, and now with all of fifteen minutes' experience under his belt and the open road ahead of him, Randalph yanked the throttle open. When he dared to take a glance at the speedometer, which was indicating 150 km/h, it felt like his skin was being torn off. It was the most exhilarating feeling he had ever had. At a set of traffic lights halfway between the two towns, an open-top sportscar drew up beside him with the driver looking at him. *Fuck you*, thought Randalph, and let go of the clutch, almost falling off the back of the bike. There was no way sportscar Fritz was going to survive this one – "Take this ya bastard!" he mumbled through tightly closed teeth. A block beyond the E5 flyover bridge where the road passed under, he slowed down to a snail's pace, letting flashy Fritz pass him and turned right, back into the family's street where he stopped the bike next to the guys. Randalph felt great, but was shaking like a leaf.

Any occasion was an excuse for the guys on the street to celebrate. When they did, one of them would be sent to get ice cream and Coca Cola, or large-size portions of 'pommes' (chips in Britain, French fries elsewhere in the world). The guys would then open fold-away chairs on the driveway of the construction company belonging to the neighbours on the opposite side of the street to cousin Peter's house, where they would gather round till sundown.

Randalph and brother Jack whiled away many a summer's evening there, feeling safe and protected by the big burly sons of the construction company owner, befriended to the other guys in the street, talking about machines, cars, horsepower and speed, and doing their best to translate into German the words of some ABBA songs that the construction guys particularly liked. For the rest of his life, every time Randalph heard *Fernando*, his memory found its way back to those carefree days in this little village of Buisdorf, his second home.

As well as high speeds on the road, until the end of the 1960s there was also high speed in the air. A few minutes flight by fighter jet from Buisdorf lay the Cologne-Wahn Airforce base. After the Second World War the field was used by the British Royal Air Force (RAF) under the name Wahn. At the end of the 1950s, the RAF left the field and the Cologne-Bonn international airport came into operation. In the 1960s the airport had a military part, which became the base of Germany's Federal Ministry of Defence Executive Transport Wing (Flügbereitschaft MBVg), which is also used today by the same Air Force and has since become one of the two garrisons of the German Air Force Headquarters.

The base was home to the infamous American Lockheed F-104 Starfighter jets, nicknamed by the Americans the 'Flying Coffin' and by the Germans 'der Witwenmacher' (the widowmaker). During the 1960s, Starfighters regularly flew low at supersonic speed over the densely populated, built-up industrial cities of Nordrhein Westfalen, frequently shattering glass windows and shaking objects off of shelves. Between 1961 and 1989, when the starfighters were grounded, the German Air Force had lost 292 of 916 aircraft, along with 116 of their pilots. The accident series peaked between February 1965 and July 1966, when on average an F-104 would crash once every two weeks. In this time frame, 46 Starfighters crashed, killing 29 pilots. Even today, this period is still infamously called Germany's

'Starfighter Krise' (Starfighter crisis). Everyone was talking about it.

The airfield was within cycling distance of Buisdorf and whenever he could, young Randalph borrowed his cousin's bicycle for the afternoon – or later his moped – and would cycle along the side of the main roads on the Fahrradwegen (cycle lanes), which ran parallel to most roads, and stand outside the airfield's fortified fence, marvelling at the rows of parked Starfighters and enjoying the deafening thud in his guts as they took off in a staggered line. Some days, as many as five would take off one close behind the other, turn while gaining speed and height, then fly back across the airfield in a V formation before disappearing with five consecutive bangs over the horizon as they broke through the sound barrier.

Back in Buisdorf, as soon as the brothers heard the loud, shattering bang as the jets accelerated into supersonic flight overhead, they would run up to their cousin Peter's bedroom to scan the sky to the north-west from the windowsill to try to spot one. On days when the sun was high and it was too hot for them to be outside, they spent entire afternoons in his room in the hope of seeing one on its landing approach, hearing another take off, seeing it fly close to the house or, better still, seeing it crash. They never got that thrill.

Back home in Scotland, the closest Randalph got to aviation thrills was Prestwick Airport, where Concorde was being tested and the occasional Boeing 707 would arrive from or take off for Canada. The Scottish Air Show was also held at Prestwick every two years, and Randalph remembers watching the English Electric Lightning duet acrobatic team there as they performed their death-defying, head-on-collision-course manoeuvre, when both planes flipped on their sides at the last second, only a few metres above the crowd and from each other. He also remembered seeing the last Vulcan bomber at the show in its farewell flypast low over the cheering spectators, making a noise louder than thunder.

In those days, when pilots broke the sound barrier low over crowded aerodromes as they performed their dangerous manoeuvres, today's crippling health-and-safety regulations would have been sneered at. Many of these pilots had probably flown operations during WWII in life-or-death situations. Men worked with their bare hands on construction sites. Ladders were fixed to walls only if absolutely necessary. If you fell into a hole, you would get your backside kicked by the gaffer (foreman). If someone dropped a brick on you it was your fault for being under the ladder. People were leaner, faster, and generally more physically able than they are today. They had to be – it was a question of survival.

As well as speed in the air and on the highways, in the summer of 1973, when Randalph – then 15 and his younger brother Jack, 13 – were driven to the Nürburgring to watch the German Grand Prix – more formally the XXXVIII Großer Preis von Deutschland – speed was also on the racecourse. To get to the event, the boys jumped into the back seat of the brand-new BMW 520/4 owned by the burly, black-bearded Hans-Peter, the elder brother from the construction company across the road from their aunt's house, while Hans-Peter's younger brother, Carl, drove an older but very classy BMW two-door 3.0 CSL with a raised wing over the boot making it look like something out of the old cartoon series Super Cars.

That day, along with the excited young boys from bonnie Scotland, the two cars were carrying a whole gang of motorsport enthusiasts from down their cousin's street who had bet ice cream, Coca Cola, Pommes (chips, or fries) and beer on how long it would take them to reach the racetrack, how fast the cars could go, and which car would get there first. Randalph would never forget that ride.

Occupying the fast lane for most of the 90 km of highway to the legendary Nürburgring the boys arrived in their 520 in less than three quarters of an hour, only five minutes after the powerful CSL. To the delight of the two young Ayrshire brothers, who'd never experienced anything like this, on one of the long downward sections their speedometer had peaked at 200 km/h (124 mph).

As it turned out, however, that day would not be remembered for German speed, but for Scottish speed. The gruelling 14-lap race was won from pole position by Jackie Stewart, the Scottish Formula 1 ace, driving a Tyrrell Ford, with teammate François Cevert, also in a Tyrrell Ford, finishing second, Jacky Ickx third in a McLaren Ford, and the five English drivers, Jackie Oliver, Graham Hill, Mike Hailwood, David Purley and Mike Beuttler, finishing in 8th, 13th, 14th, 15th, and 16th positions. Dad will love this, thought Randalph.

That day was Stewart's 27th and final Grand Prix victory – a record that would stand until 1987.

It recalled Jim Clark back in 1965. Stewart's then

world-famous fellow Scottish Formula 1 driver not only won the 15-lap Nürburgring race in his Lotus-Climax but also took pole position and registered the fastest lap of the race, leading every lap on the rain-drenched course, and achieving his 3rd Grand Slam of the season and the final one of his career.

All the way home after the race, the two brothers couldn't shut up about how great Scotland was. To them, Germany may well be the superpower, their summer-holiday Eldorado, the brave, new, shiny land of the future, but on that memorable day Scotland had won, and Scotland was the best.

The boys' jubilation would have been perfect if it hadn't been for the announcement by the Grand Prix commentators that the victor was "Der Engländer, Jackie Stewart". Once back home in Scotland, the boys related this moral injury to their parents' friends Adam and Bess Dick.

Adam McGregor Dick, who owned the Dick Brothers garage in Kilmarnock as well as the second-oldest Rolls-Royce in the world, claimed descendance from Scotland's royal past. Adam's car, which he polished and maintained to perfection and called the livery-green beauty his Old Girl, was one of six three-cylinder cars build in 1905 by Henry Royce as he was forging his partnership with CS Rolls. It was on display in recent years at the Riverside Museum on the shore of the River Clyde, near Partick in Glasgow.

When Adam heard the boys' tale he was furious and wrote a personal letter to Willy Brandt, the Chancellor of West Germany at the time. While Randalph was not yet of an age where he could understand the finer points of the letter, when Adam read it out to him it sounded like the speech of a king of old proclaiming his rights to conquered lands. A few weeks later, when Adam and Bess were visiting Randalph's parents, Adam read out the apology from the German chancellery. Randalph and brother Jack were speechless, as were Helma and Jimmy who, to remain true to his socialist identity, later nevertheless growled about politics and politicians in a less eloquent speech to the family about who was to blame for the deplorable state of the ordinary people of the world.

Uncle Adam and Auntie Bess, as the boys called them, were an old-school couple of Empire people, surrounded by trinkets and books recalling Britain's colonies and industrial achievements. They lived in an immaculately kept detached villa in Kilmarnock, with the living room to the right as you walked in and the drawing room to the left. In the corridor between the two rooms hung the wooden propellor of the Sopwith Camel, which Uncle Adam flew as a young pilot in WWI, with a clock embedded in its centre.

Randalph loved listening to Uncle Adam's stories about how he and Auntie Bess had toured continental Europe in the Old Girl between the wars, before the rise of Hitler. He and Bess took a delight in describing a second trip they did in the 1960s, also in the Old Girl, when they crossed from West Germany through East Germany at the time of the Cold War along the corridor linking West Germany to West Berlin, stopping halfway across for a picnic. In spite of their grandiose style, they remained simple people who preferred picnics to throwing money away at expensive restaurants just to be seen in public.

Uncle Adam had a soft spot for the Germans. He had befriended Helma, who worked for them as a cleaning lady when she first arrived in Scotland, and encouraged Randalph and his brother Jack to travel the world whenever they could, wherever their journey took them to. To wish them well on that Grand Prix summer of '73 he had given each boy as a gift a small notebook in a hard cover bound in the colours of MacGregor tartan.

On these summer holidays in Germany, as Randalph reached his mid-teens, his focus turned to Germany's open-air swimming pools, where the vast green lawns and common spaces around the typically Olympic-sized pools with their 10-metre-high diving boards were packed with cool teenagers, and especially with very cool blue-eyed, blonde, teenage German girls. Gone were the planes, the bikes, the cars, the machines and everything mechanical to make way for the smooth-skinned, lightly toasted, healthy, sporty, blue-eyed beauties of the Rhein. From then on, and for very many years to come, Randalph's obsession with the fair sex would lead him into the treacherous labyrinth and alleyways of emotional entanglement called love, which on so many occasions led him astray and plunged into despair. Far beyond the enthralment, the wonder, the joys, the fascination and the challenges of life itself, Randalph's focus was squarely set on chasing and catching the lassies. From then on, anything else tempting him in the supermarket of life was always on a lower shelf.

'Uncle' Adam and 'Aunt' Bess around the time they befriended Helma and took her under their protective wing.

CHAPTER 4

Bicycle Race

THE NEW EDDY MERCKX

About the same time that Jimmy was dragging him off on Saturday afternoons to football matches he didn't want to attend, Randalph had been putting together a bicycle with a frame, wheels and other bits and pieces found at the village dump (nowadays referred to as a landfill site). He had sandpapered the frame and painted it turquoise with a small tin of primer and paint begged from the hand of his dad.

Once his bike was ready for the road, Randalph discovered that he was just as fast on two wheels as he was when running for his life after playing some prank, and that he could keep up speed over a long distance. He and his classmate Cameron from the village, who was also fast on two wheels, had heard about a bicycle race taking place in next-door Kilmarnock and entered themselves as participants. The race took place in the town's Howard

Park near the river and lasted a dozen or so laps of the path around its perimeter.

Randalph had not the slightest idea about strategy, conserving energy, or positioning in corners. He just knew how to escape danger, and as soon as the starting pistol fired, he pedalled like a rabbit being chased by hounds. To his and everyone else's astonishment, he won the race, had his name engraved on the trophy as the 1972 regional champion, and found himself qualified for the Scottish Schoolboys category championships to be held later that year at Murrayfield in Edinburgh.

This was Randalph's only sports victory in his entire life. It was also the excuse he needed to never again go near a football pitch. From then on, he spent his weekends either maintaining and polishing his bike in the little wooden hut beside the family house or going on long bike rides with his new-found cycling friends through the rough Scottish Lowlands or hilly moors near the Clyde estuary, both of which routes were rich in steep inclines, bendy narrow roads and windy summits. On two wheels he felt free, and for the rest of his life he would always own a bike.

YOU DON'T MESS WITH JIMMY B.

When the day of the Scottish Schoolboys championships arrived, Randalph, along with his two new cycling mates, Alastair and his classmate Cameron, who had joined the local Wallacehill Cycling Club along with Randalph soon after his victory, set off for Edinburgh in trusty old Pag.

Luckily, the event was on a Sunday, meaning that Jimmy would not have to miss a football match.

Never having been to Murrayfield before, Jimmy turned onto a road that looked like it would lead to the stadium but that turned out to have a manned barrier at the end. This must be it, he said. As he approached the barrier, however, a guard stepped out in front of it, raised his hand, waved his finger at the car, and in an aloof, private-school, I-know-better English accent cried out "Stop. You're not allowed in here!" Jimmy stopped the car, mumbled something like "Let's see who stops who", stepped out of the car and walked straight towards the guard.

Randalph had caught Jimmy's eye and saw how his facial expression had turned black, like a starless night. He could see his chin sticking out like a bulldog's, with his bottom teeth visible as if he was preparing to rip his prey to pieces. Randalph knew the look all too well. It was the sign that hell was about to break loose. It scared Randalph when his dad got into a temper, and right now Jimmy was on fire.

In his army days, Jimmy had been a regiment boxer and harboured a deep loathing of superiority through rank. He rebelled so much against hierarchy that on one occasion it landed him in military prison. The two brothers revelled in the story told by him when one day on parade, a vicious, snooty, upper-class English officer – probably just like the one he was about to have a showdown with at the gate – was jeeringly provoking the soldiers to present their arms while he was standing so close in front of them that to present their rifles correctly would have resulted in them striking him in the face with the barrel.

Jimmy, unperturbed by the bastard, presented his arm correctly, knocking the officer to the ground with his rifle barrel and drawing blood from his face, an act for which he paid for with all of his front teeth, which were knocked out by the officer's cronies who beat the shit out of him, leaving Jimmy needing to wear false teeth for the rest of his life.

As Jimmy frequently pointed out to his two young sons when he got angry at injustice and let rip his rage: without their henchmen or an army to back them up, the inhumane, unjust, power-hungry, vicious bastards who will do anything they can to make the lives of others miserable are worth less than pieces of festering shit. Jimmy's oft-time repeated dream was to see the day when ordinary people would join together and stand up to them. On that day, he prophesied that they would simply disappear into the dust of history, leaving not even a memory behind.

As he approached the guard, Jimmy's gait quickened. As soon as he was within striking distance of the poor man, who was a whole head taller than him, bulldog Jimmy thrust his index and middle fingers forwards and upwards, bursting open the man's nose and propelling his head backwards with a bang as it crashed against the wooden side of the guard box.

The man reeled to the ground, obviously in agony, while Jimmy lectured him at the top of his voice on what happens to people who don't ask politely when they want something from him. Randalph was terrified that he'd start kicking him, but Jimmy left it at that. Visibly satisfied, he turned on his heels and headed back to the car, opened the door with a jerk and climbed in. All he said was, "He changed his mind".

Alastair and Cameron were cowering in the back of the car, speechless. The two boys later said they didn't know whether to laugh or jump out and run away. The barrier went up, and Jimmy and the boys drove through, only to end up at the wrong end of the stadium. The silence was broken by Jimmy, who was livid and growled at the boys to "Get these fuckin bikes off the roof", so that he could go for a pint.

Out of 36 riders, Randalph came in 36th, Alastair 7th and Cameron 16th. He really couldn't care less. For him, cycling wasn't about winning, it was about not going to football matches with his dad.

THE KNOCK

Randalph loved his bike. He looked after it as if it was the Crown Jewels, polishing the rims of the aluminium wheels with Duraglit wads after almost every trip. He went to school on it, raced the school bus back to the village on dry days, and got shouted at umpteen times by the bus driver, who told him not to follow so close behind the bus, warning him that if he had to brake suddenly Randalph would come flying through the back window and probably get himself killed.

Randalph didn't give a fuck. The trick was to cycle at only two or three inches distance from the back of the bus and get pulled along by the suction vortex in the space immediately behind it. Like that you could cycle effortlessly at 30 mph

(50 km/h) or more. One evening at the cycling club, the members there were talking in lowered voices about Ian, a stalwart member who, practising the same skill as Randalph on his way home from work, had indeed crashed through the back window of a bus when it did an emergency stop, and was killed instantly. To Randalph, Ian's death was just another of life's disasters. It had happened to Ian, not to him. Nothing was going to stop him from hugging the back of the school bus, or any other bus for that matter. Why pedal when you can get sucked along for free?

Ian had been one of the powerhouses of the club. Independent, determined, the silent type, and stocky, he was impossible to catch up with once he had gone off the front of the group on their long weekend rides. A few years older than Randalph and the other schoolboys, he also had more endurance as well as the tendency to lead the group further on their weekend runs than their immature energy or stamina would allow.

On one occasion, returning from the southern uplands having cycled some 100 miles (160 km) and with still 15 (24 km) to go, Randalph got what cyclists called the Knock – a painful, acute exhaustion resulting from sugar deprivation. You had to eat something sweet, and you had to eat it now. Randalph had stopped at the side of the road on the A77 between Ayr and Kilmarnock and was lying in the grass groaning. In his mind he was humming the club song "At the Nick he was found, lying dead on the ground, pushing a hundred-inch gear…".

The Nick was the Nick o' the Balloch, a cruel, steep climb on a bleak, windy, hill road somewhere in the vicinity of Beattock summit in the Scottish Lowlands. The 'hundred inches' was the distance the bike would travel with one full revolution of the pedals in top gear. Top gear – 10th gear at that time, when bikes had only two chainrings fixed to the crank set, and a cogwheel of five gears on the back wheel – would only be used for speeding downhill or on a straight road with the wind in your back. If you used it going uphill, the legend in the song predicted you would die.

A passing car spotted Randalph lying in the grass at the side of the road and stopped to ask if everything was ok. Randalph said he was starving and asked if they had anything to eat. The lady in the passenger seat asked if he would like a piece of cake, pointing to a box on the back seat of the car, which she opened and cut a slice off for hungry Randalph. It was one of those spongy strawberry-flavoured cakes with a layer of cream in the middle.

Randalph grabbed the slice, downed it in a oner, then lunged past her generous hand, seized the rest of the cake with both hands and stuffed it down his throat like a wild animal. The lady jumped back, as if scared that he would eat her too, and whimpered some inaudible comments to her husband. The couple looked as shocked as if a tiger had suddenly jumped out from between the trees and was devouring their dinner. Randalph swallowed down the entire cake in less than a minute, sat down satisfied, tried to explain himself, and said he was sorry. The good people reprimanded him on overstepping their generosity and drove off. Randalph rode home slowly, exhausted, but on a full stomach.

BOOKED FOR SPEEDING

As well as the pleasure of freedom and adventure, Randalph's bicycle tours were also an occasion for a laugh. On Wednesday evenings in summer, he and the rest of the cycle club would meet on a main road near the village of Mauchline for time trials. The trials were held on a 5-mile (8 km) section of more-or-less flat road and were usually won by cyclists like Ian, who sometimes clocked in at twenty-five minutes for the 10-mile (16 km) return trip.

For some older members of the club, the trials were followed by a stop on the road home for a pint of beer at a local pub, while the younger team members waited outside on a grass verge for their elders to come steaming out after having their beers. Just like the younger guys, the older ones also had mischief in their veins, especially when they had downed enough beers to throw care to the wind. Their favourite game was to form a single-file line of bikers on the downhill slope before the next town where police often set up speed cameras. The game consisted of building up speed with a team-racing technique, where the back rider would pedal dementedly to pass the team and get to the front where he would set the pace for some minutes before the next one came from the back and passed him. Their aim was to try to get booked by police for speeding. Being caught for speeding was an ever-sought-after prize in the minds of the club members, like being photographed catching a huge salmon or a shark is in the minds of fishermen. To get a speeding fine on a bicycle was the club's highest recognised accomplishment and would be celebrated for months to come. It was something you could stitch onto your racing shirt or shorts. Few succeeded, but those who did were revered like Gods.

CLOCKWORK ORANGE

As well as collecting fines and trophies, speeding had other, albeit less noble purposes – it was the only way to escape after the club's hit squad attacks on innocent members of the public. Looking back, Randalph was shy to admit that he actually did this, but very grateful that he was never caught at it.

Hit squad attacks happened very occasionally on the road home after the club's weekly time trial. The hits involved getting close enough to unsuspecting citizens standing in bus queues by the side of the road to be able to squirt sticky orange-juice all over them at close range, and then escaping. The attacks were as minutely planned as low-level wartime bombing raids behind enemy lines. To achieve an effective strike, each member of the squad would need to get within arms' reach of the innocent citizens standing in the queues, which were often twenty or more people long and aligned along the pavement – the perfect target, but not without its dangers.

The hit squad would be anything between four and seven bicycles in strength. The danger was that while the lead bike would create the surprise, by the time the rear bikes had passed, the people standing in the queues could react. Middle-aged or elderly ladies in bus queues usually carried umbrellas and could hit out. Burly working men who had drunk a few beers after work could launch themselves at the bikes and knock them over. If there were any thugs in the queue, they could lunge at the bikers with a knife, a razor or a bottle. The cyclists had to pedal at sprint speed.

When a bus queue had been spotted, the lead cyclist would start chanting the melody of Wagner's Ride of the Valkyries, later used in the movie Apocalypse Now, inciting the squad to speed up. At a distance of about 50 yards (45 metres), he would shout out 'Gear!' – the command to drop into 10th gear. A moment later he would scream 'Bottles!' – the order to get the attack bottles of sugary, sticky orange poised and ready, followed by 'Get the bastards!' The bomb doors were open. The blitz was coming. There was no turning back. This was not the moment to get a puncture.

If Einstein had been in the queue, he could have built his theory of relativity around the fading sounds of screaming and shouting heard by the cyclists as they shot by. Whoever was in the lead would hear the pitch of the shouting dropping a semitone as he fled to save his skin. Whoever was at the rear would hear the sounds a semitone higher as he sped towards the queue.

Imagine the scenario. The first person standing in the queue is going to be drenched by between four and seven full-pressure squirts of orange juice. As the squad passes, the pressure in the plastic bottles reduces, meaning that the last person in the queue might escape with only a few drops of juice landing on them. The danger was that the last people in the queue might also be the first to understand what was happening and react, which was why the squad had a tendency of distancing itself from the kerb where the queue stood after passing the first two or three people then splayed out from the pavement into the middle of the road, out of potential harm's way.

As the squad flew past, the orange-juice bombers were showered in insults, death threats and other prophecies about what would happen to them if they were caught. The race to safety was then on. Nobody in the squad had either the slightest desire to get caught nor the stupidity to look behind. If you were recognised, somebody, someday would catch you and probably put you in the emergency unit of the local hospital, or even kill you. There was a limit to how much you could get away with in Scotland inside your own community. Attacking another community like this was paramount to declaring war.

GET BACK ON YOUR BIKE

Every now and again, the club would organise a 25-mile (40 km) time trial or participate in this longer event at other clubs. At one such event, a club from a neighbouring district had organised a trial on a section of road parallel to a railway line. Randalph's club had entered as a team. As the club's performance would be measured by the average time of the members, everyone carried on their shoulders the responsibility of the team's success or failure.

The riders set off at one-minute intervals. It had been raining and the road surface was wet and slippery. At one point on the road there was a tight bend to the right, and at the precise moment when Randalph entered the bend, an articulated truck with an empty trailer overtook him. With no load on the trailer to ensure adherence to the road, the back end of the trailer slid outwards, hit Randalph, and sent him flying down the grassy railway embankment. Luckily, he was only grazed, with some minor injuries, and his bike was still rideable.

Once he had pulled himself together and scrambled up the embankment, he climbed back on his bike, but he no longer had the heart to continue the trial and headed back to the start. Objectively, Randalph was in no shape to finish the race. In some countries, people would have had pity on him, and someone would probably have attended to his wounds and comforted him. But this was Scotland, and the club's trainer, mad to see his team go down, pushed Randalph in the chest and shrieked his rage at him. Randalph remembered him shouting that as long as anyone was alive and still had two legs, he should get back on his bike.

CHAPTER 5

As thick as thieves

LEAVE THOSE KIDS ALONE

Randalph doesn't remember much about school, possibly because he prefers to forget it. It wasn't the subjects or the learning he didn't like, it was the bullying. Already in primary school he suffered from it, often dreading the walk home at the end of the afternoon when he might be picked on and beaten up or be threatened if he didn't give the solutions to homework to so and so. Randalph wasn't what he would call bright, but learning came easy to him and getting full or almost full marks for whatever subject he studied was usual for him.

To his credit, in June 1969, at the end of his last year at primary school, he was awarded a Certificate of Merit for Excellence in Scottish Literature by a body called the Burns Federation for being able to recite the whole of Robert Burns' epic poem *Tam o' Shanter* off by heart and explain to the class what the story was about. After his rendering he was then set upon by some of the lads from school on the road home for being a smart arse. The brawl almost ended in murder when Randalph picked up a brick and smashed it on the forehead of one of the guys, before two others dragged the enraged Randalph off his bleeding victim, who had folded like a pack of cards and lay groaning and bleeding profusely on the ground. Randalph had snapped out of his usual fears and was consumed by the sole desire to kill. He snapped like this only a few times in his life, but when he did so much bottled-up anger poured out that he would kill if not stopped by whoever was around.

Later, in secondary school, the bullying got worse. The schoolmates who pestered Randalph in the village had limits to how far they would go. They lived in the same community as him and had parents who knew each other. Enough would be enough. In the neighbouring town, Kilmarnock, however, where The Academy – the secondary school that Randalph attended – was located, some of Randalph's new classmates came from notorious neighbourhoods where violence was rife.

Until the year that Randalph went to secondary school, the three or four pupils with the highest grades in the class in his village's primary school went to the Academy, where they would be propelled towards a university career. The rest went to other schools, then later either went into vocational training or got a job when they turned sixteen.

Randalph bitterly regretted not being a year older and going forward in the old selective system. To him it made so much more sense. The new system, called comprehensive education, was based on the theory that kids of different intellectual abilities would learn from each other. In Randalph's experience and from his perspective, whoever invented it had never been in the real world and knew nothing about the rules for survival in the human jungle, where the ignorance of the masses invariably holds back the few who would naturally stand out from them.

In spite of the violence, the bullying, and the debilitating feeling of fear he felt in the pit of his stomach on so many Sunday evenings when someone or other had threatened him on the Friday before the weekend to kick his teeth in the next week or chib (stab) him with a knife, Randalph survived and learned some skills at school that he could later actually use in life. One of these was mathematics, which he was taught during his last two years (called 5th and 6th year in Scotland) from a brilliant teacher – a little man with a lame arm that he carried in a sling. He had the gift of being able to control a class of rowdy teenagers and teach them the mysteries of calculus, which he called 'the study of change', geometry, which was all about shapes, algebra, which was about operations and solving equations, and trigonometry, which was all about angles. So easy when explained so simply.

Other teachers who succeeded in sparking Randalph's interest taught him physics, engineering science, and English. The fact that he is now writing this book Randalph puts down to having spent two years in the English class of Mr. Walker, or Ronnie, as some of the students were allowed to call him during the last days of school. Ronnie was quiet, patient and softly spoken, which were rare qualities among the teaching staff, many of whom were short tempered, loud, and also had a streak of violence in them.

Teacher Ronnie was a lover of literature, not in the sense of spewing out lists of references and names of authors, but in his ability to teach how to read between the lines, where he could share his love of the written word. Randalph loved his class more than any other – it was there that he learned to read Shakespeare, Burns, Wordsworth and Milton, and how to construct, dissect, comment on and punctuate a sentence. Decades later, Randalph was able to use Ronnie's teachings during the years when he earned his living translating and editing, and later when coaching managers and executives in international organisations how to communicate effectively in writing.

When Randalph later read about human psychology and what makes individuals and society tick, he understood that the comprehensive education system would be possible only in an idealised nice-to-have world where people are taught from an early age to care for and respect each other. This, sadly, was not, is not, and never will be the world we live in, he observed on so many occasions, as long as those in charge do not want those below them to be educated in the mechanisms of mutual respect and raised with care and kindness.

Much as he was an idealist, and strongly believed in the possibility of a better world for all, throughout his life Randalph steered clear of theory and of the people who lived their lives by it or tried to shove it down the throats of others. He had no time for their bla bla, which to him was just one lengthy mind-fuck behind which they hid from the stark realities and truths of life on Earth. To Randalph, the religions, belief systems, philosophies and politics that their sponsors spouted forth would only be of benefit to society if they taught the way to peaceful co-existence during our brief lives on this extraordinary planet, which history has shown is sadly far from the daily realities of most of us.

INFERIORITY COMPLEX

He attended the once great Kilmarnock Academy, where Nobel prize laureates Alexander Fleming, the discoverer of penicillin, and John Boyd Orr from Randalph's village Kilmaurs, the first Director-General of the United Nations Food and Agricultural Organization (FAO) had been educated. There he befriended the highly eccentric Bascom, an extraordinarily intelligent social misfit who would stop at nothing for a laugh at the expense of everyone in his path.

Bascom and Randalph met in the sixth-year German studies class. While Randalph only understood anything after long nights of study, Bascom was a natural, with the gift of instant comprehension of the complexities of Teutonic grammar, which he ably used to trip up the teacher – a nasty, crooked, vindictive piece of work carved out of posh English society with an aloof tone to her voice that spoke down at all around, but not to Bascom, who she wasn't able to belittle with her sneering attitude. Instead, it was Bascom who quickly got the better of their arguments, proving that his understanding of the use of the dative or accusative, or whichever case they argued about, was actually the correct one. If you wanted to feel stupid, you picked an argument with Bascom. No one was immune to his lively wit, ridicule, probing intelligence and subtle scorn.

Bascom and Randalph struck it off immediately. Randalph was in the presence of the genius he so lacked in his very ordinary working-class surroundings, while Bascom had found an accomplice in crime – the perfect match. For the rest of that last school year, Bascom pulled off prank after prank, ever more daringly, ever more wittily. There were days when the boys thought they would die laughing.

Bascom had been brought up in a family where the father was an accomplished mathematician and countless winner of highbrow crossword competitions. On the few occasions that Randalph had sat with him at his home listening to his theorems and insights, he gathered that his father had perhaps invented or discovered secret things during the war, or at least contributed to solving complex mysteries.

Bascom had had the advantage of growing up in a stimulating environment where the stick used to thrash out disobedience or rebellious tendencies was the stick of reason, used with wit, intelligence and cunning. Bascom's elder brother Edgar was of similar ilk and had already made a name for himself in the upper echelons of academia.

After The Academy, Randalph went to university in Glasgow and Bascom to Edinburgh. At a lecture at Edinburgh University, where Randalph had joined him 'for a laugh', the visiting professor was addressing the audience on the subject of inferiority complexes. Randalph, who knew nothing about inferiority complexes or any other complexes for that matter, marvelled at how many heads were nodding, looking intelligent, and pretending to understand.

At the end of the lecture, after the applause had waned and the audience had stopped looking right and left with congratulatory expressions on their faces in mutual recognition of their superior intelligence at being there, the professor invited questions. Instantly, Bascom shot up his hand and stood tall. With his head inclined slightly backwards and a wry look in his eye, he thanked the professor for the privilege of listening to him. The Professor's speech, explained Bascom, had answered a question that had been at the back of his mind for as long as he could remember. "You see," said Bascom, "My problem has always been my inferiority complex – every day I'm confronted with it." Leaning back as if to inhale the entire room he then yelled out, arms waving in the air as if demented: "Everyone is inferior to me: you, you, you and you!" as he pointed randomly to members of the audience. "You are inferior to me now in this life, in your past lives, and in the future, to the very ends of time.". He then blurted out a whole passage of Shakespeare he had been rehearsing to prove the point.

Bascom then motioned to Randalph, commanding him in his over-confident voice using a thick French accent: "Slave, saddle my stallion. We are leaving these people of inferior brain size for greener pastures. There is naught in this room but stupid word maggots and kniggits." And out they trotted, like in the scene in Monty Python's Holy Grail where King Arthur and his band of followers are banging coconut shells together to imitate the clatter of horses' hooves.

As usual, whenever Bascom had played a prank, it took the two boys the rest of the day to return to normal from their riotous laughing, although 'normal' in the case of Bascom was always a transitory state in which anything silly could suddenly happen anywhere, at any time, to anyone.

STREET ARTIST

Like an hour after the inferiority lecture, as the two were walking down Princess Street. Bascom was permanently wound up like a tin soldier that would march off, arms flailing in all directions, as soon as you let go of the key. On Princess Street he suddenly stopped, told Randalph to watch, and flung himself to the ground, feinting agony and frothing at the mouth in an exaggerated imitation of an epileptic fit. "I'm dying" he cried out "I need a vet! Help me! Help me!" Passers-by on the pavement looked worriedly at each other. Someone asked if there was a doctor in the crowd. Someone else actually asked if there was a vet. Bascom twisted and turned himself like a corkscrew, howling ever louder, pleading with the crowd. Then, as if injected by some magical recovery serum, he sprang to his feet, stretched out his hand for coins as if he were a street performer, bowed, thanked everyone, and proudly strutted off his head held high.

TIED UP

The next day in the afternoon, and still in Edinburgh, the boys spotted a working man's club with a flashing sign over the door saying 'STRIPTEASE'. They looked at each other, nodded, paid the entrance fee and slithered quietly into the seedy environment of grubby working men in the half shadows and dimly lit velvety decor of the sleazy club drooling over enticing slender beauties peeling off their clothes on a low stage, just out of reach of their greedy hands.

One of the girls, having finished her routine, with nothing more left to cover her but a pair of frilly knickers and a garter belt, motioned to the audience, beckoning them with her index finger, and asking in an over-dramatized hoarse voice if anyone would like to tie her up. Then from a prop box on the edge of the stage she produced a long thin velvet-coloured rope of intertwined silk strands with red ribbons tied at each end and, holding it horizontally in front of her to half hide her breasts, shuffled across the stage, keeping eye contact with as many of the men as she could.

Bascom stood up briskly as if he had been called to attention and sauntered towards the stage, trying to look like the average working man. He said to the almost naked demoiselle, "It would be my pleasure madame. Where would you like me to begin?"

In between pranks, school obligations, quizzing each other about music, and occasionally helping out at home, Randalph and Bascom spent hours practicing tying knots. They had mastered those that could easily be undone, and a few others that would survive a hurricane. It was obvious to Randalph that Bascom was going to tie the poor demoiselle up with the latter, which at home, Bascom was proud to demonstrate he could even tie behind his back.

Without waiting for her reply, Bascom climbed onto

the stage, delicately removed the rope from the lady's grip and proceeded to tie her wrists together. Then, with the remainder of the rope, he tied her ankles together, leaving her on the floor in a foetus posture facing the crowd. Turning to the audience, he bowed. There was some half-hearted applause, and he stepped back down from the stage and came back to his seat next to Randalph.

A gentleman looking like a circus performer appeared from behind heavy crimson curtains on the wings of the stage, thanked 'the young gentleman' for his naughty prowess (nobody noticed the pun), and asked if there was a volunteer to untie this poor damsel in distress and set her free. Bascom, grabbing Randalph by the wrist, shot his arm upwards and cried out in a guttural voice imitating the thick local accent and echoing the gentleman's pun: "Here's your volunteer – there's not a knot in the world this naughty boy can't undo". Nobody in the audience showed any appreciation of Bascom's pun either. Perhaps they actually didn't get it, thought Randalph.

"Bastard," said Randalph, as he in turn sauntered forward. He was feeling awkward and self-conscious, caught up between the pending shame if he couldn't untie Bascom's knots and the urge to be all over the lovely wench, but not in full view of this audience. Randalph was also feeling sorry for the lady and felt a loathing for this kind of scene where women are treated like pieces of meat by a room full of uncouth roughly cut men, who would probably brutalise her if they ever got their calloused hands on her. Or perhaps they wouldn't, he thought. Perhaps deep down these rough men who earn their living in the tough working conditions of industrial Scotland would prefer to treat her nicely and look after her rather than consume her. Randalph, the eternal idealist, hoped he was right.

Bascom had tied the knots tightly, so tightly that it was hurting the lady. To the amusement of the audience, try as he might, Randalph was struggling to release the lashings under which Bascom had tucked the loose end of the rope. He was sweating, uncomfortable, embarrassed, and feeling exposed and lonely under the spotlights playing on the stage, until at last, he had wiggled the rope end free.

By the time he had undone the knots, Randalph was oblivious to the appetising flesh only inches from his hands and was trying desperately to show empathy to the lady, to let her know that he was one of the good guys, the one who came to rescue her to set her free. Bascom, meanwhile, was revelling in Randalph's discomfort and yelled out, "Three cheers to the naughty boy!" He clapped his hands, tears pouring down his cheeks.

LA CABINA

Cruising one evening along the poorly lit roads of a village nearby their homes, looking for victims to play a prank on, Bascom spotted a lady in a telephone booth. The back of the standard British Royal Mail red booth, which was solid with no windows, was facing the road. The door of the booth opened onto the pavement.

Inspired by the scary 1972 Spanish movie La Cabina, which the boys had watched days earlier (a movie in which a man gets trapped inside a telephone booth which is hoisted onto a truck by men from the telephone company then driven off to a compound, where booths are stocked in rows, and the oldest rows have skeletons inside), Bascom turned his mother's little Renault, with its iconic gear changer sticking out of the dashboard like an umbrella handle, and parked opposite the booth, on the other side of the road, so that the lady inside it couldn't see them.

Bascom then reached onto the back seat of the car and produced a WWII gas mask, a dark green workers' trench coat and a pair of long brown leather motorbike gloves that he had taken along, just in case. Out of sight of the lady in the booth, he slipped the coat on from back to front, pulled the mask over his head, and slid his hands into the big gloves. Sneaking stealthily towards the booth he then put his arms round it as far as he could and slowly passed his gloved hand over the pane of glass against which the lady was leaning her head.

The woman screamed hysterically. Bascom quickly moved round to block the door before she could get out and slammed his other hand in a stop sign against it. The lady screamed again. She was terrified, and so was Randalph, who, deep down, knew they shouldn't be doing this sort of thing to innocent members of the public.

Her ordeal lasted two long minutes. This was all the boys could hold out for without falling to pieces with laughter. Bascom shrieked like a hyena, springing backwards over to the car, and screamed at Randalph to jump in. For days to come, Randalph had misgivings about the poor girl who, he imagined, had been traumatised for life and was now receiving treatment from a shrink.

KINGS OF THE ROAD

As well as delighting in their pranks and laughter, Bascom and Randalph shared a passion for advanced driving. Bascom had a friend called Callum who was a farmer, well connected with the state Traffic Police, who taught the boys the driving skill package that the police had developed in the early 1970s to chase and catch dangerous criminals, like bank Robbers or hit-and-run gangs, without crashing their patrol cars or losing officers. The skills training had been made available to the public through an association called the Institute of Advanced Motorists – the IAM for short.

The boys learned blind cornering techniques, cornering on two wheels, critical forward traffic awareness perception, braking in slippery conditions and clutchless gear changing, passing through narrow restrictions at very high speeds, and commenting in a precisely protocolled manner everything they saw on and deduced from the road ahead. They timed themselves on stretches of farm roads, main roads, through built-up areas, increasing their average speed each time, but always within the very strictly observed speed limits of the law.

Their car became an extension of their bodies and their minds. They delighted in leaving behind flashy Jaguars or other powerful cars of the time and disappearing over the horizon ahead of them in their little Renault. For a whole year they practised and trained, many times on 800-mile (1300 km) weekend return-trips to London, leaving Saturday mornings, back on Sunday evenings, when Randalph would say to his parents he was staying at Bascom's for the weekend and Bascom would say to his that he was staying at Randalph's.

For the entire route, they practised their techniques, trying out manoeuvres, checking on each other's slightest move, interrogating and demanding each other explanations for this or that. The more they trained, with or without their police tutors, the more they became part of their four wheels. Their training entitled them to massive reductions in insurance. They were known to the police as members of the Institute of Advanced Motorists, so their version of any incident that might happen along the road would be treated as priority evidence. For both boys, the training they received would set them up for the road through life ahead and did, on various occasions, save Randalph's life.

In the meantime, there was still fun to be had. Although always vigilant and in advanced driving mode, ordinary life frequently presented enticing distractions for the duo. Among the tricks they had mastered was the one where Bascom would hang out of the driving seat window with both arms flailing in the air or banging on the roof, while Randalph was down on the floor, holding the wheel with one hand and applying light pressure to the accelerator pedal with the other. The number of bangs on the roof was a code for how much to turn the wheel. Bascom's voice indicated whether to accelerate or slow down.

Their showpiece was to drive like this round gentle left-hand bends in built-up areas, with Bascom screaming a piece of nonsense at the crowd and the crowd jumping back, also screaming, or insulting them with "Ya fuckin heidcases" or "Ya mental bastards".

The prank successfully executed, the duo had to get to safety somewhere nearby where they could stop and get out before their view become totally obliterated by tears of laughter. For many years, Randalph looked back with fond memories of the painful guts they had from too much laughing. How nice is life, he reflected, when the only aches and pains you have come from laughter.

BURNING DOG

Driving home one night, Bascom spotted an elderly lady wearing a full-length transparent plastic raincoat, holding an umbrella up against the driving rain, and trailing behind her a wretched terrier. He yanked the window down, gave Randalph control of the steering wheel and, extending his full torso out of the window, screamed at her "Your dog's on fire, missus! Your dog's on fire!"

Startled, and without giving it a second thought, the dear old lady rolled in her umbrella and started hitting the dog. It was hilarious. One of the funniest scenarios the boys had ever produced, and even if it lasted only the few seconds it took for the old dear to realise her little doggie was not on fire and begin shouting abuse at them, it had been worth it – a stroke of genius. Bascom would be remembered for this one in the big book in the sky of harmless practical jokes.

STATISTICS

As skills sharpen with practice, and experience comes with repetition, so Bascom's masterpieces of mirth at the expense of others were yet to mature. One of them – Randalph's favourite – was the sales inspector sketch where the boys would dress up in white shirts, ties and dark trousers, with Randalph carrying a clipboard, and stroll authoritatively into an unsuspecting sweet shop on some village high street.

After introducing themselves to what was usually a middle-aged or elderly lady shopkeeper from the village they were in, Bascom would explain that his colleague and himself were there that day in the role of external auditors to check on a product called Chocolate Buttons. Their check involved making sure that the stated amount of Chocolate Buttons was indeed available in each packet of Chocolate Buttons sold by the shopkeeper.

At this point, the poor old dears were already lost in Bascom's technical vocabulary. In a totally flat and neutral authoritative tone he would then ask the shopkeeper to randomly place half a dozen of the little blue-and-yellow packets of Buttons on the counter. Ceremoniously and with great attention to detail, Randalph would then open each packet, empty the contents onto the counter, count the number of individual Buttons and note down the number on the clipboard.

As the packets had been filled and sealed in a high-tech industrial environment and the numbers were identical, the trick was to push one or two Buttons from one pile to the other without the shopkeeper noticing. Bascom ably provided the necessary distraction for Randalph to deftly move the Buttons around. Looking concernedly at the results, Randalph would then invite Bascom to have a look at the numbers on the clipboard. There followed that delicious moment of silence wherein Bascom prepared his verdict and his painstakingly practised speech of condemnation.

"Madame", he would say with his head held high, his chin protruding, and looking down at the poor lady who was invariably one and a half heads shorter than Bascom as if to scold her with his glance, "It is with great regret that we have to inform you that your sale of Chocolate Buttons does not comply with the rules, regulations and requirements of our esteemed client's chocolate manufactory. Unwittingly, or on purpose, you would have sold these six packets of buttons containing 49, 53, 47, 51, 48 and 52 buttons, when they should each have contained precisely 50. We are sure you understand that this is tantamount to fraud and punishable by the law. We therefore regret to inform you that we have no other choice than to notify our client, who will send round the company inspectorate in the days ahead. Unless you have any questions to put to us, we will take our leave. We are very sorry to have bothered you and wish you good luck in explaining yourself to the gentlemen of the inspectorate."

Randalph's heart often cried out for these poor old souls who in no way suspected the mischief of the two boys and were blind to the depth of sham they had been dragged through. The remorse would maybe come later, but right then the next move was to get out of the shop before exploding with laughter. A prank like this one would take

Randalph and Bascom most of the rest of the day to recover from before they could see clearly enough through their tear-drenched eyes and calm their aching guts down to a point where they would again be able to drive. Moments like these were priceless, precious gems in the boys' gleaming treasure chest of silliness, gifts from the fertile mind of the illustrious Bascom to add colour to the hilarious memories of school year 74/75.

SCIENCE FICTION

Science fiction fuelled Randalph's and Bascom's imagination and was their inspiration for hours of discussion and daydreaming. They revelled in John Wyndham's triffids and the terrifying kraken. They journeyed with Arthur C. Clarke to *The Sands of Mars* and *The City and the Stars*. They read H.G. Wells, Frank Herbert, Azimov and Tolkien, but also the blood-chilling stories in Howard Phillips Lovecraft's books of horror fiction. They talked endlessly of space travel, the stars, distant galaxies, the moon, and the likelihood or not of life on other planets. They were mesmerised by the ominous scene in *2001: A Space Odyssey* when the ship's computer awakens. They invented their own vocabulary to express their vision of space and things not human, and what they would do to redress humanity when they became masters of the universe.

They weaved and conjured up the most far-fetched connections between the galaxies, the Holy Grail, stupid people, ABBA, spaceships, spitfires and Abbot Ale, inevitably coming up with hilarious and ridiculously implausible scenarios, spinning a web of references that only they could understand. In the company of others, whenever a word of their vocabulary was uttered by someone out of context, they would spin off into their fantasy world with mimics, quotes and antics, laughing their heads off, leaving whoever had uttered the word feeling lost, uncomfortable and not knowing how to deal with these two mad young men.

Bascom needed only the jolt of a syllable to burst into a monologue of incomprehensible, albeit intelligent-sounding rhetoric around whichever theme the syllable had evoked, and was capable of turning his observations into a belittling speech in the face of which the listener could only feel ignorant and down-trodden. No one ever argued with Bascom. There was nothing to discuss. Zarathustra had spoken.

Much as Randalph delighted in Bascom's antics, bravado and total disregard for people's acceptance or rejection of him, he had thinner skin and could easily feel awkward with the discomfort of others. When by himself, Randalph didn't have the boldness to confront the world with Bascom's brash indifference. He was concerned more about not upsetting others than about knowingly and intentionally antagonising them.

The boys were experimenting with life, sowing the seeds of their future, day by day coming one step closer to the adults they would soon become. Later, Bascom would go his way and Randalph another, but during those delicious days of shared delirium they were inseparable, partisans in the holy quest for mirth and madness, scholars of applied nonsense, convinced that they were different, better, wittier and smarter than the whole of the rest of humanity put together.

CULTURE SNOBS

Randalph and Bascom also shared a passion for classical music. Their favourites were piano concertos, in particular Beethoven's N°3 and Rachmaninov's 2nd, as well as Janáček's haunting violin sonata, the dramatic opening and powerful buildup in Shostakovich's symphony N°5, and the thundering might of the great Russian composers such as Borodin, Rimsky Korsakov, Khachaturian and Prokofiev.

They quizzed each other daily on their knowledge of classical music. One would play a few seconds of a particular piece on their portable tape recorder or at home on a record player and the other had to answer who was the composer, the conductor, the orchestra and the soloists. Bascom almost always won outright. He had a brain with much more storage capacity and cross references than Randalph's.

Their quest for the ultimate in classical music, the peak of virtuosity, the defining best, happened one day when they came across an old recording by the great Wilhelm Backhaus of Beethoven's 3rd piano concerto. Another was their discovery of the great Austrian cellist Heinrich Schiff's masterful rendering of the Bach cello concertos. On their long weekend secret drives down to East Anglia and London the boys would listen for hours on end to these old masters, quizzing each other and revelling in the wonder of their accomplishment. On the one and only occasion that

Randalph met up again with Bascom in later life, when they were both in their early fifties, Bascom presented Randalph with a recording of a symphony he had written himself. Bascom was indeed a genius, in a class of his own.

As well as their love of science fiction literature, both also had a passion for Shakespeare and would practice and repeat as best they could the famous monologues of *Macbeth, Hamlet*, and especially of Kate (Katerina), in *The Taming of the Shrew*, when she finally rallies to her husband's cause in Act 5, scene 2, pledging obedience to him and care for her man: "Fie, fie unknit that threatening unkind brow, and dart not scornful glances from those eyes, to wound thy Lord, thy King, thy governor..."

Kate's retort fitted perfectly the boys' contempt for the way society was already then turning away from traditional family supportiveness to individualism and competition, where men and women no longer upheld each other but rather used each other as a means to an end. Crazy as the boys were, deep down Randalph and Bascom were traditionalists, convinced that moral fibre was the cloth of life, that when worn it bade the wearer shelter from the storm of life.

FROGS ON BOARD

Whenever they could borrow Bascom's mother's little Renault, Randalph and Bascom would go for a drive. Anywhere. Everywhere. They would test their driving skills as they drove along, quizzing each other on their knowledge of classical music or science fiction books and permanently on the lookout for something funny to do. One of their favourite haunts was the Galloway Forest Park in what is now Dumfries and Galloway district in Scotland's southern uplands, with its hydro-electric power generation stations, rivers, lakes, lush green countryside, winding roads and country lanes pleasantly contrasting with the stark, grey-roughcast bleakness and boarded-up neighbourhoods of Ayrshire's industrial towns.

On one of their excursions there on a sultry early summer evening, Bascom suddenly slammed on the brakes and pointed ahead. They had stopped on a fairly straight stretch of narrow road, next to a pond. In front of them, giant toads in their hundreds were leaping across the road. Bascom edged forward, urged Randalph to jump out and close his door, then also jumped out, keeping his door open. Bascom then gathered together a bundle of reeds, laid it in front of his open door to create a ramp, stood back and watched in delight as the toads, one by one, hopped their way into the car.

Hitchhikers? Yes, they had to find hitchhikers! A couple of young local teenagers hitching a lift from one of the villages to the nearest town would be perfect. The instantly-agreed-upon plan was to drive around until they found them, offer them a lift to wherever they were going, deny the existence of the toads in the car, and bet on how long it would take before the couple pleaded to get out. The boys didn't need to discuss the idea further – they were synchro, as thick as thieves.

Setting off towards Newton Stewart, their first victims were easily found, and a typical pair of gormless local teenagers-in-love climbed in. "Gadz, the car's fu o frogs!" the young girl screamed. "What the fuck!" exclaimed her spotty-faced lover boy. Bascom and Randalph had already hastily driven off, paying no attention to their cries. When the volume of the shrieks of disgust increased, Bascom assured them that his mother's car did not and had never transported frogs and asked them if they had been taking drugs. "Who the fuck are you?" blurted out little Jimmy hard man from the back seats,to which Bascom replied aloofly, "We are the protectors of the forest and the night, guardians of the sacred Holy Grail".

This was too much for the couple, who probably had never heard of the Holy Grail and didn't get the joke. "Are youz boys daft? The cor's fu' o' frogs. Are ye fuckin' blind? Stop the fuckin' car and let us oot. Yer aff yer fuckin' heids!" cried out Jimmy lover boy. Randalph looked at his watch. Eight minutes. Bascom had won. Randalph had betted ten. The boys drove off in pain, mortified with laughter, the car still full of oversized, slimy, croaking toads hopping around on the back seat, on the floor, and occasionally on the dashboard.

Knowing intuitively that the fun wasn't over yet, Randalph and Bascom reminded each other of Wilhelm Busch's legendary German cartoon characters 'Max und Moritz', and their famous proverb they had learned during that last year at school: "*Dieses war der erste Streich, doch der zweite folgt sogleich*" – roughly translated as "After the first prank follows the second".

The second episode of the evening appeared in the form of a gathering on the side of the road of members of some sort of society or association outside a function room on the main street of one of the villages they were passing through. The group, composed mainly of middle-aged ladies who looked like they were babbling on about what the speakers had said or what Mrs such-and-such had replied, were standing at the edge of the pavement at the end of the tree-lined path leading to the door of the masonic-looking village function room.

Bascom pulled up, climbed out of the car with a terrified expression on his face, eyes rolling backwards, and beckoned to the ladies, crying out, "Help! We've been attacked". Randalph then jumped out, screaming "They're everywhere!" The ladies rallied round in a nervous cacophony of "Whit's rang boys? Whit's happened? Er ye a' right?"

"It's the frogs!" yelled Bascom, "They're coming to get us!" at which point he showed the ladies the inside of the car. "Ah", cried out one, "It's full o' fuckin' frogs!"

"They're coming down the road in their millions" whimpered Bascom. "They're killer frogs; we saw dead bodies by the ponds. It's horrible. They'll get us all. You'll have to go home right now and lock your doors and windows," he shrieked at the top of his voice, then added "Somebody has to sound the alarm. Call the police!"

By now the ladies had huddled together on the pavement, looking around at each other with consternation on their faces. In a last inspiration of panic-spreading, Bascom jumped into the car and yelled out "They're coming! The Daleks are coming too! Get into the Tardis, Doctor! We're getting out of here before they arrive. Run for your lives!" Then they sped off with no lights until the car was out of sight.

The boys then drove off with screeching tyres and horn honking, pissing themselves with laughter, praying to heaven above that one of the ladies would actually call the police, and role-playing the conversation she would have with Constable Whatever. "Who's this calling? What's the emergency?" "Officer, there's millions of killer frogs heading to the village, we need help!"

A little later, they chased the frogs out of the car in front of a fish n' chip shop in the next village, warning the few people on the street in front of the shop who were holding folded newspaper wrappings with their fish n' chips in one hand, their fingers picking out the greasy chips with the other, that the frogs were coming to get us all. They told them about the dead bodies they'd seen by the roadside, warning them about the end of the world, and begging them to please call the police. Then they drove off, clutching their weary abdomens.

THE FUN'S OVER

But just like in most fairytales, there comes a day when reality turns up and the fun is sadly over. It was June 1975. School had come to an end. The time had come for the boys to move on, each in his own direction, with Bascom unknowingly headed for the upper echelons of international big business and Randalph equally unknowingly on his way to a career involving twenty different jobs in twenty different countries, teasing fate nine times in close encounters with the afterlife in Asia, Africa and the Middle East.

CHAPTER 6

No Money, No Life

POCKET MONEY

Randalph was brought up in a working-class environment where people believed that money was something you got in return for your sweat and toil. That belief was so deeply ingrained in him that he unwittingly hung on to it for the rest of his life, which possibly explains why he never got rich. On his fourteenth birthday, Jimmy told him that there would be no more pocket money – if he wanted or needed cash it was up to him to earn it. Thanks Dad!

Already since he had turned thirteen, Randalph had walked around his village on Saturdays with a plastic pail full of soapy water in his hand, knocking on doors and asking people if they needed their cars washed, pocketing the sum of half a crown (25 pence today) per car from a handful of regular clients. As the car-washing jobs were irregular and didn't earn him enough to get him through the week, to avoid the misery of empty pockets, his childhood friend Donald's dad, Adamo, found Randalph a weekend job at the Creamery (cheese factory) on the outskirts of his home village, Kilmaurs, which was famous for its red Cheddar cheeses. In the main hall of the creamery, half a dozen massive stainless-steel troughs were set out in a row extending from the door at one end of the hall where Big Charly, the gaffer (foreman), had his office all the way down to the storage areas at the other end. The troughs were filled with fresh cow's milk gathered very early in the morning by Adamo and his lorry from the many surrounding dairy farms. Bacteria was then added to acidify the milk and rennet to curdle it. The curds were strained manually to separate the liquid whey, then heated to release more whey as the curds melted together.

After the curd was heated, it went through a process called 'cheddaring' where the cheese was cut into slabs that were repeatedly stacked atop one another and turned. The cheddaring process removed more moisture, acidified the curd, and gave the cheese its unique, elastic texture and pungent flavour. The curd was then pressed into moulds and left to age. Mild Cheddar was aged three to six months, while salted or extra salted cheddar was aged six to eighteen months or more.

At the time when Randalph worked at the creamery the entire process was manual, except for cutting the cheeses and packaging them, which was done by ladies who operated cutting machines in a separate room.

Randalph's jobs involved stirring and straining the milk with the added bacteria and rennet, turning and storing the cheese slabs, and carrying the dried slabs to the cutting and packaging room. In between batches, he also had the job of shooting rats with an air rifle, and sometimes even with a .22 rifle that Big Charly produced one day from inside his office. Randalph loved that part of the job, hiding like a sniper in dark corners and pinging off the rats one by one. To this day he believes that Charly kept the rifle there to shoot anyone who didn't do exactly what he told him to. He was that kind of man.

For his toils, Randalph was paid 13 pence an hour. It was a tough environment and he was shouted at by big strong working men, who cracked jokes at his expense and had a knack of making life miserable for him. But it was money, and by Sunday evening he had earned two pounds, enough to get him through the week.

After two years of exhausting and humiliating weekends on which he worked two ten-hour shifts, coming home in the evening exhausted, stinking of rancid cheese and being obliged by his parents to change into clean clothes outside in the family's hut next to the back door of the house, Randalph gave up his weekend slave labour at the creamery in favour of occasionally working on a dairy farm owned by Bascom's friend Callum, the 'advanced driver', and his elder brother Angus. From then on, instead of trudging the long cold lonely road early on Saturday and Sunday mornings to be martyred at the creamery while his family, schoolmates and most of the country was still asleep in their beds, his weekends now started on the Friday night with dinner and beer, with Callum sleeping on the couch next to the fire in the front room of his farm and getting up at 4am to help with milking the brothers' two hundred cows in the cosy warmth of their big cow shed.

Randalph loved the farm atmosphere, driving tractors, fetching in the cows from the lush green fields, the smells of the beasts, the pleasure of the big outdoors, stacking hay in summer, and the feeling of safety and friendship in the company of the two brothers who, every now and again, would squeeze some bank notes into his hand in thanks for his toil.

MUSCLE MAN – SUMMER '75

In early June 1975, on the Monday after graduating from secondary school, having hung up his prefect's jacket and school tie for the last time, Randalph began work on a building site in Kilmarnock, just down the steps from The Academy, where the old town square had been demolished to be replaced by a shopping mall and a multi-storey car park. He had talked a few weeks previously with the gaffer there, who had said he could start on the Monday straight after the end of term.

For the next three months, Randalph worked as a manual labourer, mixing cement, carrying bricks on hods up ladders to impatient bricklayers, and erecting scaffolding together with a duo of vile, lazy, dishonest layabouts who made his life as unbearable as they could, pushing Randalph nearer and nearer to breaking point. On the day that Randalph did actually break, Geordie the gaffer, thankfully, was just around the corner and heard Randalph's furious shouting as he pinned one of his two persecutors in a corner of the scaffolding and was about to smash his skull in with a length of angle iron. After the incident, Randalph was transferred to another team and never heard a whimper from the two bastards again.

From day one on the building site, school had become a luxury of the past, a paradise lost. Goodbye forever to that safe place where half the students wore enticing smiles, short grey skirts and white blouses covering their supple young breasts. Life on the site, which was also a hub for recycling goods stolen from shops on the high street, was rough, dirty and frequently violent. The only good things about it were the pay and being out in the open air.

Geordie the gaffer was a tough Glasgow man with permanently rolled-up sleeves, braces, thick baggy trousers, and a jawbone you could use for chopping wood. He could be heard from one end of the site to the other. He hired men mainly from Glasgow, as he didn't want to take the risk of having any of the local Kilmarnock thugs on the site. He was the undisputed boss – a real-life hard man. Unapproachable. Uncompromising. Cross him and two things would happen: you would be fired on the spot and your teeth would be dropping from your mouth as you crashed onto the ground begging him not to destroy your face with his steel toe-capped boots.

Geordie was aggressive and had enough rage in him to scare away an army, but he was a fair man, and in some ways reminded Randalph of Jimmy. One Saturday afternoon, a fight broke out and someone – the bad guy – was thrown through a nearby shop window in broad daylight, where he lay motionless, bleeding profusely. Above the commotion and the screams of shoppers, Geordie's voice bellowed like thunder: "Nobody moves. Nobody helps. Look and learn and get back to your fuckin' work". It was the first time Randalph had witnessed that level of violence.

Geordie the gaffer saw who pulled their weight on the site and paid wages accordingly. If you were a worker and not just a lazy bastard, you earned the privilege of working Saturdays, which paid double time. If your appetite for work went beyond the call of duty, you could also work on Sundays, which earned you triple time. Randalph was up for working seven days a week.

Mondays, Tuesdays, Wednesdays and Thursdays were 10-hour days, Friday, Saturday and Sunday 8. He was in it for the money. He doesn't remember exactly how much he was earning, but by the end of his third week he was already taking home twice as much in his pay envelope as Jimmy, who had been a foreman in a big tractor factory in the town for years. Jimmy was a staunch socialist and a Labour man and thought this wrong. He believed there should be more control over wages and overtime. Randalph had the sneaky feeling that he was jealous and teased him by inviting him out for a pint of beer.

As well as being in it for the money, Randalph, who had the energy and the stamina and actually enjoyed the work, was in it for the muscles and to put callouses on his hands. In spite of the occasional violence and the nagging on the site, he actually relished being in that environment where men had muscles, nobody wore gloves, and a punch in the face was how misunderstandings were debated.

To add to his growing physical strength from the work,

on Friday evenings Randalph went to a local body-building club, where he bench-pressed weights, trained on bars, and practised the 'clean and jerk' weightlifting technique. He had so much anger inside him and pent-up hatred for the bullies from school that he was determined that if they ever crossed his path again he would at least have enough muscle on him to make them think twice, and maybe the determination to pick up a reinforcing bar and smash their heads in. Well, maybe not, but the satisfaction of seeing their teeth spill out onto the ground after a solid punch would for him be a moment to glory in.

FIRST BITE OF THE APPLE

By the end of summer '75, Randalph had worked three full months and saved enough money to pay for the coming year at university and also to end the summer with a four-week tour of Europe on the newly introduced pan-European Interrail tickets, which could be used to travel unlimited distances by train across Western Europe, from North to South and East to West. Randalph was seventeen and raring to go. Together with John, a stocky, muscly bricklayer a few years older than him that he had befriended at the gym and who could clean and jerk 250 lb (113 kg), bench press 290 lb (132 kg), and crush an apple with his right hand, he set off to explore Europe by train.

John and Randalph travelled firstly to Bonn, where Randalph's parents were visiting his aunt and uncle, then headed south to Koblenz where, after only two days on the trains, they already had to escape arrest by jumping a slow-moving cargo train bound for Switzerland after a drunken escapade in the city centre. A few days later in Innsbruck, Austria, they were again on the run, this time being chased by a big fat 'Kelner' (waiter) with a handlebar moustache wearing a tight, bulging waistcoat over his impeccable white shirt and sporting a towel folded over his left forearm.

The Kelner was clumsy and slow, desperately yelling at all around to catch those two scoundrels, but to no avail. If anyone tried to catch them, they'd have to be able to run like the wind, but once they caught up and saw John they'd probably give up the chase. For the two lads the maths was simple. They simply didn't have enough money needed to pay the extravagant bill for the lavish cocktails they had ordered and offered all around in their attempt to impress some local ladies in a chic restaurant.

Life on the trains was one big party of young people like themselves carrying on their backs orange-coloured rucksacks mounted on tubular aluminium frames. It was a savannah of wild freedom-loving young European gazelles just waiting to be caught in Randalph's net. Randalph was in ecstasy and did his best, day in day out, to bag his prey.

Depending on their destination and the weather, the boys slept either in the trains or on the ground in big plastic bags they had 'borrowed' from the building site. Each day had its laughs. There was always something happening. From Austria they rode west, again through Switzerland, but this time on the main line that connects Lausanne with Basel. Randalph remembers looking out of the window in one of the stations trying to pronounce the place name Yverdon and wondering why everything was written in French. Had they inadvertently crossed into France? He had no idea that French was one of the three main languages in Switzerland, and definitely not the faintest premonition that one day he would settle there and raise a family.

Close to Aachen, on the German-Dutch border, they again got into trouble when they crossed a shallow stream to get to a baker's shop on the other side, not knowing that the stream was the border. The mistake cost them an afternoon's interrogation in a German border post, where the officer in charge repeatedly tried to trick them into admitting they were planning something. It was the time of the Baader Meinhof and Red Army terrorist groups and the German state was on red alert.

Freed and back on the trains, their next destination was Scandinavia. Randalph had heard about Sweden and free love and wanted to see it with his own eyes. Travelling via Amsterdam, the boys stopped off in Hamburg. Then, heading for Copenhagen, they crossed into Denmark, smuggling paperless travellers (political refugees?) under the benches of the trains' wagon compartments en route. Arriving in Gothenburg and seeing the extortionate prices of drinks scribbled on the slate on the wall of a bar they improvised a two-man con act to get free beer, repeating the sketch from bar to bar as they stalked around the city centre near the railway station. From Gothenburg they took the night sleeper train to Stockholm, where they eventually mustered up all their courage to walk into a topless bar.

Life in Scotland simply hadn't prepared them morally for this – the lads were not good at playing it cool, not looking flustered, and not staring all the time at the bar girl's lovely breasts. With a glance at each other they left before even ordering a drink, which in any case was well beyond their budget, their tails between their legs, mumbling boyish stuff about her lovely tits.

Back out in the anonymity of the streets, they came across a narrow lane lined with sex cinemas and sex shops. Having gawked lecherously at the posters and publicity above the counters of all the shops and cinemas in the row, they self-consciously plucked up courage to open the matte black door of the last cinema, which was covered in pictures of tits and bums. Once inside, they settled into big comfy fluffy armchairs in the steamy, seedy theatre, where some men were smoking and others could be heard wanking. After only ten minutes into the film, John sprang up and walked out when the lady actor's face got covered in a shower of sperm shot like a gun from the hot Latino stallion in the lead role – it was John's first exposure to the sins of Europe and he was shocked.

From Stockholm they took the night express to Trondheim. While John slept, Randalph was enjoying talking with a tall Swedish girl who was sitting opposite them, whose long red hair went all the way down her back to her buttocks, and who introduced herself as Göta.

As the train rolled on steadily into the night and the rest of the passengers closed their eyes, Göta and Randalph got friendly, ending up in their wagon's spotlessly clean and spacious rest room where Randalph enjoyed his first, very inexperienced, bite of the apple. Not thinking they would ever meet again, the two nevertheless exchanged addresses before Göta got off in Östersund, where they waved goodbye kisses to each other as the train pulled gently out of the station and Randalph sank into dreamy sleep for the remainder of the ride to Trondheim in Norway.

From Trondheim, the lads continued northwards, all the way to Narvik, then south to Lulea, along Sweden's Baltic coast, stopping in Piteá, Umeá and Gävle, before returning to Stockholm Central and boarding the sleeper to Helsingborg to catch the ferry back to Denmark, the train to Hamburg, then south to Brussels, Brugge, and Ostend, and finally the ferry over to Dover, and the last leg of the journey home via London.

THE DEAR GREEN PLACE

The lads' train travel ticket had come to an end. The time had also come for Randalph to leave his family nest and begin life as a student in Glas Caomh, the Gaelic name for Glasgow, meaning 'The dear green place', which was about as far from the reality of that grim, smog-bound, notoriously dangerous city as you could get. Randalph was not looking forward to it.

Randalph had enrolled to start a four-year bachelor's degree course in Civil Engineering at the University of Strathclyde. The course was to begin in early October, only a few days after his return from Europe. Civil engineering appealed to him because he had conjured up some dreamy notion in his imagination that it would teach him how to sling rope bridges across the Amazon jungle, measure ice floes on the British Antarctic Expedition or construct hydro power stations in the world's snowy mountain ranges.

Working on the building site that summer, however, he had seen first-hand what the daily routine of civil engineers looked like and wasn't inspired in the slightest. In spite of his desire for adventure and love for the big outdoors, he realised that if he wasn't careful, his studies might lead him to a boring office job or on some construction site where he'd be ankle deep in cement dust and clay all day. The idea sent shudders through him. There was no way he was going to end up there. There had to be something else for him out there in the big wide world…

PART 2

Out of the nest
The great escape from home

CHAPTER 7

1975 AD

1975 was the 1975th year of the Common Era (CE) and Anno Domini (AD) designations, the 975th year of the 2nd millennium, the 75th year of the 20th century, the 5th year of the 1970s decade, and the year that Randalph left school, had his first taste of earning good money, travelled central and northern Europe by train, had his first bite of the apple, left home, and moved to Glasgow to begin his studies. He was 17.

For Randalph, the highlight of that year was the "Thrilla in Manila", when Muhammad Ali defeated Joe Frazier in a boxing match in the Philippines viewed live by well over 100 million people worldwide. The runner-up in his appreciation of the year was the CCCP space mission that flew Georgy Grechko and Aleksei Gubarev in Soyuz 17 to board the Salyut 4 space station.

At home with his family in Kilmaurs, 1975 would be remembered as the year when Margaret Thatcher defeated Edward Heath for the leadership of the opposition UK

Conservative Party, becoming Britain's first female leader of any political party. It was impossible not to be aware of this fact as Jimmy raged about it passionately every day, as he also did about John N. Mitchell, H. R. Haldeman and John Ehrlichman, who had been found guilty of the Watergate cover-up. Jimmy's verdict for both events was simple: they should all be hanged.

Among the other important events of the year, Randalph had heard that Bill Gates and Paul Allen had founded Microsoft in Albuquerque, New Mexico, but didn't know yet what a Microsoft was or what it did. He was also aware that far away in Asia the Vietnam war had ended with the fall of Saigon, and that next door to Vietnam, the Khmer Republic had surrendered when the Communist Khmer Rouge guerrilla forces captured Phnom Penh, ending the Cambodian Civil War with mass evacuation of American troops and Cambodian civilians. He hadn't heard, however, that the same Khmer Rouge had raided several Vietnamese towns, eventually leading to the Cambodian-Vietnamese War.

What he also didn't know about – mainly because he wasn't in the least bit interested in what was going on in the world – was that 1975 was the year in which the last naturally occurring case of smallpox was diagnosed and treated, and that it was declared by the UN as the International Women's Year, while in the meantime its General Assembly had approved a resolution equating Zionism with racism, provoking an outcry among Jews around the world until it was repealed in 1991.

In spite of getting very good grades at secondary school,

Randolph likewise had no idea that the Council of Europe had declared 1975 the European Architectural Heritage Year, that the Dutch song *Ding-a-dong* had won the 20th Eurovision Song Contest, that Jazz pianist Keith Jarrett had played the solo improvisation The Köln Concert at the Cologne Opera, whose live recording became the best-selling piano recording in history, or that a bomb had exploded in the Paris offices of the Springer Press, with the March 6 Group (connected to the Red Army Faction) demanding amnesty for the Baader-Meinhof Group.

He was equally unaware that six Red Army Faction terrorists had taken over the West German Embassy in Stockholm, taking 11 hostages and demanding the release of the group's jailed members, and that after a referendum and seven years of military rule, modern-day Greece was established as the Hellenic Republic, with the officers responsible for the military coup in Greece in 1967 sentenced to death in Athens, a sentence later commuted to life imprisonment.

That year, many other events escaped Randolph's attention, among which were:

Carlos I of Spain became the acting head of state after General Francisco Franco conceded that he was too ill to govern; his death on November 20th effectively marking the end of the dictatorship established following the Spanish Civil War and the beginning of the Spanish transition to democracy, resulting in Juan Carlos being crowned King of Spain;

Sikkim acceded to India after a referendum abolishing the Chogyal, its monarchy;

Junko Tabei from Japan became the first woman to reach the summit of Mount Everest;

Prime Minister Indira Gandhi declared a state of emergency in India, suspending civil liberties and elections;

Founder President Sheikh Mujibur Rahman of Bangladesh was killed during a coup led by Major Syed Faruque Rahman;

Papua New Guinea gained its independence from Australia;

The term of Tuanku Al-Mutassimu Billahi Muhibbudin Sultan Abdul Halim Al-Muadzam Shah ibni Almarhum Sultan Badlishah, as the 5th Yang di-Pertuan Agong of Malaysia ended;

Sultan Yahya Petra ibni Almarhum Sultan Ibrahim Petra of Kelantan, became the 6th Yang di-Pertuan Agong of Malaysia;

Eight people in South Korea involved in the People's Revolutionary Party Incident were hanged;

Meanwhile in the Middle East, Iran and Iraq announced a settlement in their border dispute, King Faisal of Saudi Arabia was shot and killed by his nephew, the Suez Canal reopened for the first time since the Six-Day War, and in Lebanon the Kataeb militia killed 27 Palestinians during an attack on their bus in Ain El Remmeneh, triggering the Lebanese Civil War which lasted until 1990;

In Africa the South African Government announced that it would provide all Black children with free and compulsory education;

Mozambique gained independence from Portugal;

The first Cuban forces arrived in Angola to join Soviet

personnel who were there to assist the MPLA that controlled less than a quarter of Angolan territory. In response, the United States, Zaire and Zambia requested South Africa to provide training and support for the FNLA and UNITA forces, leading to the invasion of Angola by the South African Defence Force during Operation Savannah prior to the Angolan elections scheduled for November 11;

Angola became independent from Portugal and civil war erupted;

The Algerian President, Houari Boumediene, ordered the expulsion of all Moroccans from Algeria.

And while Randalph was celebrating his 18th birthday, in Laos the communist party of the Pathet Lao took over Vientiane and defeated the Kingdom of Laos, forcing King Sisavang Vatthana to abdicate, creating the Lao People's Democratic Republic, thus ending the Laotian Civil War, with mass evacuation of American troops and Laotian civilians, but effectively beginning the insurgency in Laos with the Pathet Lao fighting the Hmong people, Royalists-in-exile and the Right-wings, which ended 37 years later on March 30th 2022 when the last unorganized resistance against the Lao People's Army was finally put down.

In 1975, Randalph also had absolutely no idea that in only half a dozen years from then he would be caught up in world events in Vietnam, Malaysia, Lebanon, Sudan and Angola, escaping death nine times and experiencing first-hand the horrors of civil war. In 1975, his focus was on surviving and hopefully enjoying the next four years as a student of Civil Engineering in Glasgow.

CHAPTER 8

Student days in Glasgow

NOT HIS THING

While the world was doing its thing, in between summer jobs where he was earning money, getting around and far away from the confines of home, Randalph did his level best to study. Try as he might, however, studying was not his thing. He never found the spark that would ignite his enthusiasm or inspire him to dig deeper into the mathematics and science of engineering. At heart he was a poet, a dreamer, who resisted learning equations and theories from textbooks, preferring rhyme, the search for the truths of life, and running after his own Holy Grail.

Instead of exploring the mysteries of materials and how they stick together, during his four years at university Randalph read most of Dickens, a dozen of Shakespeare's plays, Tolstoy, Dostoyevsky, the Viking sagas, Scott, Stevenson, Plato, Socrates, Greek mythology, some poems by Tennyson and Wordsworth, *No Highway* and four other books by Nevil Shute, *Up at the Villa and The Painted Veil* by W. Somerset Maugham, and the endearing poetical works of his role model and moral guide, Robert Burns, with whom he identified and understood like a soulmate.

FIRST YEAR

Randalph spent his first year in Glasgow in a residence for students called Ross Hall, located in a wooded park in Crookston to the west of the city centre, just across the road from a gritty, crowded, noisy Glasgow pub, where you could get your head beaten in for the price of a wrong look at one of the locals.

The hall was just down the road from a sinister-looking old Victorian hospital for the mentally deranged also set in a park of mature tall trees that reminded Randalph of Kirk Alloway and the dance of witches in Burns' *Tam o' Shanter*. The place sent shivers down his spine when his mind wandered off into imagining the inhumane treatment of inmates, not so long ago, many of whom ended their days as walking vegetables, silenced through the then fashionable practice of frontal lobotomy.

At Ross Hall Randalph soon got involved with the highly strung Maggie, a suicidal virtuoso cellist who had a room on the floor above his and frequently left notes on his door to say not to come up to see her today as she was going to kill herself. Randalph couldn't handle this and turned for help to his doctor, who gave him pills and vitamins to calm his nerves.

To add to the trauma of Maggie's looming suicide, the

girl in the room directly above him wore stiletto heels and strutted around often moving furniture at all hours of the night. She was just as hysterical as Maggie, and on the few occasions when he plucked up enough courage to knock on her door and ask her to take the heels off, she shouted at Randalph to fuck off.

Randalph was miserable, confused, and becoming a nervous wreck. Before enrolling for university, he had believed that students were educated people with good hearts, up for harmless fun and open to intelligent conversation. He was shocked at the number of them who had come from money and had no notion of the nice things in life, like poetry or the classics, preferring to follow their football and rugby teams like sheep or bragging about the future careers they would soon be entering into, as if they were the chosen ones about to be canonised or blessed by God himself.

After only a few months, Randalph had already developed a profound loathing for this world of the privileged and the pampered, most of whom had never experienced life at street level and were oblivious to and far removed from the stark realities of life of the working masses, believing in their arrogance, which overflowed with social prejudice, that they were the smart ones, entitled by birth to crack jokes on the backs of these lesser mortals. This was not Randalph's world. It never would be.

In the winter of that first year, as if the gods had decided to punish Randalph for his hatred towards many of his fellow men and lack of gratitude at receiving free higher education and not yet needing to work, little warts began springing up all over his body out of the blue. The bottomless pit of self-pity, despair and anguish that Randalph fell into as the little bastards spread and multiplied got deeper and gloomier as the days rolled by. Within a month they were visible on his hands, his forearms, one even on his left eyelid, his knees, his feet, and even on the shiny skin around the crown jewel of his young masculine pride and maker of joy.

Covering himself up as best he could, pretending to everyone that came close that he had a cold and needed to stay warm, he realised he needed help to get rid of these very unwelcome invaders. But who to turn to? This was a private matter, secret, intimate, not something to discuss with his classmates or family, and definitely not with any of the young ladies who occasionally drifted in and out of his life.

Randalph resolved to consult a doctor – a male doctor – to whom he reluctantly revealed the evidence. The doctor prescribed for him a bottle of acid with which to burn the little upstarts off his hands, feet, arms and legs, but strongly recommended him to go to a 'special' clinic for the little culprits that had infected his private parts, as he had to take great care not to overdo the burning on the soft skin. The clinic he referred him to was Glasgow's venereal disease clinic – a collection of containers surrounding a one-level institutional building erected in the centre of a derelict piece of land surrounded by grim four-storey tenements in the heart of Govan in Glasgow's docklands. As he approached the clinic Randalph's heart sank as his self-esteem fell head-first into a bottomless pit of first-degree misery.

The arrows on the information board at the entrance to

the compound pointed to a waiting room where patients filled in a form, were given a number, and waited their turn to be called up. Randalph was reminded of the hilarious Billy Connolly comedy sketch describing the scene and atmosphere in precisely that same waiting room, which was full of men hiding behind newspapers and focused on looking for something they might have dropped on the floor.

There was no eye contact. No one spoke. No one was there. No one present would ever admit to having been there. Under oath or threat of torture they would even deny any knowledge of the place. "Where?" "What did you say the name of the clinic was?" "Never heard of it!" In the rows of seats sat only ghosts of shame, each with its embarrassing secret, each hoping to be more invisible than the men sitting next to them, who were so far apart emotionally that they might as well have been on either side of the Iron Curtain.

A swinging door opened to reveal a nurse in uniform with a decorative white hat who was calling out Randalph's number as she scanned the waiting area. Randalph's heart sank even further and was now at the bottom of some poisoned well, about to dissolve in the murky waters and be swallowed by the evil creatures that lived below the surface. A female nurse? How could that be? No way! How could he possibly share such a delicate confidence with a woman? He felt humiliated and small, as if someone were revealing in public his deepest secrets for all to hear.

Randalph reluctantly signalled his presence and let the nurse lead him down a corridor to a room with a stainless-steel framed hospital bed in its centre, beside which sat 'the doctor', next to whom stood his assistant – a gorgeous dark-haired intelligent-looking young lady with piercing eyes and an athletic frame, wearing a white overcoat with a clip-on watch hanging from the pocket of her overcoat, positioned as if to draw attention to her perfectly-formed little breasts.

This was too much for Randalph. There had to be a mistake. He would have given anything to be beamed up out of this horrendous nightmare that was rapidly developing into the scary part of a best-selling horror movie where everyone gets eaten by some grisly alien with poisoned tentacles and barbed teeth.

Sometimes, when he had swum in the sea on the Ayrshire coast as a kid in late spring, he had been surprised at just how much his symbol of manliness could shrink in size in the cold water. But on that desperate day, in the degrading abys of Glasgow's VD clinic, any previous records of diminishing size were being pulverised.

When Randalph took down his trousers and underpants to place his pride and joy in the delicate outstretched hand of the lovely assistant, there was nothing there. It had never been so small and never seemed so far away. Randalph felt it was no longer his, no longer part of his body. Where had it gone? He looked on in disbelief as the assistant tried to roll back his miniaturised, almost invisible foreskin. It had vanished!

Broken and desolate, Randalph replied to the doctor's questions in the third person. His eyes never met his or the assistant's. He was in total denial of even being there. It was like being in a different time zone. He was aware that they were speaking to him and telling him things, he could see their mouths move, but couldn't register what they were saying, as if his world was separated from theirs by a thick translucid membrane of shame. Could life get any worse?

With the assistant in the background looking on, the doctor – a shortish man with a bald head, a long nose, steel-rimmed spectacles and in the classic white overall of the medical profession – showed Randalph how to burn off the gnarled invaders using a pinpoint acid drop under a magnifying glass.

The interrogation, tribunal and judgement were over. The verdict had been spoken. Randalph pulled up his underpants, tucked in his shirt, fastened his trousers, buttoned up his duffle coat, mumbled an unconvincing thank you, passed by the admin desk to pick up his prescription and walked out, eyes down, trying to conceal his guilt as he left the scene of his crime, certain that the whole world was watching him and knew where he had been.

Once outside the clinic perimeter fence, he walked past the first bus stop, then the second, and finally boarded a double-decker bus heading to the town centre at the third, hoping that no one on board would ask him what he was doing in Govan. In Glasgow neighbourhoods there was always the risk that some stranger would confront you and want to know who you were. What would he say? "Oh, hi Jimmy, my name's Randalph – I've just been doon to the VD clinic to show them ma wullie." No fucking way...

Back home Randalph got to work, meticulously employing the doctor's method, and sure enough, by and by the invaders retreated. Randalph's skin lost all trace of them, and life went back to normal. He never talked about them to anybody, keeping this grim chapter of his young life hidden behind a cloak of secrecy, denied from his mind, stored in an unmarked box at the bottom of his hall of memories. From that point in time, it took some fifty years until this very day before Randalph resolved to brush away the shame and broach the subject, hoping it would at least make someone smile, or give hope to some other misfortunate martyr who found themselves in the same predicament.

GOODBYE DAD – SUMMER 76

A few weeks before the end of Randalph's first year at university, Göta, his exuberant lady friend from the night express through Sweden the summer before, turned up at his home village. Randalph and his brother Jack often remarked how much warmth and softness she brought into their home, which sadly lacked a feminine presence to balance out the protracted war raging between the brothers. Randalph's parents loved her from the first minute she walked down the garden path towards the house, all smiles, radiating happiness, and marvelling at Helma's flowers.

While Randalph was doing his best to try to study for his end-of-term exams, Göta accompanied Helma on walks and bus trips with the ladies of the village, making friends with everyone she spoke with. On her last weekend at Randalph's family home, she danced for hours with Jimmy at the annual village summer gala in the function hall just round the corner from their house.

Although Jimmy was only fifty-two at the time, the dancing had literally killed him. During that night the household was wakened by strangled cries coming from the living room downstairs, as he tried to alert the family that he needed help. Jimmy was sleeping on the floor to make room for the visitor, who was sleeping upstairs. Randalph's mother woke the neighbours next door, who had a phone, and called an ambulance. Some long hours later the ambulance arrived, apologising that they had gone to the wrong address. It was too late. Two days later Jimmy was dead.

The rest of the summer passed by as in a fuzzy dream. At the funeral, what seemed to Randalph like hundreds of family members and friends turned up to pay their respects. Many dozens of Jimmy's workmates also turned up, filling the parking space and blocking the roadside for miles. To honour his memory, Massey Ferguson, the tractor manufacture whose factory he worked in, had let the men from his tool shop attend the funeral if they wanted to wish him a last goodbye.

It was totally overwhelming for Helma and the two boys to see such a crowd gathered in silence, their heads hung low, many with tears in their eyes as they sung in choking voices the words of *The Lord's My Shepherd*. Randalph recalls feeling the numbness in his body as he watched the mourners file past in silence, nodding their heads in respect, unable to hold his emotions together enough to shake their hands.

In the 1960s, when Britain was at a standstill because of all the strikes happening across the length and breadth of the country in most of its major industries, with entire workforces downing tools and walking out for any excuse, be it legitimate or just for the sake of striking, Jimmy had stood his ground. Randalph remembers the hysterical scenes at home when he insisted on going to work and crossing the strike lines when there was a strike that he didn't see the point of. He would say to Helma not to worry, he'd be back home that night. and so he was, unscathed and unperturbed. At his funeral, several of his workmates shared with the family the respect they had for him for braving the lines.

A few weeks later, once the funeral and pension allowances had all been taken care of, Randalph, Helma and brother Jack travelled overland to Sweden to stay for some days on the Kattegat coast with a friend of Helma's she hadn't seen for years. From there, Randalph took a train north and spent a month on Göta's parents' farm in the heart of Sweden's Jämtland province. He was happy to be away from the gloom and doom of home and back in the land of endless lakes, forests and the midnight sun.

On the day he arrived, stepping down from the same night train he had travelled in the summer before, Randalph was greeted with open arms by Göta's parents, who were dressed in their traditional colourful Nordic clothes, as they welcomed him to their home, a sizeable farmstead on a slightly raised piece of land surrounded by vast fields stretching all the way to dense pine forests in the distance on the farm's perimeter. Randalph was overwhelmed by such a warm-hearted welcome. What had she told them, he wondered?

Before he got to the house, Randalph had spotted the family's dog, which was tied to a long steel running line stretching from the front corner of the house across a grassy patch to the branch of a tree a dozen metres away. Randalph was used to dogs and liked them, so he walked straight towards it.

The dog, who was obviously less naive than Randalph, backed off, tail wagging, excited, playing at being friendly until it had enough slack on the line, then leaped savagely at him as if to rip his throat out. But then the dog jumped at him with such might that its front paws sent him reeling backwards, with the fortunate result that doggy was only able to sink its teeth into Randalph's left armpit and rip off a chunk of skin.

Elk hounds are used in northern Sweden for hunting elks, as their name suggests. To kill the elk, the hounds catch it by the throat and hang on until it dies. Randalph had escaped having his throat ripped out by inches. Welcome to North Sweden!

Next stop was an emergency visit to the regional hospital, where he was sewn up and given a preventive rabies jab in the stomach, which hurt almost as much as the bite. For the remainder of his stay, Randalph never felt anything less than terror whenever he was inside the house close to the family monster. Try as he might, he never again mustered the courage to approach it again.

The little doggy incident notwithstanding, for the rest of the month Randalph enjoyed stacking hay, milking the family's half a dozen cows by hand, driving around in Göta's father's old Volvo P130 Amazon and his newer 245 station wagon through endless forests and along countless lakes, staying out until dawn at parties, enjoying traditional rural life in the far north, avoiding Göta's dad's grizzly elk hound like the plague, and all the while feeling strange in this culture so different to his own.

In his first year at university Randalph had left behind the world of classical music shared so deeply with his good friend Bascom, and embraced the world of rock. Living in Glasgow, and out in the city most Friday and Saturday nights, he had enjoyed many live concerts at the city's famous Apollo Theatre and also at the Students' Union building. He had seen Queen, The Rolling Stones and Deep Purple live on stage, as well as Elton John, Supertramp, The Moody Blues, Uriah Heep, T. Rex, Status Quo, 10cc, Leo Sayer, Leonard Cohen and many of the lesser-known local bands that played in the city's pubs. Randalph loved the city's musical vibe, knocking back pint after pint of beer to the sound of electric guitars and drum solos.

In that summer of 1976, the local bands that toured around north Sweden and played at the various venues transported their gear in big Mercedes vans that had windows on the upper half of the two rear doors on which they stuck posters of their band. The bands all looked the same, typically with four musicians wearing waistcoats, white billowing shirts below, drooping moustaches, big blue-eyed smiles, resembling more like a happy family of brothers visiting their favourite aunty at her birthday than a rock band. When you heard them playing, they were even further removed musically from what anyone could ever call a rock band.

Randalph remembers arguing with Göta about why they played these ridiculous songs that sound more like country and western instead of trying their hand at Pink Floyd or Led Zeppelin. She couldn't answer – this was her culture, and she didn't really know what Randalph was talking about. At that time countries had their own culture and their own identity. The 'global village' of many decades later where everyone listens to the same shit and believes the same lies had not yet been invented.

In spite of the excitement of discovering the far north, for much of that fateful month Randalph felt miserable. He was madly in love, but he knew deep down that summers never last. Sooner or later, he would have to leave. Sooner or later, he would be back in Scotland, missing Göta, and missing the pale blue all-day-long horizon of Scandinavia's northern wilderness, where the sun never sets.

Having arrived back home in Scotland, broken by the sadness of love lost and the misery of having been propelled to the status of 'head man of the household', Bascom's father took pity on him and offered him the job of constructing low-level dry-stone walls, as part of a project to landscape their garden. Randalph loved the job, as he could use his hands, learn a skill, be creative, and see tangible results at the end of the day. Why the fuck had he ever signed up to become a student, he wondered?

Randalph worked diligently in Bascom's family's garden all summer, scraping together enough money by the end of August to buy another interrail ticket for September, and this time travelled south through Italy all the way down to

Sicily and on to Malta by boat. This was his first experience of life in southern Europe.

Having travelled through Germany and Switzerland in a sleeper carriage bound for Italy, Randalph changed trains in Genoa, where he remembers the bustling crowds and street vendors selling anything from pizza to porn. He was struck by the stylish looks of the Italians. Even workers looked like they had stepped out of a fashion-shop window, contrasting sharply with the shabbiness of the British crowds and the handyman look of the men in Germany, where many people wore dusty working overalls and had pockets and belts bulging with tools.

He remembered hanging his head out of the window and feeling the southern heat as the train he had caught in Genoa pulled to a standstill in Naples after chugging slowly through the poorer quarters of the city. Randalph had looked on uncomfortably at prostitution and other dealings going on in broad daylight between the railway line and the old abandoned and rundown industrial buildings that lined the railway line in Naples' suburbs. His gut was telling him that it would be safer to stay in the station than to venture out to have his usual look around – Naples looked dangerous.

Randalph's next train was headed for Palermo in Sicily, passing through Messina, where it pulled in at 3 am in the heat of the southern night. Randalph had heard about Palermo and the mafia there from his father, who had taken him to see *The Godfather* some years previously in their local cinema in Kilmarnock. He remembered vividly Brando's famous line when he makes an offer to one of his enemies that he can't refuse. He thought it best not to go to Palermo and got off in Messina.

When the train pulled in to Messina Centrale in the middle of the night the station was dark, ominous and silent. Where to go, Randalph wondered? He had hardly had time to think about the answer when an impeccably dressed elegant gentleman in a dark suit with classical Italian features and manners asked him if he was looking for a place to stay. Tired and totally naïve, Randalph replied with a 'yes', to which the gentleman invited him to follow him.

After a few turns left and right along dismal, smelly streets, they arrived at what looked like a shoddy hostel, where Randalph was shown into a grubby room with a tall ceiling, a high window and a noisy ceiling-fan. In a thick Italian accent, the gentleman said something like "Signor can sleep here. Signor will give me his passport. Signor will pay the bill in the morning".

Like a good trusting citizen Randalph handed him his passport, which the gentleman snatched and slid expertly into an inside pocket. Then he turned around with almost a pirouette, exited the room and closed and locked the door behind him.

It didn't dawn on Randalph straight away that he had just been taken prisoner. In the morning, however, when he woke and wanted to get up and be on his way, the penny finally dropped. After banging on the door of the room and calling for someone to come, two other gentlemen turned up and unlocked the door. While one stood squarely in the doorway, the other stood behind and slightly to one side of him, as if to block any chance of escape.

In very limited English but in terms that left no doubt in Randalph's mind as to their intentions, the man in the doorway said he was here to sell him his passport. "How much?" ventured Randalph, trying to look cool. "All" was the reply. "You give all", the gentleman suggested politely, "and signor is a free man". Much as Randalph would have loved to have had the guts and the ability to take on the two men like some super-hero in the movies, he realised he had just been given an offer he couldn't refuse.

"Il tuo portafoglio, per favore – your wallet," barked the man in the doorway. Luckily for Randalph, most of his money was in travellers' cheques, which they weren't interested in – they wanted only cash. "Pantalone! Tasche! Borsa! Pockets, Bag!" he called out, apparently used to talking about pockets in these different languages. Randalph had some loose change in his trouser pocket left over from when he had bought a slice of pizza in Genova, and that was it. Apparently satisfied that they had stripped Randalph of all his cash, they handed him his passport and in an ill-fitting gesture of hospitality bade him "Welcome to Sicily".

Randalph was shaking and shattered. He licked his wounded pride, walked around cautiously until he found a bank, exchanged some cheques, and took the first train out of Messina, heading south along the coast to Catania. By mid-morning he had reached Taormina, which looked small and picturesque enough to be safe, and got off the train. Terrified at the thought of being ripped off again, he grabbed some slices of pizza and a bottle of cheap red wine in the main square and decided to climb the hill behind the town to look for a safe place to spend the night. There was no way he was going to risk another night in a hostel or in lodgings.

Unlike the previous summer when he had had a big plastic bag to sleep in and the company of his mate John, the muscle man from the building site, this summer he was travelling alone and had only some clothes and a lightweight rain jacket. While shepherds might feel comfortable sleeping under an olive tree on a steep hillside under the stars, it scared the shit out of Randalph, who jumped up, startled at the slightest sound. His imagination was running riot with him. The next morning, he packed up his few things just before dawn and scampered back down to the town, with the sole intention of getting the hell out of there on the next train.

A few hours later he stopped off in Catania and was enjoying a leisurely stroll through the old port when he saw a biggish motor launch with massive outboard engines pull up alongside one of the quays. Half a dozen rough-looking guys were on board with tattooed arm muscles and long hair. A truck appeared from somewhere and parked next to the launch. Two of the guys set up a perimeter and were scanning the horizon in all directions while the others hastily unloaded the cargo and put it into the truck.

Randalph did his best to try not to stare directly at them, but he couldn't help noticing that the boxes looked exactly like those you see the baddies unloading in the movies. Guns? Munitions? Drugs? Bullion? Randalph was in no mood to hang around to find out and decided it was time to move on. Soon back at the station, he jumped the next train to Siracusa. By then he had had enough of the Sicilian spooks and wanted to get away from there.

In Siracusa he called his aunty Eileen's sister-in-law, who lived in Malta, and bought a passenger ferry ticket for Valetta. It was Randalph's first ever night on a boat in the southern seas, and his first taste of warm spray as the ferry ploughed its way into the southerly winds and waves. Randalph spent the entire crossing on the bridge deck, revelling in the warm air and stormy skies. He didn't realise then just how significant this crossing would be in shaping his life's choices in the years to come. Unknown to him at the time, in a couple of years Randalph's path would soon be leading him south again across the seas to countries far, far away.

SECOND YEAR

After the premature death of Jimmy in the summer of '76, Randalph agreed to spend his second year as a student at home to keep Helma and younger brother Jack company. He had now become the eldest male of the family – a position he would willingly have traded for anything that took away the feeling of responsibility that the position implied. The decision to return home for a year turned out to be a nightmare for Randalph, a step backwards that entailed the relinquishing of the freedom he had found the previous year away from home, and it also meant travelling by car every day to Glasgow.

Driving backwards and forwards on weekdays to the university, he would arrive home tired, often late, and have to deal with Helma, who never seemed to understand that he needed solitude, peace and quiet to study. Helma had other plans and often wanted him to drive her to events in town in the evenings or to visit her friends.

The bitter war between mother and eldest son that had already been raging for years worsened, with both sides ever deeper entrenched in their positions, giving no quarter to the other, and lashing out with injustices and injury whenever the fighting reached a new peak. Randalph was miserable. He had to get out. This would be his last year at home.

During that year of freedoms lost, Randalph's only escape was to stay overnight or over weekends with a family that had adopted him and lived in a village to the north of Glasgow. He had had a romance with their eldest daughter, which had led to a life-long friendship, but nothing more. Her parents had welcomed Randalph into their midst, as had her four younger brothers and sisters. Randalph loved them all. They were kind to him and fed both his body and his soul. He could have intelligent conversations with them, enjoying the music of their lilting Highland accents, going for walks with them in the Campsie Hills to the north of Glasgow, or for drives along the country lanes to either Stirling in the East or Loch Lomond in the west. He had discovered another part of Scotland that his romantic heart could relate to, and a family he loved dearly.

Meanwhile at university, Randalph was struggling. He had no head for subjects like soil mechanics, hydraulics, structures, finite elements, and all the other components of his Civil Engineering course, which to him were dry and lifeless labyrinths leading to intellectual frustration and forever highlighting the limits of his abilities. The only subject that interested him was sanitation and sewage treatment, which introduced him to the world of bacteria and the other microscopic living things that swam around in human excrement, which he was able to associate with the manure he used to shovel on the farm where he worked and the compost heaps he looked after in his parents' garden.

To whet his appetite for new horizons and satisfy his need to escape the narrow world of engineers and engineering, every now and again Randalph would slip into lectures in the Architecture or Modern Languages departments and talk with the students there. In addition, on many days before driving home in the evenings he regularly headed for the first floor of the students' union building for a beer and the thrill of a game of snooker or table football with three classmates he had befriended. They became his buddies, forever together, and always aside from the rest of the class.

As Bascom had been his partner in crime at school, Simon, his closest friend in the gang, became his bosom friend at university. Simon's riotous laughter and ready spirit for harmless mischief fitted Randalph's needs for fun and distraction perfectly. Simon reminded Randalph of Rabbie Burns' character Souter Johnie in Tam o' Shanter: "And at his elbow, Souter Johnie, His ancient, trusty, drouthy crony: Tam lo'ed him like a very brither; They had been fou for weeks thegither".

Simon and Randalph had indeed been 'fou for weeks thegither' (English: drunk for weeks together) and been banned umpteen times from the students' union and on several occasions also kicked out of Simon's village pub. When it was impossible to see straight enough after a night at his pub to drive home, Randalph would sleep on a couch at Simon's parents' house. Sometimes, Simon would do the same at Randalph's house when the boys got drunk in their favourite haunt in Stewarton, a small town near Randalph's village. They were inseparable. In the two years left ahead as students, and in the months thereafter when Simon had moved south to a job in London and Randalph was packing to leave for Nepal, their pranks grew in daring and their laughter in delirium, while their tears of joy flowed like rivers.

On one occasion in that first autumn after university, Randalph was travelling through London on his way home from Germany to re-sit his final exams and stopped off to spend a weekend with Simon, who had borrowed his father's car while his parents were travelling somewhere. Delighted to have four wheels at their disposal, the two cronies went for a pub-drive around town.

Pissed out of their minds and getting hungry, as it was getting late the lads spotted a fish and chip shop on the other side of the road they were driving down. Oblivious to oncoming traffic, Simon swerved over to the other side of the road to a symphony of honking horns and screeching brakes and headed for a free space to park the car along the kerb. While the space would have easily accommodated the car, Simon had forgotten to hit the brakes hard and stopped with a crunching bang as his father's car demolished the rear bumper of the car parked ahead.

Unperturbed, Simon pushed the gear lever into reverse, accelerating backwards until he hit the car behind, again stopping with a metallic bang, then climbed out and headed directly to the chip shop. Inside, a young guy was showing off his prowess at burping, unaware that Simon was the undisputed deep-burp champion of the world. To the amusement of the rest of the customers and the staff behind the fryer who were clapping and laughing, Simon and the guy got into a delirious burping competition from which Simon effortlessly emerged the winner.

By now full of beer and fish n' chips, it was time to go for a stroll and think about how they were going to break the news of the damage to Simon's father's car. The thinking was interrupted a few steps further on down the road when they spotted the dimly lit doorway to a night club set in a recess with a small round window like a ship's porthole opening at eye level. "Let's see if they sell any fags (cigarettes)" said Simon and started banging on the door.

When the window opened, the face of a bald gentleman with mean-looking little beady eyes wearing a bow tie and a suit appeared. Simon stuck his face to the opened window and asked – not impolitely but slurring and with wafts of alcoholic breath from which the gentleman reeled backwards – if the gentleman had any fags. "Fuck off", came the answer, "This is a select club. We sell cigars, not fags, and not to drunken juvenile punks like yourself. Go on, fuck off".

Just as he was about to close the window, without waiting or thinking of the possible consequences, Simon thrust his hand through the open window and ripped off the gentleman's bow tie. There was no need to discuss what to do next, as the two lads broke one Olympic record after the other as they raced up the street, with Bow-Tieless and some other evil-looking angry thugs that had spilled out onto the pavement trying to catch them.

The chase went on for no more than five or so minutes, by which time Bow-Tieless and his gang had run out of breath and had stopped to hurl abuse and death threats. Also stopping, but at a safe distance ahead of them, Randalph and Simon then sent a salvo of insults at them, goading them on by saying that they couldn't catch them because they were fat old fuckers full of shite. "Come on ya bastards. Show us yer feet, ya fat slobs!" they yelled, along with other select pieces of Glasgow street language until they collapsed with laughter.

The night, however, wasn't over: they had to find their way back to the car and get out of there in one piece before either the club guys or the police got a hold of them.

For four entire long years, their friendship and shared carefree happy moments of ecstasy had made the drudgery of study bearable for Randalph. It was a bond he would cherish long after university days. When Simon's wife contacted him forty years later to tell him that Simon had died, something in Randalph died too. How could it be that this thing called death could tear apart such treasured trust and friendship?

MIDNIGHT SUN – SUMMER '77

To add some spice and new horizons to the drudgery of his engineering studies, during the winter of 76/77 Randalph had started to learn Swedish, trying to convince himself that his future lay in the far north, in the lands of the midnight sun. Hoping to find work in Sweden, he had approached a number of construction companies in Stockholm, one of which offered him a summer job starting in July.

About the same time, Bascom, who had by then settled in the windswept Shetland Islands, had called him to ask if he would be interested in coming up for some weeks to work alongside him as a manual labourer in the plasterer's company he worked for. They could spend the summer mixing, shovelling and supplying a gang of plasterers with cement, earning substantial amounts of money, and generally taking the piss. Bingo! With a job on the Scottish islands in June and in Sweden's capital from July onwards, Randalph had found work for the entire summer.

While working alongside Bascom inevitably meant a summer of nonsense and fun, sharing the same living space with him for a month might prove to be challenging. By the summer of '77, Bascom had abandoned university life in Edinburgh and life in general in mainland Scotland, opting instead for a barren existence in a caravan parked on a bleak hillside on a windswept island as far away as you can get from city life. There, he had found a job as a manual labourer in the local plasterer's company that Randalph was about to join. At the time when Randalph joined him, Bascom was already known across the length and breadth of the island as a raving lunatic, albeit a harmless and extremely hard-working one, who was tolerated, accepted and already endeared to the local community.

The plasterers' gang that Bascom was working for drove around the bleak island from building-renovation site to building-renovation site in a Ford Transit van. The gang's favourite pastime was to bet money on events. Any event. In that particular summer, the gang remarked that several couples of Scandinavian tourists had been seen walking the island's desolate tracks or climbing through the bogs to get a view from the top of a hillock. Wearing bright red or yellow rain gear and colourful bonnets, they could easily be spotted in the bald, treeless terrain of the island.

Sure enough, on the way home from work on some weekday, on a windy ridge to the west, the gang spotted a likely couple and a plan for abundant amusement at their expense was sprung. Bascom was to sit in the back of the van, loosely tied to the vertical struts of the partition separating the back compartment from the driving cabin, and play the part of a gentle but severely mentally deranged village idiot. The upper part of the partition had sliding glass windows that allowed the driver and the passengers in the front to look over their shoulders and see what was happening in the back.

Just as with the frogs a couple of years previously in the Scottish Lowlands, money was wagered among the team on how long the tourists could endure Bascom's mentally instable antics before demanding to be dropped off. Five minutes? Ten? Fifteen? Twenty? Each put a fiver in the kitty and the bet was on. Bill, the driver, stopped the van at the end of the track where the unsuspecting Scandinavians were just about to arrive, rolled down his window, beckoned to them, said they were heading down to the town and asked if they wanted a lift.

The tourists' lilting sing-song positive reply in good but not perfect English already had the rest of the team almost in fits. Bill said they could sit in the back with Bascom, and explained that although Bascom was nuts, he was harmless, and not to mind him. Randalph's role was to sit in the back beside Bascom, calm him down when he got out of hand, and reassure the tourists that there was nothing to worry about. The tourists jumped in and sat on the floor near Bascom, the guys checked their watches, and the van drove off.

Bascom's initial antics were indeed harmless; he stared blankly at the couple and gave out the occasional sigh, wearing a sheepish grin. When the van drove over a small bump in the road, however, he shrieked and started banging the back of his head against the partition. The couple looked at each other, unsure what to say or think. Pete, one of the masons, slid open the window and told them in his thick island dialect not to worry, Bascom was tied up and couldn't harm them.

This was the cue for Bascom to start tugging violently at the ropes around his chest and lunging towards them. In true Bascom style, he had masterfully entered into his role and began swaying from side to side, crying out with piercing sounds of anguish and pain, stretching his arms towards the pair, then howling like a lone wolf on a mountain top. If you listened and watched carefully you could hear the team in the front trying to suppress their laughter, not daring to look at each other, and fighting with their emotions to keep a straight face.

Bill the driver leaned over and shouted to Bascom to behave himself and leave the people alone. "Good people" he said, "Nice people". The effect on Bascom was like an electric shock. He screamed out something that sounded like "Nice people", wheeled around on his rear to the right, fell over onto his back, lifted his right leg and started kicking the partition with the reinforced toecap of his boot, making a noise like thunder in the back.

"Stop!" cried the big blond Scandinavian man. "Please let us out! Your Bascom is a mad man. He will kill us all." "No problem", replied Bill apologetically, "We'll drop you at the crossroads." Bill was cheating; he had bet fifteen minutes. Right then they were closer to ten. Pete, one of the plasterers, piped up with "Let them out now Bill, right now. If the idiot gets loose, he'll eat them". Pete had bet ten minutes.

The Scandinavians picked up on the threat of being eaten and started screaming "Stop! Stop now! Now!" All the while they were mumbling incomprehensible stuff between them as they shuffled towards the back doors, as far away as they could get from the by-now frothing Bascom. Enough was enough. Bill slammed on the brakes, jumped out, swung nimbly round towards the back of the van, opened the doors, and was almost knocked over by the couple as they sprang out of the back like frightened sheep as if the van was on fire and about to blow up.

Bill marvelled at Bascom, who by then was in a fit of total hysterics, gnashing his teeth, tearing at the ropes and screaming at the top of his voice "Eat nice people! Eat them!" The tourists disappeared like light disappears when you switch off a light bulb at night. "Fifteen," said Bill. "Fifteen my arse," replied Pete, "You cheated. You didn't stop when they wanted out."

The two got into a furious argument as the van trundled down the road, heading to the local pub, where the winnings and the argument soon vanished as the men gobbled down endless pints of beer, bellowing out "Eat nice people" in between their tears of laughter.

Immersed once again as they had been previously in their world of classical music and masters, Randalph and Bascom shared a deep dislike and disdain for some of the lesser pop stars of the time who were earning stardom – and lots of money – with a handful of guitar chords, gaudy clothes, lots of noise, and provocative lyrics which, when read as text, told hollow stories of a world of drink, drugs and often violence. To the boys, there was no beauty, no finesse, no depth. They had to stop this. As well as terrifying innocent hitchhikers, they had to rid the island society of this scourge.

Bascom, somehow, had gotten his hands on two twelve-bore double-barrel shotguns and kept them hidden in his caravan, and from somewhere else he had access to an endless supply of cartridges. The boys discussed the issue and came up with a plan. After dismissing the extremely nonsensical idea of pleading with the Monty Python God cartoon figure to throw a burning meteorite at the Top of the Pops recording studio or capturing a submarine to sail close to the next Eurovision Song Contest event and lobbing a nuclear warhead at the stage, they settled for an achievable goal.

They chose a group – the Bay City Rollers – and decided to buy up all the recordings they could find on the Island of their songs and obliterate them with their shotguns. The plan secured in their minds, they drove off to the island's main and only town to map out possible sales points. The town was small compared to mainland standards and populated mainly with active or retired deep sea fishermen and a handful of quaint ex-brigadiers and other wild-weather romantics from the British mainland. The island was not a thriving hub of pop music and urban culture. Nevertheless, it did have a stationery shop that sold music cassettes alongside a small collection of newspapers, pens, pencils, all the items one might need in the home office, and a shelf tucked away at the back of the shop with half a dozen glossy porno magazines.

Bascom strode in, made a beeline for the counter, greeted the stocky shopkeeper on the other side and announced that his colleague (Randalph) and himself had been sent by the Cultural Cleansing Department to buy up all and any music cassettes of songs by the Bay City Rollers. The songs, he explained, had been classified as detrimental to the development of the human brain and must at all costs be kept away from the ears of children, adolescents and young adults. "You're having me on, boys," retorted Willie, the wily shopkeeper, with a wry look in his eyes – Islanders were known for standing their ground and not being easily manipulated by nonsense.

Bascom raised the stakes and launched into an eloquent plea on behalf of the plight of parents struggling to educate their young in the current climate of social rebellion and family disintegration, placing the blame for young-aged delinquency fairly and squarely on the shoulders of Pop music. "A nice story, son, but you're not foolin' me, boy. What is it you're up to?"

Bascom, foiled by the gentlemen's intuition and stubborn refusal to enter into his game, relaxed, took a step back, and in a perfectly normal voice explained to the old man that Randalph here had bet him a pint of beer for every Bay City Roller cassette he could shoot out of the sky with one barrel, and that he (Bascom) had returned the bet.

Satisfied, Willie the shopkeeper produced two boxes full of cassettes and suggested the boys might find what they were looking for, adding wryly "If you find any by Andy Stuart, you might want to shoot them too". To the boy's disappointment, there were only half a dozen Bay tapes, but around a dozen ABBA tapes. They bought up all of both, thanked Willie for his kind help and headed off to the armoury store.

Bolstered once more with his habitual stage aloofness, Bascom opened up a conversation with Fergy, the old gunsmith, beginning with some small talk about the weather he then asked if he knew where we could buy a tank. "A tank, Bascom?" Randalph could tell this was not the first time Bascom had joked with old Fergy. "Not this week", he replied, "I'm afraid, we sold the last one to your old neighbour who was complaining about the noise coming from your caravan. If you're at war with the old bugger I might have a look in the back of the shop for a rocket launcher. Would that do the trick?"

Bascom and old Fergy were struggling hard to suppress their grins. Despite the bleakness of the landscape, the poverty of the soil and the harsh conditions of life on the island, which might lead someone to think that islanders were just poor country folk, they were witty, steadfast, gifted with a rare sense of humour, and not easily caught off balance by someone pawning nonsense.

"I was thinking more along the lines of a cruise missile," replied Bascom, "but I would need a

submarine to launch it. You don't happen to have one moored in the bay?"

"Russian or American?" continued Fergy in a perfectly flat voice.

"I'll take both," said Bascom, adding "Oh, and two boxes of twelve-bore cartridges when you're at it, please. If you could wrap them up with the submarines, I'll make some space in the boot of the car."

The two big boxes of cartridges cost a week's wages. The bets won or lost on shooting down the cassettes would cost another week's. But fun was priceless, and the joy of shouting "pull", throwing the cassettes up into the air and doing your utmost to hit them was gold.

And so it came to pass, on a long summer's evening in the year of our Lord 1977, that all traces of ABBA and the Bay City Rollers were removed from potential public possession, leaving the islanders free from moral contamination. It also left Bascom's old neighbour thundering insults and threatening with his hand in a pistol imitation from his single-pane, one-foot square kitchen window to blow the boys away if they didn't put their fuckin' guns down.

On a bend in the road at the bottom of the dirt track where Bascom's caravan was parked stood a 30 mph (50 km/h) sign. This was a great offence to the two boys, who could comfortably corner the bend at more than 70 mph (112 km/h), and on one unusually warm dry day even managed to round it at 80 mph (128 Km/h). The boys reckoned that something had to be done to get rid of the sign, and came up with a plan. Betting against each other on how many shots it would take to knock the sign over they bought another couple of boxes of cartridges, borrowed the tractor from the farmer next door, attached its front loader scoop, and stood side by side on the scoop, a few feet from the sign, and started shooting at it. By the time they had downed the sign they had been deafened by the relentless shooting and were nursing their shoulders, which by then were bruised black and blue. To the locals who passed by in their cars, there was no sign of surprise or alarm – it was just Bascom.

The month drove on with pranks and laughter, but also with hard work and lots of cash to show for it. By the time they parted, when Randalph set off for Sweden, it was as if they had exhausted their reserves of boisterous fun. The game was over. Life was calling. It was time to say goodbye.

Randalph and Bascom finally parted company, not by choice but blown in opposite directions by the unpredictable winds of life on earth. Randalph continued his studies of Civil Engineering for another two years, later doing his best to avoid the world of engineering altogether, moving from job to job and country to country, while Bascom became a stalwart manual worker who worked his way with intelligence and determination to the top of Scotland's then booming fossil fuel industry.

The boys met again only one more time, some twenty or more years later when Randalph was touring Scotland with a friend of his, his youngest son Timothy and a friend of his son. As they approached Bascom's little cottage, Randalph felt uncomfortable. He knew that the silliness-at-the-expense-of-others chapter of his life no longer held any appeal to him. He had turned that page long since. What would it be like to meet Bascom again after such a long time? Would they still be friends? Would they still have a laugh?

Randalph's three companions de route never forgot the encounter as they sat spellbound listening to the boys' tales of past bravado and silliness, all five with tears running down their faces. It was good for Randalph to see Bascom again. Today he hopes that Bascom is well and happy, wherever he is, whatever he's doing, and whoever he's enjoying life with.

After waving goodbye to Bascom, sailing back to the mainland, picking up his gear back home, and heading off by train to Newcastle and the ferry to Gothenburg, Randalph set sail for part two of summer 77 in Sweden. As instructed in his introductory letter and contract, Randalph turned up for work at the offices of his next summer employer in Stockholm early on the first Monday in July. Mr Jörg, or whatever his name was, said he should report to the road maintenance team who were based in the outskirts of the city and handed him an address.

With only a paper map and a bus route timetable to guide him, Randalph eventually found the depot, where he hung around until the maintenance team got back from their day's work repairing holes in Stockholm's roads.

Randolph's heart sank when he saw them. They were an unkempt bunch clothed in checkered workers' shirts half tucked into their tar-stained jeans, and half-hanging over their pouting beer bellies, with filthy handkerchiefs tied round their necks like sailors and worn-out head bands presumably intended to stop the sweat pouring down their faces. Not one spoke a word of English and Randolph, despite trying to learn Swedish the previous winter, could only muster up a few sentences.

It was too late in the day for Randolph to do anything other than say hello, and so they parted, the asphalt gang tapping insistently on their watches to impress on him that he should be there tomorrow at 4.45am – the truck left the depot at 5 am sharp.

Randolph's sole reason for coming to Sweden was to be with his lady friend Göta from the far north. The job in Stockholm was no more than a stepping stone to that end. Sadly, his dream was not to be. Göta had other plans for her life and wanted freedom – it was too early for her to be tied up in a relationship, she said. Besides, she had admirers with big motorbikes, plans to live in a kibbutz in Israel, and talked about crossing the Atlantic to Argentina with a Danish 'travelling high school' in an old three-mast schooner. Her dreams were far beyond the narrow world of Randolph's limited experience, involving things he didn't even know existed. During the two months that Randolph spent in Sweden, they saw each other only once. Randolph was heartbroken. After work he would walk the streets of Stockholm's old town, crossing the bridges from one side of the city's many islands to the other, staying away from the cafés where people met, too sore to sit down and face his loneliness.

Although Göta came to see Randalph several times during his remaining two years of study in Glasgow, and although she kept up contact with him, Randalph was never able to heal his wound. Something had broken inside him. Their story was not to become the fairytale romance he had once believed in.

His job gave him little satisfaction but paid well. In the early morning, his team would drive to an asphalt plant in the suburbs, load on to their truck a dozen tons of hot asphalt and half a dozen shovels, and hitch the low-loader trailer carrying a road roller, a narrow-gage asphalt paver, and a hand-held asphalt paver, and head for whichever holes they were to repair that day.

On his third day on the job, they asked Randalph if he could drive and showed him the truck's gears and hydraulics. Randalph had a UK car driving licence, no insurance, and only the experience of the previous summer driving on the right side of the road in Göta's father's old Volvo, but he also had a year of intense 'advanced' training under his belt and a strong desire to take up the challenge, so he said yes. From then on, and on every working day for the next two months, he drove an articulated Skandia truck with a total load of around 40 tonnes, totally illegally, through the streets of the city, swinging the massive Skandia from right to left as he negotiated corners, bends and roundabouts. It was his only pleasure, and he exploited it to the full.

Now that the gang had a driver, they could focus freely on drinking beer. On many days, especially towards the end of the week, by around eleven o'clock in the morning the three asphalteers were already so drunk that they could hardly stand and would sit around sweating, burping and farting, crushing empty can after empty can of Pripps Bla beer under their feet. With the exception of their gaudy, raucous outbursts of sneers and gritty laughter, presumably at some coarse joke or remark, the men were sulky, impolite, coarse, unfriendly and stinking of stale sweat.

Summer dragged on. The city was getting Randalph down and reminded him of the world of Orwell's *1984* with its stark concrete and glass facades, drunks lying around by the dozens on street corners, and taut, humourless faces who would not exchange a friendly glance with strangers.

One day, as if sympathetic to Randalph's desperate need for some humour and fun, the gods conjured up the appropriate scenario. The gang had emptied more than half of the asphalt in the tipper truck's bin by early morning and had arrived at a road maintenance site where they needed the rest of the load. By then, the bin's base had become sticky and had to be sprayed with solvent so that the mass of asphalt could slide down freely onto the road surface. Although Randalph had tilted the tipper upwards, the asphalt refused to budge.

Swearing loudly and shouting at Randalph to lift the bin even more, Sven, the leader of the three asphalteers, climbed into the bin, stood with his heatproof boots on the asphalt, and started clawing at the mass with a pick. All of a sudden, the hot asphalt began to slide downwards, tipping Sven over backwards and landing him on his bottom on the sticky black mass of burning stones coated with steaming liquid bitumen. The few seconds that it took him to slide out of the bin and land on the road were enough to burn through the seat of his jeans and scald the skin of his bottom.

Randalph couldn't contain himself. He was roaring with laughter watching Sven jumping up and down like a circus clown with his two hands clutching his scorched bottom. In his native Scotland, anyone who witnessed Sven's antics would have burst out laughing; bystanders would be wetting themselves, but not in Sweden. The gang turned on Randalph, cursing him, shouting "det är inte roligt" (it's not funny), and gave him some hefty kicks and a slap on the head. Swedes, Randalph concluded, have no sense of humour, and a land with no humour was no land for him.

By then it was already mid-August. Randalph had had enough. His Swedish bubble had burst. The next morning, he went to the company's office and handed in his notice. On 1st September he would be gone, resolved never to return to this land of the humourless.

On his train journey southwards and away from Sweden, somewhere between Copenhagen and Hamburg, Randalph enjoyed another short restroom romance, this time with a young German Fräulein, and resolved to go and stay for the remainder of the summer at his aunt's family home near Bonn.

A few days after he arrived, he was invited to a party on his aunt's street where he met and danced with the very classy and much-sought-after divorced Rote Rosie who lived with her daughter next door to his aunt's family. He promptly jumped into bed with her, fuelling a scandal that shook the village for the whole month of September.

Rosie was twenty years older than Randalph, had time on her hands and cared nothing for what the people were saying. She had a sky-blue VW Beetle in which they spent carefree days driving around and exploring the Rhineland. You lose one, you win one, thought young Randalph with the wind in his hair at the wheel of Rote Rosie's iconic little car.

THIRD YEAR

Having spent the first half of the summer on the Shetland Islands and the rest in Sweden and Germany, there was no way Randalph was going to return home to the domestic chaos of life with Helma. To secure his escape, he had applied for and been accepted for a second year at the Ross Hall students' residence where he had stayed during his first year.

Remembering the long hours he had spent during that first year travelling on public transport to occasionally come home for weekends, this year, his third year, he decided he would have his own transport, so as not to have to rely on buses and trains. During the couple of weeks he spent at home immediately after returning from Germany, and before moving back to the halls, Randalph grabbed the opportunity of purchasing a second-hand Yamaha 250 CC motorbike from someone in his village.

With the intention of turning his Yamaha into a racing bike, like the ones he had seen on TV or talked about with friends, he got rid of everything heavy on the bike he considered superfluous, stripping the machine down to the bare essentials. This included getting rid of the kick start, which he thought he didn't need as he could bump start the bike. As usual, Randalph knew better than the people around him, whom he didn't bother to ask for advice, and set about the bike with hammers, screwdrivers, pliers and a hacksaw.

In truth, Randalph had never owned a motor bike and had no clue about what he was doing, nor about the price he was about to pay for his ignorance and arrogance. Once the bike was stripped down and looking sleek and fast, Randalph wheeled it to the end of the lane behind their family home, slipped it into third gear, pushed with all his might and, when he thought he had enough speed up, jumped onto the bike. It slowly ground to a halt with a coughing sound as its two pistons exhaled oily air. He tried again in third gear and then in second, but still there was no sign of the engine igniting.

The last option was to try in first gear, but if the engine caught, he knew he would have to be very quick to pull in the clutch. A racing biker would know the trick, as would his good friend Donald from the village, who had moved on from scouring the countryside with Randalph to repairing motorbikes for a living and doing stunts for films with trial bikes. Randalph had only heard the trick talked about and seen it on television, but knew nothing about how to actually perform it.

Less sure of himself by now and in spite of the voice he heard inside his head telling him to be careful, he once again pushed the bike as fast as he could and, as he leaped on, dropped the clutch as if it was made of red-hot steel. Instantly, the engine roared into life. The unbridled centripetal force of the back wheel spinning and whipping up gravel drove the bike forwards and lifted the front wheel off the ground until it was almost vertically above the back wheel. Randalph, who by this time was clinging desperately to the handlebars and flying at about 45 degrees to the ground behind the bike as it accelerated and sped forwards had let go of the clutch altogether and opened the throttle fully, propelling the bike ever faster forwards on its back wheel.

At the end of Randalph's family garden stood a wooden garage where the family car slept behind double wooden doors opening onto the lane. On that day, Randalph had parked the car along the pavement at the front of the house and the garage was empty. As fate would have it, the bike, by now probably travelling at around 30 mph (50 km/h), swerved uncontrollably just in front of the garage and crashed straight through the lightweight wooden garage doors.

Randalph, the new Flying Scotsman, was protected by the mass of the bike, which took the brunt of the crash and continued on by itself to the end of the garage, smashing its way through the glass windows Randalph's father and himself had added a few years before his death. At the moment of impact he let go, landing on the wooden floor. He rolled over and was gathering himself up when he heard Helma screaming. From the kitchen window she had heard the crash and seen the glass flying and was now running up the garden path with a knife and fork in her hands crying out "Jimmy, Jimmy" – she sometimes confused Randalph with his dad. The ensuing commotion, emotional outbursts, chiding, and tears reinforced Randalph's deep conviction that his decision to leave was the right one.

The next day he repaired the doors and wheeled the bike up to a country house at the top of a hillock in a park in the centre of the village where the owner – the father of brother Jack's girlfriend – said he could store it until it was repaired. Unfortunately, the owner's goat got to the bike before any repairs were made. It chewed up the saddle and the cables and pushed it over on its side, sending it to its final resting place on a grassy patch next to an old oak tree.

Randalph promised to pay back to his mother the £144 she had lent him to buy the bike, called the warden at Ross Hall to ask if he could come earlier than planned, packed his bags, jumped on the next bus to Glasgow and never came home again for weeks. He was off.

When he arrived at Ross Hall, he was two years older than when he first set foot there at the beginning of his first year. The suicidal Maggie had gone, as had the bitch with the stiletto heels. The residents seemed more civilised, gentler, and he sparked off a hilarious friendship with the warden, the very illustrious Dr J.

As if in preparation for his fourth and final year at university, which was to be one of the most enjoyable years of Randalph's life, his third year was totally uneventful. No pranks, no mischief, not much fun, no new girlfriends. As the only antidote to the boredom of studying, he sharpened his aim on the snooker table, read more and more of 'his' books, increased his consumption of beer, put on weight and joined in tournaments of table football. In occasional moments of lucidity and fear for the future, he began to seriously wonder about what he was going to do with his life after his studies were over.

Now that his third year was coming to an end, the time had come for Randalph to find a serious summer job that would count as points towards his degree and would therefore need to be work that fell under the broad umbrella of practical training in Civil Engineering. After months of writing begging letters to the nation's better-known construction and consulting firms, Randalph was invited for an interview at a reputable consultancy firm in Cambridge where, to his astonishment, he was offered a summer job with a reasonable salary and an allowance that would cover his lodgings and one return trip home. Randalph in Cambridge in the land of the toffs? He already felt uplifted and superior to his classmates, who, for the most part, had opted for jobs closer to home, having not yet severed their umbilical cords with their native Scotland.

Although he felt stuck in the cul-de-sac of a subject he couldn't muster up a flair for, surrounded by classmates who somehow got it, outside university Randalph was on the move. Unquestionably a lesser engineer than any of them, Randalph did nevertheless hold the upper hand when it came to mobility. Entice him with the name of some far-off city and before you knew it, he would be heading straight for it on the next train. Randalph had not the slightest second thought or hesitation about taking a summer job in Cambridge, and straight away signed on the dotted line.

STARSKY AND HUTCH – SUMMER '78

Randalph liked Cambridge. He loved the greens, the river, the grandiose architecture of the colleges and their courtyards, the old pubs, and the centuries-old streets where great men like Sir Isaac Newton had once walked. He discovered there that he also liked rowing, and for three months on end he got up early most mornings to take his seat on the company's octuple sculling shell – an eight-person rowing boat, which was stored in the prestigious St. John's College's Lady Margaret Boat Club on the bend in the river opposite Jesus Green.

Randalph cringed when he remembered trying his hand at rowing the previous winter on the oily-brown frothing waters of the polluted River Clyde in Glasgow, where you had to look out for thugs on the bridges who took a delight in dropping bricks or other heavy objects on the boats, while also keeping your eyes on the river to avoid landing your paddle on floating objects, which could be anything from wooden chairs and tables to the carcases of dead dogs.

The reputable firm of consulting engineers where Randalph had landed had opened two positions for students that summer. One was the job that Randalph had somehow been entrusted with and the other was the position given to Harry from Manchester, who was soon to become Randalph's bosom partner in mischief and misdemeanour. On meeting for the first time, the two boys struck up a friendship like it was love at first sight, and it was not long before they were roaming the streets together in the evenings, looking for fun and distractions.

1978 was the summer after the release of the John Badham film *Saturday Night Fever*, and the pubs and bars by the river in Cambridge where the young crowd gathered were full of John Travolta imitators, one arm outstretched reaching for the stars, the other pointing rigidly to the ground, head cocked back, feet jiving, body spinning on its heels, wherever there was space enough to dance. You hardly heard an English accent. The privileged sons and daughters of noblesse, royalty and the fortuned had returned to their castles for the summer. The young people there were for the greater part summer students from all over the world, drawn to historical Cambridge to learn or build on their knowledge of the Queen's English. The atmosphere was electric, young, all smiles, an all-summer party.

Randalph and Harry would remember this summer forever for their improvised game of Starsky and Hutch and the night it went horribly wrong. Zigzagging in between parked cars on each side of the inner city's narrow lanes after a few beers, they got their greatest kicks from springing out, one from each side of the line of parked cars, squatting low, legs splayed out, and pointing their hands in imitation of handguns at oncoming traffic, like David Soul and Paul Michael Glaser in the TV series.

At every single holdup the car approaching them would slam on the brakes and you could see the frightened look of the driver and the front-seat passenger, sometimes covering their eyes with their hands. Randalph Starsky and Harry Hutch would then run like the wind down to the river and disappear along the narrow lanes leading back to the centre to lie low somewhere and laugh their guts inside out.

One night their act went wrong. Blue lights lit up on the roof of the car they had held up. Like Tam, the hero of Randalph's favourite Rabbie Burns poem who startled a dance of witches on a dark and stormy winter's night in Alloway's old haunted church, this was not a time to hang around and see what happens next. And just like Tam, who was being chased by a hellish legion and the very devil himself, the boys ran for their lives.

They ran and they ran and they ran. Down by the river, along the banks, back into town, then back to the river and finally under a steel girder bridge, where they spent most of the night, firstly clinging to the upper girders upside down like bats in a church spire, then squeezed between them like wedges, their hands and arms aching, grimly holding on. There were police everywhere with their sirens wailing and you could hear their distant chatter on their radios.

Randalph and Harry were shitting themselves. This was not just a prank gone wrong, this was prison for a long time if they got caught. As the night drew out, the police withdrew, and by the time the summer sun's first rays were sparkling and dancing on the water's surface the coast was clear. To avoid all suspicion, they still had to get to their respective homes, change, and be at the office on time. Looking back, Randalph sometimes thought about the laws of the universe, what people today call karma, wondering why it is that some get caught and some run free. He never found out.

Undeterred by their narrow escape, but with their Starsky and Hutch prank abandoned forever, Randalph and Harry needed to find another outlet for their insatiable appetite for fun. The perfect next victim in line was one of their colleagues, a frightfully proper too-well-educated elite-private-school-type golden boy built like a stick insect with long spindly arms and legs who had the exasperating habit of putting on an admiring smile and saying something condescending whenever one of the bosses walked by. Randalph and Harry had nicknamed him Rodney Butter Boy.

In the 1970s, before the advent of computers and mobile phones, the working day for office staff began at 9 am and finished at 5 pm. Only the extremely zealous stayed on a minute longer. Lunch and coffee breaks were included in the eight hours, and it was common to start the day with a cup of tea and a chat with colleagues inside working time. Despite the occasional anti-sports outburst from Randalph's department head, one of the few staff members with a beer belly, who upheld the point of view that sports should be banned, staff like Randalph, who were part of the company rowing team, had permission to turn up at the office at 9.30am. Outside these eight hours, the firm could be reached via a telephone voice recorder with messages picked up by Bentje, the big boss's personal assistant, who was Dutch, smart, trilingual – she also spoke German – and was married to a marine biologist who studied sharks.

Randalph and Harry were disgusted by Rodney's habit of licking the boots of passer-by bosses and came up with a plan to embarrass him. In the evenings, now that they had been immunised against playing at Starsky and Hutch, once they had downed a few pints they would squeeze into a telephone booth down by the river and call the company's answering phone. After the 'please leave your message' prompt, one of them would announce in a posh English accent spoken into a handkerchief as in gangster films that he was Rodney from the dams department, and continue with a message for Mr McKenzie, the Managing Director, saying how much he enjoyed working for his wonderful company and underlining his unwavering loyalty and total commitment to its success.

This went on relentlessly for weeks, until one day at about mid-morning Bentje put out a call for the boys on the department intercom asking them to come up to the directors' suite on the top floor. The directors' suite was a plush lounge beyond two swinging doors with stained glass windows and polished brass doorhandles where both boys had been welcomed on their first day by their respective department heads. To get to the suite you had to pass in front of the very alert Bentje, who manned her desk as if it was Checkpoint Charlie. Beyond the suite was the MD's office.

Not sure why they had been called for, the boys tried to chat up Bentje to get some info before meeting the MD but were met only by a dry "It's about the messages". This rang in the boys' ears like a death sentence. They looked at each other and then at Bentje. Harry smoothly switched into defensive mode and asked innocently "What messages?" Bentje just smiled, saying "I'm sure you'll be able to explain them to Mr McKenzie". Holy fuck! How had she found out?

Like lambs heading to the slaughter they crossed the suite, knocked timidly on the MD's door, waited for his sign to come in, pushed open his door, then ventured into his spacious office awaiting further instructions. "Have a seat," said Mr McKenzie in a friendly tone. "Bentje told me you wanted to see me. What can I do for you?"

They had been had. Bentje was having her revenge. The silence that ensued seemed to last for an eternity.

"Well?" said McKenzie, looking the boys questioningly in the eyes.

"It's about the messages," piped up Harry, who was always a step ahead of Randalph when it came to cheek.

"What messages?"

"The phone messages, sir."

"What phone messages?" The boys were trapped, caught in the nets of the prosecution, standing naked and defenceless before their executioner.

Harry took the lead, trying to explain that it seemed that someone was sending messages to the company and that Bentje thought we might know something about them. McKenzie promptly called in Bentje, who had rehearsed her lines and came out with a story about anonymous phone messages, suggesting that as the boys were students and not on the permanent staff, they might be able to shed a light on who the culprits were. For a moment it looked like three heads were going to roll, but McKenzie was no fool and it was plain to see that he intuitively knew what was happening. With a "Thank you Bentje, I'll handle this from here" he turned to the boys.

McKenzie's expression had changed from that of a friendly old geezer to the frown of a supreme-court judge about to sentence a gang of thugs to death by fire. "Now listen here, chaps, I don't know what's going on and don't want to," he bellowed, "But if you're up to some mischief or other, I'll have you thrown out of this office headfirst down the stairs and you'll never set foot in it again. Is that clear?"

With their sentence reduced from death to a suspended sentence of banishment, the boys apologised, promised it would never happen again, and walked out like beaten dogs, past Bentje, who was beaming at them with a victory-day smile on her face, and headed for the lift.

After the Starsky and Hutch chase and now this humiliation, it took the boys a full week to recover from their wounds before plucking up courage to hit the road again. Their next and final lark was to run down the back lanes of the old town between gardens with their trousers down, flashing their bums at startled householders and leaping to safety over the perimeter wall with its glazed fireclay coping stones before anyone could catch them or call the police.

Their endless tears of laughter after this, their latest gem, quickly erased the memory of the chase and the scolding by old McKenzie as they each downed half a dozen well-deserved self-congratulatory pints and staggered home, their hearts ablaze with the camaraderie of partners in crime.

Before the summer came to an end, Randalph accepted the offer from his house mates – Bill and Ben, as Harry and Randalph called them – for a lift back with them to Scotland for a weekend. The two Flowerpot Men came from Kirkcaldy and could drop Randalph off in Edinburgh, where he could catch a train to Glasgow and then the bus home. Sitting in the back of the car and looking out at the increasingly drab, grey, damp, inhospitableness of Bonnie

Scotland, he was reminded of the sadness that had gripped him so often as a kid at the end of his summer holidays in Germany as he drove with his parents across the Scottish moors in pouring rain after weeks of sunshine and the easy life in the heart of continental Europe.

In a few weeks he would have to return to Glasgow for a fourth year of study. One more winter to survive. He had no idea where he would be heading to after that but knew it would be somewhere south. Randalph looked out at a flock of miserable sheep, huddled together on a rain-drenched hillside under a tree bending in the wind. He wondered if they knew that if they were to walk southwards for a week or two, they could dry out, start a new life, and enjoy blue skies and sunshine, as Randalph was going to do as soon as he could.

FOURTH YEAR

In his last year as a student, Randalph shared a posh Victorian flat in Queen's Drive, on the edge of Queen's Park on the south side of Glasgow, one of the city's most distinctive examples of Victorian architecture and designed by Scots architect William McNicol Whyte in the 1880s.

The flat had been bought by the very learned Dr J., the previous warden of Ross Hall, whom Randalph had befriended. Dr J. was a renowned professor of German literature and culture, and he would join the flatmates when they pissed themselves laughing watching anything funny on television, and in particular the John Cleese Fawlty Towers series during which Dr J. used to shout out "It's us, they're filming us". He would invent hilarious similarities between the Fawlty Towers crew and his flatmates as he slid off of his armchair onto the floor, tears streaming down his cheeks.

The other two flatmates were Nathan, an extraordinarily likeable Aussie motorbike mechanic with no formal education who had a remarkable attention to detail and understanding of how things worked, and Kazim, a Turkish Masters student who cheered something in Arabic every time Randalph brought home a lassie for the night.

Nathan was passionate about industrial archaeology. He drank a crate of their favourite Bellhaven Beer with Randalph almost every Friday night listening to Dire Straits and Bob Dylan. To the disgust of the local academia, he was awarded an honorary PhD in recognition of his devotion, knowledge about and contribution towards the subject.

Later, when Kazim moved out, they were joined by Kevin, a self-indulgent English snob with a posh accent whose wife used to spend hours in the bathroom in the evening, leaving the lads no other option when their beer-inflated bladders reached bursting point than to piss out of their third-floor kitchen window onto the courtyard below.

"Indecent exposure," said the two coppers (policemen) who turned up on the doorstep on one occasion on a summer evening and marched Randalph and Nathan down to the Victoria Police Station where they got a bollocking (were reprimanded), a booking, and some free education about Scottish presbyterian morals, learning that hanging your wullie (dick) out in public was as much an offence as beating up some poor bugger half to death.

Nathan and Randalph became close friends. On Thursday nights they used to go out for a pint together at a nearby pub, then head down to the old cinema on Victoria Road to watch the Clint Eastwood movies that were showing there over the winter. It was the highlight of the week, and after another few pints on the road home they'd be doing Dirty Harry imitations, reliving the spaghetti Western showdowns, or playing at being Clint.

One night on the way home they strolled into a pub just round the corner from Queen's Drive, with their noisy imitations in full swing. Apparently they were too loud and boisterous for local tastes. In Glasgow, rule number one was 'don't draw attention to yourself'. They got to the bar and were about to order when they were approached by a grim, stalkily-built, grisly middle-aged working man with a cigarette in the corner of his mouth, a loosely-hanging tattered tweed jacket on his back, rough-looking hands with bloody knuckles and a no-mercy look in his eyes. He grabbed Randalph by the lapels, pushed him up against the bar and growled at him like a dog about to bite, saying: "You're the bastard that buys me pints. Right?" He was absolutely right. Randalph was the bastard who, that night, was going to buy him pints. Lots of pints. And he was going to keep buying him pints until the last-orders bell rang just before closing time at 10 pm.

It was one of those cold, wet nights where the rain somehow managed to get inside the back of your coat lapels and dribble down your sleeves. It could have been a night for moaning and groaning in self-pity about being put in their place by the rough guy in the pub, but the boys were still alive and standing, with only their pride knocked down a rung or two which, in Glasgow at the time, was tantamount to a miracle.

Freed at last by the 10 o'clock bell announcing last orders, Randalph and Nathan left as soon as the last beers were paid for and made a beeline for home. Happy as they were to be unscathed, they were nevertheless hungry for revenge. If they had had more courage or were typical Glasgow guys, they would have kicked the shit out of the guy in the pub, as Clint would have done, but as they were both softies at heart they had to settle for a gentler form of vengeance.

With the rain showing no sign of abating, the wind driving spray from the puddles in the street, and the streetlamps lighting up the streaks of marble-sized rain drops as they battered down from the black skies, it was a perfect night for a favourite prank Randalph and Nathan had already played a few times before.

Stopping at the local fish n' chip shop on the corner of Victoria Road to buy two big portions of greasy chips wrapped in yesterday's copy of the *Daily Record* newspaper, the boys prepared their retaliation. As they walked along the elegant sweeping curve of Queens Drive on the way back to their apartment, there were cars parked along the kerb. Making sure no one saw them, they firmly squeezed two or three squashy chips onto the wiper blades of half a dozen of the cars. Then they kept on walking past the entrance to their flat and on round the corner by the church before doubling back through the back yard of window-pissing fame. They sneaked quietly through the back door and up the stairs to their flat, where they cracked open a celebration can of beer, giggling like schoolgirls in anticipation of the scene they would witness the next morning.

The last beer downed, the boys then set their alarm clocks for 7 am and went to bed relatively early. The next morning they got up when the world was still asleep, dressed, put the kettle on for a cup of tea, then took up their positions hiding behind the heavy draped curtains of the front room and peeked out through the pouring rain, waiting for their first victim to show.

Sure enough, a dark shadow could soon be seen walking quickly towards the parked cars, lapels held high, carrying an umbrella. He opened his car door, shook the rain from his coat, sat down in the driver's seat, started the engine, put the lights on, and – the moment of truth – switched on the windscreen wipers. You could almost hear the squish, squish of the blades as they smeared the cold, greasy chips across the windscreen.

The intensity of the atmosphere inside the apartment was unbearable. The boys were holding their breaths, as if a bomb was about to go off. Any second now all hell would break loose.

The car door opened. The driver got out and scraped away what was left of the chips from the wipers. His fingers would be covered with cold grease. "Ya fuckin bastards. I'll fuckin kill ye, ya wee shites!"

Randalph and Nathan ducked down, revelling in the rain-muffled shouting, swearing and abuse they could hear coming up from the street. The driver stomped off, presumably to get a cloth or a rag from home, appearing a few minutes later raging like a tied-up tiger. It would take more than a piece of cloth to remove the streaks of grease from the windscreen.

Immediately after, a second driver appeared and followed suit, adding his abuse and anger to the curses of the first.

Randalph and Nathan were by then lying on the floor, clutching their sides, gutting themselves with laughter, drowning in tears of mischief. They knew full well that if they were ever caught they would probably be killed or beaten to senseless pulp on the street, but this had not deterred them. In Glasgow, you got your kicks where you could. An eye for an eye, violence met with violence, ignorance by ignorance. The innocent victims of the hard man in the pub the night before had become perpetrators of the misfortune of others. Looking back, Randalph could still enjoy the memory of the fun, but knew deep down that his acts had not contributed to making a better world – he was as guilty as anyone else for the deplorable state humanity was in.

Just around the corner from their apartment and along the street were the dormitories and bedrooms for the night staff of Glasgow's Western Infirmary. On their various sorties in the neighbourhood, Randalph and Nathan had observed that this foreboding pile of grime-blackened sandstone was in fact a four-storey-high stronghold full of lots and lots of young nurses. Could there be a way in, they wondered…

After successive failed attempts to get past the night guards and having run out of plausible stories to fool them with, Randalph and Nathan changed tactics. If they couldn't get in through the front door, they'd get in through a window. Hiding behind parked cars and the few trees that lined the road behind the hospital they spotted a 4" (100mm) diameter gutter pipe that drained the rain from the roof down past a first-floor window that was often open and regularly lit. A toilet window perhaps? They checked it out, all the while exchanging with each other their raunchy daydreams about what they would do with all these juicy young girls in their tight, smart nurses' uniforms. They decided to give it a try.

Committed to having a go at climbing the gutter pipe and trying to squeeze through the open window, the lads rehearsed their lines about what to say in the very likely event of being caught. Then one dark night, having drunk enough beer to pluck up the courage to scale the pipe, they climbed up, pushed open the window, and found themselves in a ladies' toilet on the first floor, where they promptly locked the door. Behind the door, they could hear nurses' chatter from inside the toilet block and beyond. Hoping no one would knock on their door, they waited until the coast was clear.

In a lull in the chatter, the lads gingerly unlocked the toilet door, peaked their heads out to check for danger, tiptoed out of the toilet, crossed the toilet block to the main door and stepped out into the corridor. They knew it was suicide, a plan destined to fail, but what the fuck. Hurrying to get as far away from the toilets as possible before being spotted, they were halfway along the long corridor when a door opened and two nurses stepped out.

Randalph opened up the conversation with "Eh, excuse me ladies, we're very sorry, we're here to check the plumbing in the changing rooms. Could you show us where they are?" The girls looked at each other. This was a ladies-only zone. Besides, it was night, and the two would-be plumbers definitely didn't look the part. It took the girls only a startled second to work out that something was not right. "Get the fuck out of here ya filthy bastards or a'll cau the police!" screamed one of them. "Come on love, we're just here for a laugh. Gee's a smile," ventured Nathan in an attempt to defuse the bomb that was about to blow up in their faces.

There was going to be no smile, no welcome glitter in the eye and no invitation to join them in their room to play at doctors and nurses. When Glasgow girls get upset it's best to stay clear, and these two were ready for war. The only course of action left to the lads was to run like fuck, and keep running until they were clear.

As they soon found out, it's not easy to run when you're half pissed, in stitches with laughter and at the same time terrified of being caught. Randalph, however, was fast on his feet and on many occasions in the past running had saved him.

Once at the end of the corridor, running the gauntlet past a dozen doors, some of which were opening as the nurses' reserve detachment answered the war cry from the two front-liners in the corridor, the lads hurled open two heavy swinging doors and almost dived down the central stair well. At school, Randalph had practised jumping half a flight of stairs at a time, touching the ground only seven times as he hurtled down the four-storey school building to get out first at break time or away from whoever was out to catch him. Here, in imminent danger of being captured and probably beaten to a pulp by twenty or more angry nurses, one leap swallowed up the first ten steps and the second landed him on the floor of the giant hall that led to the exit corridor. Nathan, who was also quick on his feet, was right behind him.

While the lads were escaping at Olympian speed from their certain doom, the sound of the commotion and the cries of "Stop the bastards!" had already reached the doorman, and security people who until a moment ago had been sitting on chairs under the stairs having a smoke began converging on the main entrance. The lads needed inspiration, and they needed it now.

This was one of those moments when only the hand of God could save the day, and it looked like the Almighty had heard their plea. "There's a bomb!" screamed out Nathan, "Run for your fucking lives! There's a bomb!" Randalph joined his voice to Nathan's, imploring everyone to leave the building: "Get out!" he cried, "Everybody out! Open the door and let the people out!"

It was a stroke of genius. As Randalph recalls the scene, dozens of people were running behind the lads, echoing their cry about the bomb, fleeing to safety. All hell had broken loose. Randalph would remember this night as the fastest and furthest sprint of his life. The lads darted out of the hospital grounds like hares escaping from a pack of hounds. They zigzagged their way to the park nearby, ran halfway round it, skipped over a gate, jumped behind some bushes growing around a big tree on the mound in the centre of the park near the pond and collapsed, gasping for breath in thigh-high sodden grass, crying their eyes out with laughter, the adrenalin still pumping furiously in their veins in case they needed to make another run for it. "There's a bomb!" would be their rallying cry for years to come.

Enjoying his last year at university to the full, Randalph decided to throw a massive party to celebrate his 21st birthday and rented the student's union function room on the fourth floor on Union Street with his classmate Henry, who also had his birthday in December. About seventy of their classmates turned up. Once everyone had been accounted for and had had a drink, somebody in the crowd produced a big carpet and rolled it flat onto the floor. Randalph's morale sank into a bottomless pit. Shit – it looked like the guests were going to give the two birthday boys 'the dumps'.

This was when somebody celebrating their twenty-first birthday got either twenty-one hefty hits on the back or, as was about to happen, something even worse. Randalph was grabbed by a dozen classmates, thrown onto the carpet and tossed twenty-one times into the air to the applause of all in the room, who seemed to revel in his screams as he crashed to the floor. An observer writing about Glasgow would remark that there couldn't be fun in the city without somebody getting hurt. The crowd seems to relish cries of pain.

Henry, the other birthday boy and next in line for floor bashing, was much smaller than Randalph and probably only half his weight. Accustomed by then to the effort needed to toss Randalph up in the air, the carpet gang launched poor Henry with the same force, propelling him straight into the low-hanging plasterboard suspended ceiling, which came crashing down in a cloud of dust and pieces of asbestos all over him and those holding the carpet.

The howls of laughter that burst out in unison across the room could probably be heard on the street outside. The scene was indeed hilarious. The same observer would also remark that the misfortune of others is perhaps the greatest source of mirth in the city, and so it came to pass that this epic episode with featherweight Henry crashing into the ceiling was given a special place in Randalph's big book of amusing disasters.

While the guests found it funny, the janitors, who in the meantime had turned up, didn't. In fact, they were so pissed off that for a moment it looked like all seventy or so guests were going to be thrown over the banister and end up in a pool of blood on the floor of the entrance hall four levels below. The janitors were not well versed in diplomatic speak and their threat came over in language that left no doubt to their intentions. "You! The fuckin lot o' you! Yer gonna pay for this, ya bunch o' stupid useless shites. Every fuckin one o' you!"

The room fell silent.

The janitors consulted for a few minutes, looking up at the ceiling and down at the mess on the floor, then one of them pronounced their verdict. "Each an every fuckin' one o' you's gonna cough up a fiver. If you don't, yer deed. D'you hear me?" The silence deepened. "We'll kick the fuck out o' anybody who doesn'y chip in and throw them ower the banister."

The absence of smiles on the faces of the guests suggested

that everyone had heard and understood the verdict. To make sure they had, the janitors repeated it: "A fiver each, or we'll kick the teeth oot o' the fuckin lot of you – you bunch o' stupit fuckin' bastards!"

When extreme violence is promised in Glasgow, extreme violence happens. There's no way out of it. The city was a dangerous place for anyone ignorant enough to believe you could negotiate your way through threats of grievous bodily harm. The price was set. The fun was over. One by one, everyone present dug into their pockets to pay the furious janitors their estimated cost of repairs. It was time to go home.

As birthday presents, Randalph had received five or six bottles of cheap whisky. It was now up to him to find a way to get the bottles safely home. It was too risky to take one of the late-night buses that left at the half hour all through the night from George Square, just down the road from the student union building – the bottles wouldn't last a minute. Randalph was too mean to pay for a taxi ride. Nobody who had a car was driving back in his direction. Walking was the only alternative.

The walk was not an easy one, not because of the distance or topographical challenges, but because of the danger. Randalph would have to cross the river Clyde footbridge, stay away from groups of drunken men hanging around outside closed pubs, cross the derelict wastelands of what was left of the Gorbals neighbourhood after the clearances, and get past the street corners on Victoria Road, where gangs of young guys sometimes hung out.

Randalph was used to the walk in daytime, early in the morning, when nobody bothered you. At night it offered a scarier perspective. But too pissed to be bothered by the danger, Randalph opted for blind bravado. He would give it a try. Besides, it was pouring with rain and the streets were empty.

Having safely crossed the bridge and cleared the gloomy riverside buildings, he made a beeline through the streets of old tenement buildings on the outskirts of the Gorbals wasteland, got as far as the Y-junction on Victoria Road, headed towards the infirmary and relaxed. He was almost home and, revelling in the relief of having made it so far, upped his pace.

That was the last thing Randalph remembered. Sometime at about 2 , 3 , or 4 in the morning, somebody had struck him over the head with something blunt and knocked him out. Who it was, Randalph would never know. Nathan, who had not heard him come home, was worried and went out in the early morning to look for him. He found him only a couple of hundred yards from their apartment lying face up in the rain in a garden, covered in piss and coming slowly back to life.

The whisky – the subject of Randalph's first question – was gone. The bitterness quickly also went when Nathan asked him if he had been hit by a bomb and laughed. "Bastards!" What the hell, thought Randalph. He was alive, a little bit smelly, unscathed except for a lump and a cut on his head that needed four stitches, but with a story to tell to anyone who would believe him.

NO JOBS FOR BOYS – SUMMER '79

As the year fled by, the spectre of having to find a job when university was over was drawing nearer. It was clear in Randalph's mind that he would not be applying for a job in Civil Engineering. Not in Scotland, nor in England, nor anywhere else. But what, and where?

On TV he had seen a documentary about the British Antarctic Expedition and thought he would give it a try. A few weeks after having sent them an eloquent letter suggesting that he was born to adventures and challenges of this type he got a letter back thanking him and filling him with hope, only to drop him into a ditch when they asked him to send a copy of his honours degree.

Another destiny that appealed to him was working as a guide for the summer at the exotic Inverewe gardens up in Scotland's bleak north-west. He wished he had kept the application letter he wrote to them in which he had waxed lyrical about everything he knew about gardening. Again, at first appearance the reply spoke highly of his desire to work there, then buried him under a heap of manure with the question of what he knew about botany and the life cycle of the semi-tropical vegetation in the garden. Fuck all, thought Randalph, and fuck them too.

Randalph's third and last attempt to get a job was in answer to an advert posted by a rock quarry who were looking for an experienced stone cutter to build 'dry-stane dykes' – stone walls between fields constructed without using cement. Bingo! This is it, believed Randalph, as he recalled the job his friend Bascom's father had given him three summers previously to build low-level dry-stane dykes in his garden.

The thank you letter this time didn't waste any ink on niceties, opening with "Thank you for your letter", then going straight to the point with: "This is a job for men and not for boys". Although it was a slap in the face, Randalph loved the candid attitude of the writer and wrote back to him to say that when he came of age he would apply again.

It looked like destiny was telling him something. He wasn't sure what. End of term was just around the corner and, as he listened to the enthusiastic bragging of his classmates who, it seemed, had all landed jobs with reputable firms, Randalph was seriously wondering where his life was taking him. What next, he thought, as he gave up trying to find a job. Let the job find you, Nathan had said to him once upon a time in a moment of beer-inspired wisdom, which is precisely what Randalph decided to do.

ACADEMIC SUICIDE

Randalph's last two weeks at university had been bliss. In a U-shaped bar on a Friday night in Glasgow city centre where he was having a few pints with his Turkish flat mate, Kazim, and some friends of his, he caught the eye of a stylish lady, possibly in her forties, sitting at the opposite side of the U. The lady was eyeing him up with an uncannily bold and confident expression on her face. Unsure of himself, Randalph looked away, ordered another beer, then looked again. Her focus had not wavered an inch. Randalph felt like he was looking into the telescope of a sniper. Another

Randalph in May 1979 in a last desperate attempt to study for his finals

beer provided him with the courage he needed to go over and say hello to her.

Still desperately unsure of himself, he approached the lady with a friendly "Hi". To which she boldly replied "You took a long time to make up your mind. Hi, my name's Rebecca. My friends call me Beckie." That instantly removed from their encounter any space for unnecessary small talk. Destiny, in its mysterious way of putting in your path situations that will change your life, had played its trump card.

Beckie was a writer and an amateur painter, indeed in her forties, mother of two sons a little older than Randalph and wife of a sea captain who she dismissed with an unconcerned wave of her hand towards nowhere in particular, saying he was riding the waves somewhere on the other side of the planet. Randalph was bewitched. He was as soft as putty in the hands of the potter, ensnared like a fly in a spider's web, as helpless as the victim of a hypnotist. There was no need for questions, introductions, flirting or games of any kind. It was as if they had known each other forever. Next stop was Randalph's bedroom. No need to pass 'go'. Randalph's dice had rolled a double six.

The next two weeks were end of term at university, the time of the final exams, the last step before liberation from studies and crossing the threshold into the big wide world beyond. Randalph was dreading the finals. Although he had studied as best he could, he was in no way ready. His rebellious mind did not accept that his future would be judged on his ability to answer theoretical questions about stuff he would probably never encounter in the real world, and besides, he now had Beckie on his mind.

On day three of the finals week, half way through his third exam, as Randalph was inwardly cursing the irrelevance of a laboratory question on soil mechanics that he couldn't get his head round, he stood up and flattened out his exam paper on his desk. This was it. Randalph had had enough. He walked to the front of the exam room, turned round to wave goodbye to his classmates, opened the door, turned right down the main corridor of the old Victorian university building, headed for the telephone booths in the entrance hall, called Beckie, pushed his way through the heavy revolving door, and set off to meet her at Glasgow Central Station.

Randalph had just committed academic suicide. He knew it, but didn't give a shit. This was his jail break, his first step to freedom. For the next five years he would walk on the wild side, choosing adventure over security, risk over safety, the unknown over the familiar. Jobs found him, tricky jobs, dangerous jobs, and so did all sorts of shit that most people never have to deal with.

Randalph would soon be experiencing the terror of being at death's door several times and see the world through the lens of refugee camps, the smouldering remains of battlefields, and smell the nauseating stench of decomposing human flesh. By the time he would eventually settle, it would be in another country and speaking another language. In those years of travel, discovery, and waking up to the harsh realities of this world, he never once regretted his decision.

After spending the next week with Beckie roaming around the islands of Rothesay, Arran and Bute, he packed his bags, caught a train for London, the boat train to Dover, the ferry to Ostend, and the legendary Wien Express to Köln HBF (Cologne Central), where he got out, put his bags in a locker, climbed the 533 steps to the top of the towering Kölner Dom (Cologne Cathedral) and smiled. He had done it. He might have failed his exams and thrown away four years of studies, but he had followed his heart.

That night he turned up at his dear aunt's house in Germany. Surprised, she asked him what he was doing there and showed him to his usual room.

Kölner Dom (Cologne Cathedral) photographed from Köln Deutz on the East side of the river Rhein, where Randalph's mother was born back in 1928.

The following Monday morning he turned up early at a big building site within cycling distance of his aunt's house and was hired on the spot for a job labouring with a team of concreters, putting up shuttering and setting steel and vibrating tons of high-grade concrete. His workmates were for the most part Turks and Greeks who had only a spattering of basic German, but were intent on impressing the foreman with their willingness to work hard.

Except for during the previous summer when Randalph had enjoyed the cushy environment of an office job in Cambridge, he had spent the three summers prior to that working hard outside on construction sites in Scotland and in Sweden. West Germany, however, was not the north, and the Kölner Bucht (The lowlands along the Rhine valley) was a notoriously warm and clammy place in the summer, where the sun was hot and daytime and night-time temperatures frequently hovered around the mid-thirties.

Three weeks into his job, Randalph collapsed with heat stroke. He had been trying in vain to keep up with the pace of Greek and Turkish workmen who were used to the heat, and to whom the summer temperatures were considerably cooler than those in their home countries. Not knowing what to do with him, someone from the site was assigned to drive him to a first-aid post and then to the company's head office in Cologne, where his future would be decided by 'Der Chef'.

'Der Chef' was Herr Dr Ingenieur Wilhelm Bachmann, an authority-wielding self-indulgent always-right technocrat who strutted around correcting everyone and everything, and insisted on being called by his title, as was common then in Germany, where people stuck their credentials to their names even on their letterboxes. To Randalph, who came from a country where people were called by their title only when they were being reprimanded or handed out a jail sentence, Der Chef's name would be Willy. On that first day, however, Randalph acquiesced and thanked the Herr Dr Ingenieur for giving him the opportunity to work in the office.

There are people in this world who are destined not to get along, and so it transpired that from day two onwards, Willy and Randalph were at war. Willy had no respect for the Greeks and the Turks, and even less for the Scots. Every day at lunch time in the vast office canteen he would crack a joke about 'Die Schotten', probably believing that because people laughed, it was funny. Randalph didn't mind, as by the end of the first week he was shagging Willy's personal assistant, who used to pick him up in her VW Beetle after work, just like Rote Rosie two years previously, and take him for a drive in the countryside.

In the office, Randalph's immediate colleague was Claus, a young, elegant, effeminate German guy Randalph's age with a heart of gold, patter that could chat the clothes off of even the most reserved woman, a liver that could hold eight pints of beer, and a spare bedroom at his parents' flat where Randalph could crash out after their raucous nights in the city. Claus and Randalph instantly struck up a lively friendship and just as quickly became known to the Kelners (waiters) of the bars in Cologne's pedestrian streets where they spent most Thursday and Friday nights and weekends drooling over the local talent, downing endless glasses of ice-cold Kölsch beer, and contributing generously to the prosperity of the premises' owners.

One particular night, with both boys unstoppably happy and Kölsch flowing like a river of golden delight from one glass to the next, Claus said something so funny that Randalph bit into his beer glass, which disintegrated into a dozen pieces, spilling beer and broken glass over the table in front of them. Panicking at what had just happened, Randalph sprang to his feet and began spitting out fragments of glass from his mouth in all directions. It must have been a disgusting sight for the other customers, who were looking on with reprimand written all over their stern faces and shaking their heads. The moment was saved and eternalised by Johann, the Oberkelner (head waiter), who appeared, towel in hand, his handlebar moustache all smiles, and invited the boys to drink from the glasses and not to bite them. As the bomb scare had brought Nathan and Randalph together forever, so "Trinken, nicht beissen!" became the rallying cry for Randalph and Claus.

The remainder of summer '79 passed by uneventfully, except for the merry wedding of Randalph's Aunt Eileen's and Uncle Ronnie's youngest daughter and being fired by Willy towards the end of September on the day that Randalph humiliated him in front of the entire workforce at lunchtime; Willy accused him in writing of "gross insubordination, racial cheek and degrading remarks to senior personnel".

Stopping off for a weekend in London to see his university friend Simon on the way home to the wedding, Randalph went back to Glasgow in October to re-sit his finals and this time managed to get a degree, albeit an ordinary degree, and could now append BSc to his name if he so wanted. With his degree under his belt, not much to lose, no job in sight, and still no desire to have one, he took a night bus to London, where he had heard about a charity organisation that hired young graduates on a volunteer basis for two-year assignments in what was then called the "third world". Rather than risk refusal to a letter, he chose to knock on the organisation's door and take it from there.

The knock on the door paid off. Randalph was passed around from desk to desk, asked questions, and within that same afternoon given the opportunity to sign up. When asked where he would like to go, he replied Thailand. It was clear in Randalph's mind that he wanted to go to a country with warm turquoise sea water, sandy beaches lined with palm trees, sexy local girls, and delicious food. Instead, the organisation gave him the opportunity to go to Nepal. Where the hell was Nepal?

A few weeks later Randalph found himself participating, along with two other volunteer guys heading for Nepal, in a month-long cultural and language preparation workshop held at the very stately Hengrave Hall in Suffolk. The course came to an end a few days before Christmas, allowing him the time to travel home, pack his bags, say goodbye to everyone, and be back in London early on 2nd January 1980 for his flight to Delhi, then onwards to Kathmandu and whatever life would have in store for him there. Destiny had rolled Randalph another double six.

CHAPTER 9

Jai Jai Nepal

Randalph was looking out from the left-side window seat in the ten-abreast economy bay of a Boeing 747 Jumbo Jet bound for Delhi when the captain announced that alcohol consumption was not allowed during the flight time across Iranian airspace. The passenger next to him was reading an article in *Time* magazine about the US Embassy in Islamabad attacked by a mob and set on fire. At his briefing for his two-year volunteering stint in the land of the one-eyed yellow idol to the north of Kathmandu, someone had spoken about Tibetan rebels and a no-go zone on Nepal's northern border. Another spoke highly of the fearless Gurkhas.

Somewhere in the back of his mind Randalph had heard about Mahatma Gandhi and Mother Teresa but it hadn't clicked that Calcutta and India were only a bus drive away from Kathmandu. Randalph rummaged in his cabin bag for a book recommended on the course about India titled *India: A Wounded Civilisation*, written by a guy called V.S. Naipaul. He knew nothing about the part of the world he was travelling to, and even less about the world in general. As he turned the pages and the miles flew by, it was becoming clear to Randalph that the world he was familiar with was fading behind him on the western horizon as his flight neared this new world he would soon be landing in.

While Randalph was embarking on whatever was waiting in store for him in Nepal, elsewhere in the world in that first week of January in 1980:

The International Decade of Water & Sanitation had begun.

U.S. President Jimmy Carter had asked the Senate to delay further consideration of ratification of the Strategic Arms Limitation Talks (SALT) II Treaty – the second US and USSR agreement to limit the number of nuclear missiles.

U.S. President Carter had also proclaimed a grain embargo against the USSR with the support of the European Commission.

At least 29 Iranian civilians were killed in rioting against the Ayatollah Khomeini's efforts to suppress all opposition to his government rule, mostly in fighting between Sunni Muslims and the ruling Shi'ite Muslim faction in the cities of Bandar Lengeh, Tabriz and Qom.

A 6.9 magnitude earthquake struck the Azores.

Massachusetts became the last of the fifty states of North America to permit drivers to turn right at a red light.

A mob had stormed the Russian embassy in Tehran.

British steel workers had gone on a national strike.

Indira Gandhi's Congress Party had won elections in India.

U.S. President Jimmy Carter had authorized legislation to bail out the Chrysler Corporation with a 1.5 billion dollar loan.

The first day of Global Positioning System (GPS) time had begun.

And in Saudi Arabia, 63 Islamist insurgents were beheaded in eight different cities for their part in the siege of the Great Mosque in Mecca on November 24. The leader of the siege, Juhayman al-Otaybi, was decapitated in public in Mecca. Other public beheadings took place in the cities of Riyadh, Medina, Buraidah, Dammam, Abha, Ha'il and Tabuk.

HAND IN HAND

In the 1970s, men in the city of Glasgow, where Randalph had studied, did not walk hand in hand. In fact, to do so would have been as decisively suicidal and just as bloody as jumping off the roof of a tower apartment block. But in Nepal they did. Gopal, Randalph's Nepalese culture and language teacher, knew this and it sent him into delirious fits of high-pitch laughter every time he stretched out his hand to catch Randalph's, who pulled away with a look of horror and disgust on his face. By and by, as the language lessons progressed and Randalph's narrow-minded outlook on life stretched to accommodate the observation that the rest of the world was not like home, he acquiesced.

After only three weeks into his cultural and language initiation, the day of the hand-in-hand walk through the streets of Kathmandu had come. To Randalph, who hated confrontation and the kind of attention that could threaten his safety, his discomfort was equivalent to the feeling he would have had if he was standing naked in a Glasgow street with garlands of flowers round his neck hurling insults at a gang of thugs armed with knives. This was most definitely not a day to bump into anyone he knew in Kathmandu. It was, however, the first day of his long struggle to free himself from the straitjacketed, blinkered belief that Randalph had learned at home and had held as the absolute truth about how people should behave, dress and act.

Some months later, Randalph also learned to accept that men in Nepal often sit with their legs folded across a friend's legs and their arms around their shoulders, looking like they had just been married. Randalph began to wonder why, in the English-speaking world in particular, physical contact was such a taboo. He was touched by the open friendship these local guys so publicly displayed, and a little jealous of it.

Apparently oblivious to danger, they would sit like this for the length of an eight-hour bus ride across the Himalayan foothills, happily chatting, laughing and endlessly smoking 'bidis' (local cone-shaped cigarettes), while their ornately-decorated wooden-superstructure Tata bus adorned with bright orange flowers, Ganesh images and incense sticks swayed recklessly, its oversized steering wheel spinning from left to right and right to left, bend after bend, foot to the floor, hand on the horn, around blind corners carved out of almost-vertical rock, a thousand feet above a sheer cliff, and not bat an eyelid.

The bus ride finally over, Randalph stepped out into

what would become his new home in the picturesque little city of Pokhara, in the heart of West Nepal.

MY STUFF – YOUR STUFF

Amongst the many cultural differences Randalph was being subjected to, he observed that ownership and possessiveness of material things was not such a coveted right in Nepal as it was in the West. Walking through Pokhara's fruit, vegetable, meat and anything-else market with its haphazard stalls, flies, barking dogs, fresh puddles of blood, cheeky local girls, nauseous smells, naked kids, colourfully clad tribespeople and the occasional fierce-looking mountain men from the then-restricted Dolpa region, with their hand-carved silver knife sheaths proudly and provocatively sticking out from under their red and black robes, he spotted someone wearing his jacket.

His jacket – there was no mistake – which he had left in his room, was draped over the shoulder of a local gentleman wearing a horizontally-striped short-sleeved wool pullover over his traditional daura suruwal, a ceremonial Dhaka topi (Traditional Nepalese cap) on his head and rubber flip-flops on his feet. Uncommonly, he was carrying a walking stick. Who the hell was this?

Fortunately, Randalph had been told in his initiation that people in Nepal sometimes borrowed other peoples' clothes. In his understanding of what was right and what was wrong he believed, however, that people should ask first before walking off with someone's stuff. The gentleman walked straight past him, not recognising Randalph, and obviously oblivious to the scathing finger-pointing criticism and blame he would have loved to have showered on him. After all, Randalph believed strongly that he was in the right.

Randalph later found out that his landlord's relative had dropped by, poked his nose into Randalph's room, spotted the jacket, asked the landlord if he could borrow it, and walked off proudly sporting his new garment. A few days later, as if by magic, the jacket reappeared, draped over the back of a chair in the yard. Sometime later, Randalph's camera also went for a short vacation in town with its new temporary owner. Just like the jacket, it too found its way back home, unscathed and still in working order.

Despite his failings as a student, Randalph had a natural faculty for adaptation and the ability to blend in and soon felt comfortable in this country where behaviour and social norms were so different from home. Cultural heritage, however, runs deep, and the voice deep inside him never stopped nagging about his jacket and the camera: they should have asked him first. Didn't they understand that it was his and not theirs?

GIVE ME YOUR CIGARETTE

About six months into his assignment, Randalph was sitting on the roof of a bus that went over the edge of a cliff, killing half of the passengers. He had been thrown clear and landed on his side with a deadening splash, uninjured, in a paddy field. From where he landed, he could see the bus spilling over into the Kali Gandaki River gorge, with luggage, animals and passengers flying through the air, splaying out like the colourful points on the tail of a peacock as it spreads its feathers, hurtling downwards to inescapable destruction. Randalph could hear the terrified screams of the people trapped inside. Numbed by the horror of so much violent death, for the remainder of his stay in Nepal he never rode inside a bus again.

As in any learning experience, there is always an initiation to the next level. Randalph's learning curve hit a steep incline as he was riding another bus along Nepal's hot and sticky Terrai region on the Indian border, heading down for a weekend in the sultry plains of India. It was hot. It was smelly. The sixty-seater bus was carrying well over a hundred passengers with their bundles, hens, goats, sticks, boxes, a handful of babies, and an old lady propped up against a haystack she had somehow managed to lift onto the roof of the bus.

Randalph was also sitting on the roof, with his lower back propped up against the low stainless-steel railing that surrounded the roof on all four sides on roughly the same spot at the back of the bus he had sat on in the crash some weeks before. Here, he reckoned, he would stand the best chance of survival in the event of another crash. He had not forgotten the crash – every time the bus swerved, his heart missed a beat.

Randalph's legs were stretched out in front of him. Suddenly, in a scuffle of hands and feet and people shuffling to get comfortable, his legs found themselves under the legs of a local farmer, who was using them as a seat. Be my guest, thought Randalph, who found himself on that thin cultural dividing line between acceptance and repulsion. In the traditional Nepalese way, the farmer bade *namaste* to all around, then, once settled comfortably on his perch, fumbled under the grimy cloth of his tunic, took out a squashed packet of crumpled bidi cigarettes and started to ask around for a light.

The light came from another bidi held out with the toil-worn grimy sinuous hand of another farmer sitting nearby who had tied his goat to the outside railing of the bus with its backside facing the road. There was no need to exchange exaggerated thanks and gestures. Someone needed something; someone else handed it to him. In rural Nepal if someone needed a puff, it was not uncommon to see someone else take a cigarette from their mouth, have a few puffs, and put it back. It was the way with these people who have so little. Randalph looked on. He wanted a smoke. He was feeling brave. Could he do it?

Leaning forward, Randalph stretched out his hand, took the bidi from the mouth of his perched passenger, had a few puffs, exchanged a glance of mutual human recognition and put it back between his lips. No fuss. No ceremony. No problem. He had done it. He was in. With his rucksack, western T-shirt and shorts – the archetypal white man – Randalph had just plucked a cigarette from a stranger's mouth, smoked it, and put it back into the man's mouth without batting an eyelid. Back home, this simple gesture could have cost him his life. Here, it brought him one step closer to blending into daily life in that distant mountain Kingdom perched on the top of the world.

NOT ON THE MAP

Turning up in a mountain village in rural Nepal at that time as a young, bearded, blue-eyed, fair-skinned Westerner with thick red-brown hair must have been as quaint a sight to the villagers as a green alien with tentacles stepping out of a flying saucer would be back home.

On one of his first tours of duty by himself, Randalph had sat down on the ground in the shade of a luxurious peepul tree. Laughing kids were swarming around him like bees around honey. Shy young girls were smiling at him while covering their mouths with their colourful headcloths. Older women, their ears and noses adorned with golden rings, proud defiance in their eyes, backs upright, clad in the deep blood-red cloth of their traditional apparel, stood around at a distance. Boys were taunting, laughing, a few shouted "kuiary ayo" (the white man's arrived). Some men were looking on sternly also from a distance.

Randalph was in Gurung country – one of the mountain tribes from which Nepal's tough Gurkhas are recruited. Some of the men proudly wore a khaki-coloured topi (hat) bearing the crossed kukris (traditional Nepalese knives) of their fearless order like the badge on their regimental cap. Some of the cheekier women approached. One touched Randalph's hairy arm and drew back in a shriek of laughter. Another did the same. Randalph felt like a monkey in a zoo. "Where from?" said one of the men, who had probably learned English in his years as a soldier in the British Army. "Scotland," replied Randalph, "Ma belayatabata hum" (I'm from Britain). Everyone burst out laughing at the young foreigner who spoke a spattering of Nepalese.

Randalph had an idea. He would show them where he was from on a map. He spread a folded map of the world on the ground, pointing to Scotland. Except for the men who had served abroad, no one had any clue what Randalph was trying to explain. The kids and women looked on bewildered. One old lady sneeringly spouted out "Nepal kaha cha?" (where is Nepal)? Randalph in his innocence pointed to Nepal on the map. The old lady barged forward, spread her crackled hand brusquely over the place where Randalph had said Nepal was as if to feel the terrain then blurted out "Nepal china!" (not Nepal!) "Nepalma himal cha." (In Nepal there are mountains). It was one of those moments where nothing you can say or do will have the slightest effect on the other person's point of view. Randalph looked up at her. She was right. The map was not Nepal. He was beat – checkmate.

HOLY MAN

However far removed Nepal's villages seemed from the culture and society of Randalph's world, the people there did, nevertheless, show great respect for learning and the written word, especially from the scriptures. While learning the Nepalese language and about the country's culture back in Kathmandu at the outset of his stay, Randalph had found a thick black tattered hardback edition of the works of Shakespeare in a tourist shop in the narrow alleyways of nearby Swoyambhu Mahachaitya, Randalph's favourite Buddhist temple. Whenever he had a free moment, he would wander off to the temple through the squalid streets, avoiding spitting and dishwater being emptied on him from windows above, to spend an afternoon in relative peace there under the all-knowing golden eye of the Buddha painted on the stupa.

Swayambhu Mahachaitya, an ancient religious complex atop a hill in the Kathmandu Valley, west of the city, Randalph's favourite spot in Kathmandu.

When he spotted the book on the shelves of a dark, dank bookshop lit by a small oil lamp on a table in the middle, he thought of his own collection of books he had given away before travelling to Nepal. Randalph loved to read and felt the pang of homesickness as he remembered curling up safely in bed day-dreaming his way *through Cider with Rosie, The Sea for Breakfast, The War of the Worlds, No Mean City, Shoes were for Sunday,* and *The Taste of Too Much* – a story about Glasgow that had him laughing with tears streaming down his cheeks.

When he saw the big church-bible sized edition of Shakespeare, he remembered his English teacher in Kilmarnock Academy explaining Macbeth to his class of heedless morons. Mr Walker, his teacher, had said something about language structure, punctuation and rhythm. Randalph remembered him talking about semicolons. He picked up the book, bargained the price down to a few rupees, put it in his backpack and felt safe. Shakespeare would be his armour and shield from the muddy streets, toilet smells and squalor of this haphazard city of barking dogs, street vendors, noise, clatter, and the mystic practices and ceremonies of religions and beliefs he could not begin to understand.

As with many things in life, the book had a secret purpose, to be revealed at a precise moment in time. The works of the Bard had found their way into Randalph's hand for a reason. On his next tour to the villages, Randalph had again found himself surrounded by a crowd of sniggering kids and taunting villagers fingering his hairy arms and plucking at his beard. Only old men in Nepal have any hair on their chins, which is invariably black and never reddish-brown.

Feeling uncomfortable and vulnerable, he tried his best to smile. He was feeling miserable, just wanting them to go away and leave him in peace. He was thinking of stuff he wanted to write to his friends and family back home, and he would have given his right arm to have a quiet place to write. He took out a blank, blue, wafer-thin airmail letter envelope, of the kind people used then to write letters home. He needed a flat surface to lean on and took out the big black book from his skimpy rucksack.

In an instant, the mood of his tormentors had changed from provocative teasing and laughter at his expense to pious solemnity. The only people who ever carried books to these far-flung outreaches of this forgotten country, where distance is measured in days of walking, were the serious and foreboding-looking Hindu gurus with their long white beards, flowing white and yellow robes, on their foreheads an over-sized, bright-red bindi pasted in the centre, and carrying in one hand their three-pronged holy Shiva trishulas as if they were Merlin the magician, about to cast all unbelievers into the endless pains of hell.

"Hajurko keetab?" (your book), the kids asked. "Padhna sakcha?" (you can read). Relieved by the sudden respectfulness, Randalph opened the book at Macbeth and replied "Hō, ma padhna sakchu" (yes, I can read). The kids sat down around him in silence. Some women made signs to others to come and see. Someone rang a bell. A few others were looking on from behind the kids. Randalph the holy man? This was unbelievable. He had to play the part.

Randalph began to read out loud his favourite passage, and the only one he remembered off by heart: "Tomorrow, and tomorrow and tomorrow", you could hear a pin drop, "Creeps in this petty pace from day to day", he caught his breath, raised his finger to the sky "To the last syllable of recorded time; and all our yesterdays have lighted fools the way to dusty death".

Randalph looked up, scanned the men gathered in the back rows, cast his hand dramatically downwards towards the ground as if to signal the end of all things, raised his voice, and lifted both hands to the sky as if to implore the judgment of God. Continuing in a dramatical voice, he recited "Out, out, brief candle; life's but a walking shadow, a poor player that struts and frets his hour upon the stage, and then is heard no more". More drama in his voice: "It is a tale told by an idiot, full of sound and fury..." Randalph chopped the air with his hands, thumping them onto the ground, "Signifying nothing".

The silence was delicious. The looks of mesmerised awe on the villagers' faces were a delight. For the rest of the afternoon, and on his subsequent visits, Randalph enjoyed the reverence and privilege of eminence and dignity. He had found his stage and his audience. He just had to figure out a way to make sure he was never accompanied to this village by anyone from his organisation or his counterpart from Nepal's Ministry of Rural Development under whom these village water supply upgrade projects were being carried out. This was too good to be taken away from him in scorn.

HOME SICK

Randalph's first six months in mystical Nepal had triggered in him a mixture of strong emotions. In Kathmandu, he was amazed at the carvings on the pagoda temples and the city's many colourful religious ceremonies with people getting covered in blood-red powder and bright yellow flowers, but disgusted by the squalor, the noise, the smells and the filth, and wary of the gangs of aggressive stray dogs that prowled the streets at night.

Outside Kathmandu, he was stunned by the rural scenery

with cultivated rice terraces climbing thousands of feet in height on steep mountain sides everywhere he looked, and was speechless as he ascended for the first time the steep valley past the western flanks of Machapuchari – the fishtail mountain that watches over the mountain people of West and Central Nepal – to enter into the 'sanctuary' of the Annapurna Mountains and see there the icy-crisp shining skyline of white mountain tops set against a jet-black starry sky.

On a personal level, he was exhilarated by feeling every day fitter on his days-long treks out to the tribal villages on the footpaths of the Himalayan peaks, satisfied with himself that he had lost so much weight in so little time, and thrilled that every now and again he had that special feeling of 'home' inside him, when he felt he was where he should be.

Confronted with the way Nepal's public administration functioned, Randalph was often angry and frustrated at the slowness, the corruption, the privileges of the few, and disgusted at the surprising tolerance shown by the locals to the leftovers of the drug-abused wasted hippy crowd with their lazy-life, baba-cool attitude and the debauched image they portray of Europe. If Randalph was king, he would have them all kicked out and sent back to their countries with the word 'scum' tattooed on their foreheads.

Randalph also had to deal with the jabbing pain of homesickness, his craving for friendly banter and a drink with people of his own ilk. Also lurking in the depths of his secrets was a deep-seated loathing he had developed for one of the other volunteers in town. Sven was cocky, bold, self-righteous and outspokenly critical of drinking, smoking, womanising and any other pursuit outside his narrow moral boundary lines. Sven clamped down heavily on any argument in support of these 'vices', all of which Randalph excelled at and revelled in. From day one of their meeting, Sven became Randalph's private enemy number one. Randalph hated him. Above all, he hated not having the courage to tell him what he thought of him. Instead, Randalph developed the indelicate art of avoiding conflict by speaking behind Sven's back and would rant on for hours to his colleagues about Sven's failings, taking comfort in any sign of compassion, understanding or agreement they showed him.

Sven and Randalph were assigned to designing and supervising the construction of gravity-flow water supply systems in a handful of villages in Nepal's Annapurna foothills. Sven had already been doing the job for over a year; he knew the ropes and was to be Randalph's initiator. In reality, his initiator was Govinda, the Nepalese counterpart from the local government office who occasionally teamed up with the two European volunteers.

To get things done in Nepal you need tact, the trust of the people you are dealing with, and the ability to read between the lines of what is happening. Govinda, a local, had all of these qualities. Sven, despite his bravado attitude, outspokenness and self-confidence, had none. Randalph could sense that he never actually got close to the locals, who remained wary of him and had not opened the doors of their hearts to let him in.

In the same way that Randalph had imagined some years before that students would all be good, thoughtful, cultivated and open-minded citizens, here, in this context of social and cultural immersion in such a fascinatingly different world, Randalph had believed that volunteers would naturally be culturally sensitive, interested in the people around them, and open to the many differences in the world they had been plunged into. The blatant lack of social intelligence and the unwillingness of Sven to embrace the day-to-day realities of life in this exotic setting upset Randalph. Just like the hippies, he would have sent him home too.

After only a few months of putting up with Sven, Randalph breathed a deep sigh of relief when he left, secretly wishing on him a future rich in disaster, failure and humiliation. Many years later, Randalph learned that Sven had died from gun wounds during a period of social upheaval and revolution that later scarred Nepal. He was unable to feel any remorse and thought of all the other bullies from his early years whose deaths he would have been pleased to learn of.

THE RESERVOIR

Apart from the thrilling experience of being in a grass-roots environment in mountain villages with neither electricity, running water, proper sanitation nor roads, this exotic-sounding job in this mythical setting far, far away was a never-ending test of patience and perseverance, and a total no-brainer in some of its practical aspects. It was also a test of how you were able to deal with the good-hearted teasing and joking by locals who had never seen a westerner.

When Sven's term came to an end, Govinda, their Nepalese counterpart, was not around. He had been absent for some months on family business at the other end of the country, from where he was expected back 'bholi' (a similar word to 'mañana' in Spanish, indicating an uncertain time in the future).

At that time in Nepal, Government employees took months off for marriages, births, deaths, festivals or whatever. They turned up again for work when they were ready. In the meantime, Randalph's projects were in full swing, and materials, such as cement, needed to be procured. Moreover, plans for the delivery of the materials and the organisation of a workforce needed to be made.

The problem with getting stuff procured or making plans was that whenever one of the international staff asked about procedures and dates, the locals would shy away. In a country where the future is believed to be held in the hands of the gods, how could anyone be so arrogant as to suggest they knew better than the gods or what they want? Cement will arrive when it arrives, God willing. Govinda will be back when he is back, God willing. The project will be completed, God willing. Tomorrow? Next month? Never? The future, like everything else, was in the hands of the gods.

In spite of the logistical challenges resulting from their absence, with Govinda absent and Sven gone, Randalph could at last travel by himself to the villages. One of the projects he was assigned to supervise had reached the phase where they were going to build a reservoir by the stream above the village. Trenches had been dug, pipes laid, tap stands erected, pressure-reduction vessels constructed, and amazingly all the materials they needed had arrived on the backs of donkeys, reportedly "at the last full moon".

That particular village lay high up on the steep foothills of the snowy Himalayas and was home to the Buddhist Gurung tribe. Unlike the villages in the south of the country inhabited by more argumentative and tricky-to-deal-with villagers from the Hindu tribes, the Gurungs were fiercely proud, cooperative, tough and raring to show off how hard they could work.

Easy, thought Randalph as he contemplated how to go about constructing the reservoir. He would lay out the foundation, check the tools and the materials, and make sure the village workforce knew what to do and when to do it. He would then piss off into the mountains for a few days, and when he came back down he would celebrate the completion of the new reservoir with the villagers in the traditional manner with music, dance, food, and enough local *roksi* (rice alcohol) to knock out a regiment.

Satisfied with his elaborate plan, Randalph sat with the village elders, drew diagrams on pages torn out of school jotters, pegged out the first row of stones needed for the foundations, went over the various steps with the men, made sure they knew how and when to mix the cement, then packed his rucksack, wished them good luck, picked up a tent at a local trekking outpost, and headed north along the trail.

Certain that everything would be fine in the village, Randalph spent the next two days on a trek up to the

Annapurna Sanctury – the home of the legendary snow leopard, and by then his preferred spot on Planet Earth – where he camped out solo under the stars for another two nights, revelling in the splendour and natural beauty of this mythical place. He liked it so much that a few months later, when he was diagnosed with a potentially deadly tropical water-borne disease, he wrote a letter to his close friends and family asking to be buried there if he died.

As Randalph approached the village on his way back down from the mountains, exhilarated at the experience of being by himself under the star-light Himalayan sky, in the distance he could see 'his' reservoir, standing tall on the outcrop of rock dominating the village where he had set out its foundation dimensions the week before. The villagers spotted him and came running to greet him, beaming with pride and anxious to show him their prize accomplishment.

Randalph was ecstatic – what an achievement! The closer they got to the reservoir, the more solid it looked. Big stones, hand-hewn from the rockface interlocked with each other in a homogeneous mosaic of rustic architecture. It looked fantastic. Randalph couldn't believe his eyes. What a party they would have that night.

Once up close, however, a vital detail revealed itself to him like a rusty dagger slipping out from beneath a golden cloak. His heart sank deep into that abyss where hearts sink into when they lose everything. There, on the corner where he was standing, as if inserted by the gods to remind him of where he was, a massive design flaw was staring at him. Instead of constructing the walls as a continuous construction with interlocking corners, the brave, tireless, hard-working, well-to-do tribesmen of this little village at the foothills of the world's highest mountains had erected the reservoir's four walls individually, as four separate elements. Between the sturdy, well-constructed walls they had left wafer-thin gaps, running from top to bottom, where the water would simply pour out.

How could anyone be so stupid, thought Randalph, as his mind raced to find a way out for himself. How the hell was he going to broach the subject to them? It would be a crime to crush their enthusiasm under the cruel cudgel of reality, but he would have to do it.

Lost for words, Randalph suggested filling the reservoir with water. It only took a few seconds for everyone present to understand that the water would flow out of the cracks. In an instant, the mood of the crowd changed from jubilation to shame, blame and anger.

This was Randalph's fault and he knew it. It was his mistake – a masterpiece of egotistical irresponsibility. The proud culture of these noble mountain tribesmen, however, would not allow them to identify Randalph the engineer, the white man, the guest in their country, to be at fault; at least, not to his face. Instead, they insulted each other, shouting, pointing, spitting on the ground, with everyone accusing everyone else of being a *"latto manche"* (a stupid man). Although no one would ever say it to him, everyone knew that the stupid man was Randalph – he should have stayed with them to guide them through the job. What a wanker.

But the gods are generous: sometimes they bring you down to build you up again. The gaps between the walls were just wide enough for the men to introduce a trowel on its side and deposit cement to fill up the cracks. After only a few hours of hectic activity, daylight could no longer be seen peeping its cheeky eye through the gaps. Three days later, once the cement had completely dried, the reservoir was filled with water, and to Randalph's immense relief, not a drop flowed out. The job was done.

Ceremoniously, walking together with the entire village from one part of the water supply system to the next, the valves were opened, the flow was checked, all fourteen tap stands were tested and blessed, kids danced around, women wore smiles, men argued about who had worked the hardest, and the entire village got blind drunk, celebrating the success with local roksi, a few slaughtered chickens, the usual rice, lentils, spinach and potatoes, and music that went on all through the night and most of the following morning. As the great Shakespeare said: "All's well that ends well".

CEMENT ON THE DAM FLOOR

In another village in the same region, one of Randalph's colleagues had supervised the construction of a small gravity dam. He had told the people to mix cement and spread it on the bottom of the upstream side of the dam. Like Randalph, he had buggered off to enjoy the hills for some days, only to come back and find that the work-gang had mixed the cement and sand to make the appropriate mortar, then poured it behind the dam, but unfortunately into the water that had already gathered from the small stream. All the cement was lost.

Sacks of cement reach that part of the country on mule trains or on the backs of porters who carry them all the way from the nearest roadside to the village, which can be as far away as five to eight days' walk. Randalph often watched the porters pass by, leg muscles tensed, veins protruding, not an ounce of fat, usually barefoot, sweat pouring out from under the woven head straps that held their loads, traditional kukri knives tucked under the overlaps of their ragged cloth tunics, as they made their way slowly but steadily along the often steep and slippery stone paths that link these remote hill villages to the modern world of trucks and buses, culturally a thousand light years away to the south.

Some of the porters carried two bags of cement. Others took six twenty-litre drums of heating oil securely lashed together with locally made hemp ropes. Imagine for a moment carrying one and a half times your weight on your back up and down mountain trails for eight to ten hours every day, under blazing sunshine, barefoot. Their daily wage was twenty rupees, enough for two hot meals, some tea and biscuits and a bed for the night. On the artfully presented postcards of Nepal, these hard-working, incredibly resilient pillars of survival in that harsh terrain were depicted as endearing subjects romanticising the simplicity of rural life. Their life expectancy at the time was said to be around 40. You were considered to be 'old' if you reached 50.

SRINAGAR DANDA

Randalph's preferred project supervision tours started

on the trail that led north at the end of the main market street at the top end of Pokhara. Heading straight into the mountains, he would reach his first village after two eight-hour days of walking. Another day would take him to the second village. West for two days more brought him to the third. All three villages were the homes of Buddhist hill tribes.

Another tour led south from Pokhara, down to the predominantly Hindu villages on the lower foothills between the town and the plains on the Indian border. That tour started at a drop-off point on the road to the historical city of Tansen, and India beyond. Whenever possible, Randalph would stop off for a night in Tansen to enjoy the magnificent panoramic view from the top of nearby Srinagar Danda of the Kanjiroba, Dhaulagiri, Annapurna, Mansiri, Ganesh and Langtang Himalayan mountain groups, sometimes daydreaming about what it would be like to drop every tie to his life back home in Scotland and move permanently to Nepal.

A long time ago, Tansen was the capital of the Magar Kingdom in Palpa, one of the most powerful regional principalities before the rise of the Shah dynasty. It even came close to conquering Kathmandu in the 16th century under the leadership of Mukunda Sen. Later, Tansen became a Newari bazaar on the important trade route between India and Tibet via the Kaligandaki River and Mustang.

Because it was a district administrative centre of the Kingdom of Nepal, Maoists targeted Tansen several times during the Nepalese Civil War, between 1996 and 2006, which saw countrywide fighting between the country's Government and its Maoist Communist Party, including a major assault on the historic Durbar (palace) compound in Kathmandu in 2006.

A CUSHION FOR MY HEAD

In one of these villages on his south tour, Randalph had been introduced by Sven to a local family who fed him during his stays and let him sleep outside on the dried-mud veranda of their modest two-storey village hut. The hut was made of wood, mud and straw with large, unevenly-shaped stone slabs on the roof. Randalph liked it there. The people were kind and simple and always wore the unassuming, lowly smile of humbleness. With just a little bit of culinary knowledge, the food, however, could have been greatly improved. As could the basic hygiene.

On his stays there with the family, at around 10 am and at 5 pm, just before sundown, Randalph would sit cross-legged on the floor of the smoke-filled kitchen to eat from a metal plate with his right hand a heap of steaming-hot rice, spicy lentils, a few leaves of spinach boiled into submission, and on rare occasions an egg. To wash it down, there was a glass of hot sweetened milk.

Randalph, the visitor, ate first with the father. Once he had finished, he would rinse his mouth with water poured from a spout by the mother, then stand up and go outside to prepare his place to sleep for the night while the mother and children ate. In these outposts of humanity, with no electricity, and lamps lit with oil that was carried by porters from India and therefore extremely expensive, people went to bed at sundown and got up just before the dawn.

The family Randalph stayed with on one of his project supervision tours in Nepal's southern foothills.

What Randalph didn't know initially was that on each of his stays, one of the family skipped a meal. The family's cow and meagre vegetable patch did not produce enough to feed the family and also entertain even one guest. On his last tour before leaving Nepal, he asked the father what he would like Randalph to bring him as a gift if he ever returned to his country. The father said he had heard that cushions are nice to rest your head on when you sleep; he had only ever slept on a wooden bed.

It was difficult for Randalph as a Westerner to imagine that the family's wealth did not stretch far enough for them to buy a cushion for an old man to rest his head on. A year later, on his way home from his next assignment in Malaysia, Randalph brought him a cushion. He would have loved to have brought comfy beds and cushions for the entire family and never forgot the look of sincere gratitude in the father's face and the affectionate tear in his eye.

COCKROACHES

On one stay with the family, disaster struck. Sitting on the kitchen floor as usual, Randalph was lifting a mouthful of piping-hot rice scooped up with the fingers of his right and was about to propel it into his mouth with his thumb – a skill he had learned by watching how the villagers ate – when he heard the scurrying sound of insects somewhere above him. He looked up. The ceiling was covered in a thick, copper-brown creeping carpet of cockroaches clinging upside down to the smoke-blackened wooden planks, crawling over each other, antennas swaying to and fro like those of aliens in a freak film.

Randalph was nauseated. As when you catch the stench of excrement or bile, he felt his stomach wretch and his mouth fill with the disgusting taste of vomit. He tried to swallow it down but couldn't, and in spite of himself he threw up everything he had eaten over the plate and the floor in front of him. The mother of the house looked on in shock and sprang back like a cat surprised by a snake. In Nepal, many objects are considered holy. Food, and the places it is prepared in are among them. In his uncontrolled spewing up, Randalph had defiled a holy place. He had crossed a deep-rooted cultural red line.

In the eyes of the mother and the father, who by now were consoling each other, he could feel the unspoken disgust and hurt. To this day, he has no idea about just how far reaching his insult was or how much shame it brought on the family, but within less than half an hour a crowd had gathered outside. Holy people clad in orange and yellow flowers and powder had turned up and were anxiously chanting, ringing bells, lighting incense, and carrying out a 'Puja' – a holy ceremony of cleansing and worship. Tattered kids clinging to their mothers' arms were looking on expressionlessly. Some men had come back from the forest or wherever they were busy and stood silently as if at a funeral. No one was laughing. Not even the kids would let out a smile. What had he done?

On his next trip to the village a month or so later no mention was made of the incident. Had the evil spirits been ousted? Were the gods appeased? Randalph would never know. His gift of apology was accepted, but his lodgings had moved to the house next door.

OFFERINGS TO THE GODS

Randalph's favourite anecdote of these two years spent in the Himalayan foothills was a story told by Peter, a fellow volunteer. Peter, who had been assigned to two projects in the area south-west of Pokhara, took delight in telling the story of how he turned up in his village on a local holiday that was to coincide with the inauguration of the new village water supply. At the ceremony, he was ushered over to a table where food was being served, like at a wedding. Platefuls of local fare were being dished out from steaming bowls of rice, spinach and lentils. Everyone got an egg, and there were even spicy pieces of chopped-up chicken. People wore colourful necklaces of flowers. Kids were plastering each other with tika powder and running amok among the colourful crowd, chasing after chickens, hounding dogs away with sticks, and avoiding the chiding hands of adults who did their best to keep the kids from knocking over the food.

A sort of band was marching around playing out-of-tune horns in an even more out-of-tune cacophony of notes and sounds that took a lot of imagination to qualify as music. The 'tune', as Peter described it, sounded vaguely like the one played at the time to announce the news on Radio Nepal, something like the trumpet section of a brass band warming up, when individual band members are each practising their own part.

Randalph had experienced a similar event in another village. He remembered wanting to shout out at the band to get their fucking act together. The effect of the deafening din on both young Western volunteers had them cringing with distaste and criticism – how could anyone call this music?

According to Peter, he was sitting on the ground with his plate enjoying a for-once-more-lavish dish when the music suddenly stopped. A holy man had begun chanting and performing a holy ritual on a makeshift altar in the shade of the village's central peepul tree with various plates, jugs, incense sticks, flowers and what looked like pages ripped out of a book. The villagers thronged around him.

The band kicked up again. When Peter told anyone he met who would listen about what happened next, tears used to run down his cheeks and he would cough himself into an uncontrollable fit of laughter.

If Peter's story is indeed true, a solemn procession of men then approached the altar bearing gifts. The usual stuff: some fruit, vegetables, flowers, sugar, a terrified squawking chicken in a wickerwork basket, a collection of metal rice bowls, and to Peter's dismay, various pipe fittings, a tap, a drain, and the vertical pipe that connected individual water points to the system. Grateful for the gift of water in the village, those obviously in the know about what the higher powers needed as thanks had massacred one of the tap stands to offer the various constituent parts to the gods.

On hearing the story, Randalph imagined taking his old toilet seat to his village church back home in Scotland to offer it to the minister in thanks for the council workers repairing the plumbing in his bathroom. Randalph loved the story. It didn't matter if it was true. Nothing he had heard in those two years better highlighted the deliciously immense cultural gap between his culture of rationality and the mystical intrigue and societal surprises of the endearing Himalayan Kingdom of Nepal.

THERE'S A WATER BUFFALO IN THE BEDROOM

Randalph's base was a two-storey L-shaped brick building with a tin roof and an inner courtyard next to a coarse gravel road close to Phewa Lake at the bottom end of the town of Pokhara, the capital of Gandaki Province and today's 'tourism capital of Nepal'. The city, which at the time Randalph lived there was home to some 43,000 souls, now, in 2024, had grown to a population of some 600,000 inhabitants.

According to the 2021 census, while three-quarters of Pokhara's population spoke Nepali as their first language, others spoke Gurung, Magar, Newar, Tamang, Bhojpuri, Hindi, Maithili, Tharu, Urdu, Kham, Rai, Thakali, Bengali, Bhujel, Chantyal, Limbu and other languages. In terms of religion, some 80% were Hindu, while the remaining 20% were Buddhist, Christian, Muslim, Bon, Prakriti, Kirati and some others.

According to Wikipedia, the same census established that in terms of ethnicity/caste, the population was composed of Hill Brahmins, Gurung, Chhetri, Magar, Kami, Newar, Damai/Dholi, Tamang, Sarki, Gharti/Bhujel, Thakuri, Badi, Musalman, Sanyasi/Dasnami, Rai, Tharu, Kumal, Thakali, Chhantyal, other Dalit, Kalwar, Kathabaniyan, Sonar, Teli, Bengali, Dura, Gaine, Ghale, Hajjam/Thakur, Halwai, Koiri/Kushwaha, Limbu, Majhi, Sherpa, Sunuwar, other Terai and Yadav, and a handful of foreigners. When Randalph compared this to his hometown, indeed to his home country – which at the time had one common language and basically one religion divided into two belief paths – his mind boggled. How did all these different ethnicities, religions and native languages get along with each other, he wondered, when in his homeland the two different paths of their one religion had been tearing each other's throats out for centuries.

Randalph shared his base with two other colleagues from the same volunteer organisation. Both had arrived before him and had taken the two bedrooms on the top floor. The bedrooms opened onto a balcony that ran the length of the courtyard and was accessed by concrete stairs at the field side of the building. At the street side was a common room and a kitchen. Randalph had a room below the kitchen on the street side on the bottom floor. In each of the other two rooms on the ground floor lived an entire family with kids and a blaring stereo radio.

Both floors had a squat toilet connected to a cesspit. The families downstairs shared an outside water tap. The boys upstairs had the unusual luxury of a kitchen sink with its own water tap. The ground floor doors opened onto a courtyard with a haystack in the middle and a big water buffalo tied by the nose to a post. The owner, 'Gurung Ji', lived with his family of three kids in a thatch-roofed mud hut behind the haystack.

Sketch by Randalph looking from the door of the common room of his accommodation at the bottom end of Pokhara, a few minutes' walk from Phewa Lake.

Gurung Ji, his family, and the endless procession of relatives and neighbours that passed through the yard in daytime shared the water tap with the other two families. To enjoy the company of his colleagues and not have to deal with the daily bombardment of questions from curious locals who had the irritating habit of bursting into his room downstairs, sitting on his bed, asking him questions, and keeping him company, Randalph often slept on the cloth futon-type cushions his colleagues had laid out on the floor around the walls in the common room upstairs.

On one occasion, as Randalph turned the corner of the yard to head for the stairs, Gurung Ji was running around all flustered and upset. He was crying out "Baishi ayo! Baishi ayo!" (the buffalo has come) and frantically pointing at Randalph's bedroom. Sure enough, somehow the family water buffalo had found its way into Randalph's bedroom, where there was hardly enough room for Randalph to walk around in, never mind a buffalo. Gurung Ji was in a panic about how to get it out. Somebody would have to go inside and try to scare it backwards, he said, but not Randalph. The Baisi didn't know him and it might gore him to death.

He was damn right it wasn't going to be Randalph. Eventually, Bindi, Gurung Ji's tiny daughter who had the lively energy of a shrew, scurried in beside the beast and waved and shouted at it while Gurung Ji pulled it by the tail. By then, a small crowd had gathered and were peeing themselves with laughter as the poor old Baishi struggled to get its horns and wide flank through the door. Then as with almost every mishap in Nepal, a local priest turned up to sanctify Randalph's room and cleanse old Baishi's wayward spirit. It was one of those hilarious moments in life that should be captured on film.

After the cleansing, Gurung Ji explained to Randalph that the priest said Baisi was sad and was looking for company. The story became an epic, "Randalph and the lonely Baisi", told a hundred times to travellers and anyone else passing through, on each occasion reducing them to tears of laughter. When asked years later what his favourite animal was, Randalph would always reply the water buffalo.

STRAY LADIES THIS WAY PLEASE

To Randalph's delight, many single Western ladies with rucksacks and baba-cool colourful baggy batik-printed leggings, some with flowers in their hair, passed through Pokhara on their way to the mountains or just to hang out by the lake. All told stories about being pestered by local boys trying to peer at them through hotel windows or trying to fondle them, bumping into them in the crowd, or jeering at them on the streets. Poor girls, thought Randalph, how could he help?

Randalph's lodgings offered a safe haven to these poor damsels in distress and lured them into security away from all these dangers. Randalph also knew a few words of German, which impressed many of the Fräuleins, and by then he could also bargain on their behalf in basic Nepalese at the local market or with street vendors passing by, which impressed them even more and got them fresh fruit, cigarettes, or souvenir trinkets at a good price.

The lure was completed by offering the stray ladies a place

to sleep upstairs in the front room, where the cushy comfort of the futons with 70s music playing in the background on the boys' portable tape recorder was the perfect lady trap. Very soon, Randalph became known to the landlord, the families downstairs, the staff at the office, and probably the entire street and neighbourhood as the 'Deri cheekni manche', literally the 'very fucking man'. Randalph liked the nickname, and only wished it were closer to reality.

Young Randalph in his accommodation in Pokhara, Nepal.

CLOSE CALL

With his flatmates at their lakeside den in Pokhara, and with all the other volunteers, travellers and foreigners he met, the conversation would invariably come around to talking about shit. Diarrhoea, dysentery, giardia and worms crept into every discussion. According to the World Health Organisation (WHO), in the 1970s Nepal was the cesspit of humanity, where domestic hygiene was quasi non-existent and water-borne diseases were rife. Everybody got the skitters, and everybody talked about them. Having solid shits for five days in a row was almost suspicious. More often than not, someone in the room would have giardiasis and would let rip the most foul-smelling farts ever to flutter past the human sphincter. The smell was disgusting. Vile. Putrid.

To counteract the army of alien magots that had invaded their intestines, Randalph and his flat mates ate raw garlic and raw onions, making the stench even more unbearable. When one of them got infected, they joked about capturing the farts in bottles and selling them to the military as munition for chemical warfare. Not only did the maggots create the most nauseating smells, they also bloated the stomach to a point where the infected person would feel almost pregnant. To top it all, farting in Nepal was taboo – the thing you just didn't do.

While giardiasis and dysentery were common and could be cured with a five-day course of the medicine Flagyl, other more dangerous diseases lay lurking in Nepal's murky waters. Unknown to him, Randalph had caught one of them, called 'tropical sprue', and began losing weight rapidly. Believing he had caught another bought of dysentery, he picked up a dose of Flagyl at the local 'pharmacy' – a road-side hut selling an assortment of various drugs over the counter from aspirin to Belladonna. Tropical sprue was a rare disease that infected the intestine, killing the intestine membrane and reducing its ability to absorb nutrients to zero. Flagyl, which killed off unwelcome bacteria in the intestine was precisely the drug not to take to cure it.

Day by day Randalph was losing weight, getting thinner and weaker. After two weeks or so he no longer had the strength to reach the toilet and had to be carried there by his colleagues. Anything he ate went straight through him, coming out the other side intact. He was shitting whole tomatoes and potatoes. Not having succeeded in finding a local doctor who recognised the symptom, Randalph's colleagues lifted him onto the back of a truck bound for India and asked the driver to drop him off at the famous United Mission Hospital in Tansen. Established in 1954 as a partnership between the people of Nepal and a coalition of 20 Christian organizations on four continents, Tansen hospital was recognised as the place to go to when all else failed.

Upon his arrival there, propped up between two passengers from the truck, an American doctor took one look at Randalph and knew instantly that he had contracted the sprue, a rare acquired malabsorption syndrome characterized by chronic diarrhoea, weight loss, and malabsorption of nutrients. "There's a one in a hundred thousand chance of catching it," he explained to Randalph, and proceeded to feed him drops of folic acid. "Yep" he exclaimed in his American slang, "All you need is some drops of this and in a day or two you'll be right as rain." Sure enough, three days later Randalph was on his way back to Pokhara, no worse for wear.

Randalph was a preferred target of the dysentery bugs and prided himself at having caught it more times than any of the other volunteers. The problem with dysentery is that it can be so painful that you need painkillers, as Randalph experienced on his way back from one of his project supervision tours. Clutching his stomach in agony he turned up at a local medical post in Baglung village and saw the doctor there, who prescribed for him the usual Flagyl, but also a dose of Belladonna.

Randalph would never know if it was the doctor or the pharmacy who got the prescription wrong, but instead of two tablets of Flagyl three times a day and one tablet of Belladonna every two days, the labels had been switched round. Randalph started his treatment straight away, swallowing his first two Belladonna tablets with a glass of filtered water at the pharmacy and downing one of the Flagyl tablets. By the time he had taken his second dose at midday he felt dizzy. In the evening after the third dose, he passed out.

Two days later, when he regained consciousness, he found himself in Baglung missionary hospital with tubes up his nose and a drip feed in his arm. The witty English nurse there explained to him that if he had taken another two of these little buggers – pointing to the Belladonna – he would by now probably be flying home in a wooden casket. Randalph smiled and told the charming nurse not to worry, it would take more than Belladonna and tropical sprue to get rid of him. Looking back at his reckless life so far, he actually believed it…

STEAM TRAINS IN INDIA

Volunteers serving in the organisation that had sent Randalph to Nepal were allowed an annual four-week vacation. And so, halfway through his assignment, Randalph, Robert and Harry, his two flatmate colleagues from Pokhara, decided to spend their time off visiting India. Travelling by bus to the Indian border, then by train to Gorakhpur and Patna, their first stop was Calcutta, where Randalph remembers standing twelve hours in a queue to buy tickets for the mainline train south along the eastern shores of the Bay of Bengal to Madras.

On the wall in their common room back in Pokhara the boys had hung a large-scale map of India and spent hours day dreaming about this mystical subcontinent, imagining stories of the Raj and the Indian kingdoms of long ago. The journey to Madras, which was scheduled to take a day and a half, eventually took a day longer. The train was so crowded, with people breathing into your face, that after a few stops Randalph decided to climb onto the roof. This was one of the better decisions he had made in his life, because, except for relief from the scorching heat, it treated him to breathtaking views of the endless Indian landscape of villages, fields ploughed by buffalo, and tropical vegetation.

From the roof of the train as it trundled southwards, he could smell ripening mangoes, and at some moments catch glimpses of the sea. Luckily for Randalph, their carriage was towards the rear of the 20-wagon-long train and most of the smoke from the belching steam locomotive passed by overhead. Randalph was in his element and loving it.

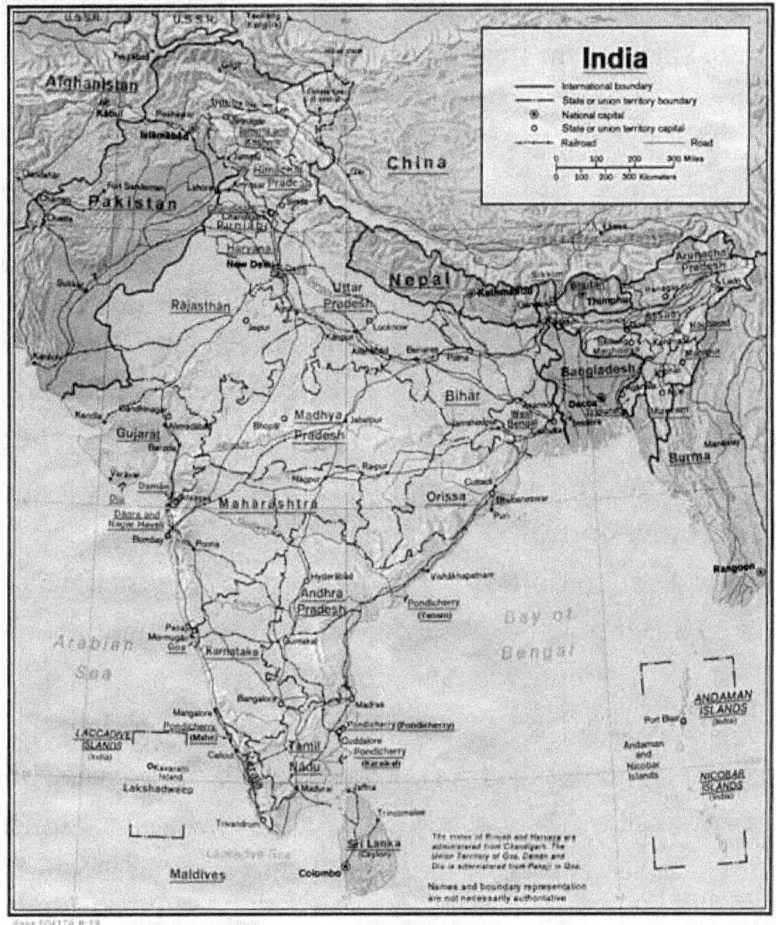

Map of India, akin to the one that hung on the wall of Randalph's shared common room in Pokhara.

Once in Madras, the three musketeers found the shabby remains of a once grandiose imperial mansion, which now carried a worn-out sign above the entrance archway trying to trick people into believing it was a hotel. Just around the corner from the 'hotel' was a public swimming pool and baths, where little Miss Fortune had apparently heard about the young white boys' arrival and was preparing some fun at their expense.

Delighted to have found a place to wash, but revolted by the slimy scum floating on the pool's surface, the boys undressed, hung their clothes in lockers and opted for taking only a shower. They would have a real wash the week after in Sri Lanka when they reached the sea. While they were relishing the warm water and soapy suds in the showers, little Miss Fortune, meanwhile, had emptied their lockers and run away with their clothes, leaving them with only their swimming trunks to cover themselves. Luckily, their hotel was just around the corner. But still, parading in swimming gear in the bustling centre of a crowded and conservative Indian city drew more than only stares and they had to fend off a barrage of jeers and insults, which looked like it might turn to violence at any moment.

Back at the hotel, and by now dressed again in clothes but feeling cheated and determined to set India right, the musketeers set off to report the incident to the police, who, as luck would also have it, manned a station on the other side of the road opposite the hotel. To cut a long story short, the police, in their infinite benevolence, had heard about the incident and were prepared to sell the boys' clothes back to them at a very reasonable price.

After their loss of face in Madras, the trio headed south via Madurai to catch the ferry to Sri Lanka in Rameswaram. Stepping out of the train and heading for the pier, they could see that the queue for the ferry, which seemed miles away, was endless. Randalph made a quick assessment of the situation and reckoned it would be impossible for all the people to get on board. On their walk from the station to join the queue, he remembered seeing a clothes shop selling pompous-looking uniforms and had an idea: Robert and Harry should take their place in the queue while Randalph went back to the shop to buy an outfit that might get them to the front of it.

An hour later, Randalph reappeared wearing a double-breasted tunic with shiny buttons and golden lapels, black trousers with red stripes running down the outside leg, a ceremonial cap with a bright red tassel that could have belonged to a military regiment, and shiny black boots with stainless steel buckles. With his furry red-brown beard bristling from underneath the cord that held his cap on Randalph could have been anything from a brass band member to a general on parade. To complete the disguise, he was brandishing a stick with a shiny knob on the end.

"Don't laugh," he said to the other two. "Watch." Scanning the crowd, his eyes landed on a porter wheeling luggage towards the ferry. "Excuse me sir, we are first-class passengers, can you take us to the ferry?" The poor porter, who was more than likely from a lowly caste and accustomed to serve those above him, looked at Randalph as if he was Donald Duck. You could see that he wasn't fooled, but at the same time he did not dare to take the risk of offending someone who, in the extremely unlikely event, might be important.

The porter's expression changed to happy compliance when Randalph slid a fifty rupee note into his hand, and off went the quartet, luggage trolley in front, General behind, and the two gentlemen in waiting taking up the rear. There were thousands of people in the queue and hundreds of hippies in their orange and yellow robes with drugged-looking drooping eyes, all lined up between two rows of metal riot-containing fences. Some of the more awake hippies had seen what Randalph and the gang were up to and started jeering. "Fuck them," said Randalph to his crew, "They're just a bunch of wankers. Don't look at them. Just walk." The porter, who had just earned two day's wages, caught the gist of what Randalph was saying, balanced his head from side to side in the delightful way the Indians do when signalling agreement, grinned, and said in his guttural Tamil accent, "Sahamat, Sahib. Fuck them".

As soon as they stepped onto the ferry, which cost young Randalph an extra hundred rupees in backhanders, the race was on for him to get changed back into his normal clothes before somebody in the queue recognised him and threw him overboard. Remembering a promise he had made to the guard on the Nepalese/Indian border, Randalph carefully folded away the uniform – this would be the gift to the officer there to make sure they got comfortable front seats on the bus back to Pokhara. When in India, do as Randalph does – everything has its price, he thought with a satisfied grin.

The boys' stay in the beautiful tropical island of Sri Lanka was uneventful. Most of the time it rained. The beaches they visited were stormy and threatening. The elephants they hoped to see must have heard they were coming and were in hiding. Only the breathtaking views of the train ride from Kandy through the tea plantations remained engraved in Randalph's memory.

On their last day, luck piped up, and on a stroll along the waterfront in Colombo's busy commercial harbour, the crew of a tugboat beckoned to them to climb on board for a ride through the harbour.

In those days the restrictions and security phobia the world is suffering from today had not yet infested all of its countries. Citizens could walk into a port, like this one, totally unhindered. Workers could scale ladders, even long ones, without needing to attach them or themselves to it. People could cross shunting yards at mainline stations, if doing so shortened their path. The more adventurous could travel by land across southern Europe and Turkey into Syria and Iraq, then, until the end of 1979, on through Iran, Afghanistan, and Pakistan to northern India. It would have been impossible at the time for governments to enact the Covid clampdown of 2019. Although not necessarily richer or in better health, in many parts of the world people had more freedom of movement. Big Brother had not yet taken control.

ANNAPURNA SOUTH

In March 1981, the weather in Nepal was getting hotter as summer approached. This was the last moment for expeditions to the mountains. For Randalph, who had never climbed before, it was time to give it a try. Down by the lakeside in Pokhara he had struck up a conversation with Cale, a muscly fitness-first Australian Crocodile Dundee type experienced in climbing who had his mind set on scaling Hiunchuli. Undeterred by Randalph's total lack of experience, he invited him to join him. The would-be mountaineers laid out their riches, made a budget, and duly hired a dozen Sherpas for what they believed would be a two-week ascent.

When they set off from Pokhara, weather conditions were excellent. With not a cloud in the sky it took them only three days to arrive at the last outpost on the trail before turning west beside Machapuchari, Nepal's holy 'Fish Tail' mountain, into the magical Annapurna Sanctuary. But

Annapurna South and Hiunchuli (above) photographed from Ghandruk in October 1980

The Annapurna Sanctury photographed in November 1980 on one of Randalph's treks into the mountains and used by the two apprentice mountaineers to plan their base camp.

then, as if lying in waiting for the enthusiastic climbers to arrive, all of a sudden the skies turned black and the gods spat out their wrath in a blinding snowstorm. Randalph, who had been to the Sanctuary three times previously and knew the terrain, took the lead.

To avoid avalanches or being snowed under in the steep valley at the entrance to the Sanctuary, they had to cross its snow-filled floor and get to the plateau to the west. For four hours nonstop from the moment they turned into the Sanctuary, the group plodded on relentlessly, walking at a brisk pace, heads down, snow building up all around them. On the way, they passed an already encamped expedition of French climbers who looked on in disbelief as Randalph's gang marched past. Randalph was feeling strong. He smiled at them. For once out in front in life, he was making the pace.

By the time they reached a safe spot out of reach of possible avalanches and could start setting up their tents, night had fallen. The temperature was -35°C. While the Sherpas were struggling to set up and secure the camp and make a fire to boil some water on, the two dived into their sleeping bags, huddling together under the thin red skin of their flimsy tent. Worried that they would suffocate under the deepening blanket of falling snow, they took turns at staying awake, ensuring that there was always a funnel of air leading to the tent. With the noise of the howling wind that had picked up and the crashing sound of snow and ice cascading down the steep slopes all around them in avalanches from thousands of metres above it was impossible to sleep.

To immortalise the event, once back in Pokhara Randalph documented their arrival in the Sanctuary on the office typewriter in a story that went like this:

```
What began as frosty crispness in the darkness of the morning has grown to
through a spell of burning shafts of sunlight bouncing on the snow, to clou
skies and now to almost blizzard in a perfect white-out. It is early in the
afternoon. My memory of how this road looked back in October in the autumn
of last year tells me that we must go on and upwards if we are to reach our
chosen campsite. On we trudge in to the driving freezing snow, determined
cold and wet and angry. I am shouting at the porters now who want to turn
around and go back down or stop near here under a rock, screaming at them to
go on for just another hour then another tand another; they complain, quite
rightly so: the meagre pittence and discomfort which we offer them for
helping us is hardly worth the danger and the blind obidience they must
subject themselves to, but they are strong and still they come. The wind
picks up a little and our effort needed is a little more. We form ourselves
in to a slowly moving steady group. The tension and the anger are removed,
there is no cold, no fear, no nonsense: if I live or die means nothing to me
now. The only feeling that pervades me now is force, and for half an hour I
am privileged to leed our sodden misserable troop with measured step. No
turning round to look and count, no thoughts of what might be or was or ever
is, no nothing.....unity.

Here among the highest mountains of the world among the snow and ice and
spleandour lies a road to freedom. Freedom from the rigours of the towns and
cities of our world, freedom from the pressures of society. Here reigns a
peacefulness, an absolute absorbing wilderness and calm so powerful that we
need no longer fear for love or man or death. Here we may have freedom from
ourselves.
```

Extract from Randalph's typed account of the walk into base camp at the west end of Annapurna Sanctury on 20 March 1981.

By the following morning, the skies had cleared. The sun was cutting wedges of melting ice in the mountain slopes to the north, which groaned and cracked under the fiery torture. The tops of the camp's red tents poked out shyly in the brilliant white desert like poppies in a corn field. While the guys had made it so far, Randalph, who had valiantly led the team through the blizzard, was exhausted. It would take him days or even a week to recover. To add to the exposure problem, the Sherpas, who were wearing only minimal clothing, were freezing and their mood was bleak.

Undeterred, Crocodile Cale, who was angry at Randalph for being tired and at the Sherpas for feeling the cold, had only one thing on his mind. He made it clear to Randalph that the next day, tomorrow, at dawn, they would head off by themselves on a two-day, two-man attempt to climb the 6,441 metres of Hiunchuli, the little sister of the mighty Annapurna South.

If Google had existed then, they would have learned that the time frame they planned for was completely unrealistic. The 2000 m (6561 ft) climb from their base camp to the summit was not a Sunday afternoon stroll, and totally impossible to do in only two days, unless you were a Sherpa, born and toughened in the inhospitable wilderness of the high Himalayas, or Italy's Reinhold Messner, who climbed Mount Everest that same year without supplemental oxygen.

Nevertheless, Commander Cale's bravado and total disregard for common sense got the two would-be mountaineers as far as the cusp of the ridge between the two summits, from where they enjoyed the momentary pleasure of marvelling at the sight of India far to the south and the procession of peaks stretching as far as the eye could see to the west, the north and the east. It was a wonderful sight, and although they had reached an altitude of only around 5,500 metres, to Randalph it felt like they were on top of the world.

The next morning, after they had dug themselves out of the freezing snow where they camped that night on the ridge, Randalph realised that he had overstayed his welcome in the high mountains and was stricken by altitude sickness so intense that he lost any idea of where he was or what he was doing. Cale, who was enraged, knowing that he would have to attempt the climb to the summit on his own, sent

Randalph back down to base camp.

On his way down, Randalph slipped and landed in a shallow crevasse, disappearing from Cale's sight. Cale's last glimmer of hope of going to the top was over. From his perch on the ridge where he was arrogantly smoking a cigarette, as if in defiance of the altitude, he came charging down the mountainside, reluctantly helped Randalph out of the fissure, swore at him, then set off at his own pace down to base camp, where he bade goodbye to the Sherpas and headed off out of the Sanctuary alone, never to be seen or heard of again. The last time Randalph had seen someone so totally pissed off went back to his cycling days when he and his cycling friends had sprayed innocent members of the public at a bus queue with sticky orange juice.

A ROYAL TOAST

Randalph's favourite exploit by far in Nepal, which became his claim to infamy and was recorded in a short story he wrote that was read out by the illustrious Dr J. to his university PhD students in Glasgow, was so controversial that Randalph feels it wiser not to say too much about it in his memoirs. Suffice it to say that he had escaped arrest by the skin of his teeth in the Royal Palace grounds in Kathmandu during a royal banquet at which he, and all the other Brits in Nepal, were invited to attend a visit by a member of the British Royal family.

Twenty years later, at the morning coffee break during a conference in Geneva where Randalph had bumped into an ex-volunteer who had been in Nepal at the same time as he was, the story came up again. The two didn't immediately recognise each other, but as they wandered together down memory lane, they realised that the ex-volunteer had been a nurse in the Baglung missionary hospital when Randalph had been taken there unconscious, after his overdose of Belladonna.

Puzzled, she suddenly asked: "Would you be the guy who pulled away the chair of the wife of such and such during the toast?" He was. Randalph's little playful indiscretion had caused such a stink in the room that he had been marched out under guard and confined to a locked room on the first floor.

There are times in life when you hang around, confidently waiting for the next step. This was not one of them. Filled with just enough alcohol not to worry about consequences, Randalph had leapt out the window of the first-floor room he was being kept in, crossed the lawn, scaled the perimeter wall, ran like an athlete through the streets of Kathmandu, heedless of the barking dogs chasing him. He hid in the shadows at the bus terminal waiting for the first bus to Pokhara in the morning, and was never again seen in Kathmandu for the remainder of his time in Nepal.

HOPELESS LOVE

Randalph's adventure in Nepal ended with a broken heart. On the way down from his last trek to his beloved Sanctuary, he joined up with a group of French trekkers who were also on their way down from the mountains. One of them, the delightful, blue-eyed delicate and discreet Juliette, had a sparkle in her eye that set Randalph's heart on fire. Without saying a word to each other, Randalph – who at that time didn't speak a word of French, and besides didn't want to risk breaking the spell he was under by saying something stupid – just smiled, and dreamed, and dreamed, and smiled.

Once back in Pokhara, he offered *les français* accommodation at his place, which fortunately was deserted as the other colleagues were all out of town on supervision tours to their projects in the villages. For a couple of days Randalph lived in a bubble of bliss. His smiles were met and returned and his eyes twinkled every time they met Juliette's.

Sadly, the smiling and the dreaming came to a painful end on the day when Juliette and her friends flew back to their homeland. Randalph took them to the airstrip and made sure they had tickets on the weekly flight to Kathmandu and good seats near the front of the Air Nepal Twin Otter. There was so much he had wanted to say, but of the dreams he had wanted to share there was nothing left. As autumn turns to winter when migratory birds take to the sky and head south, so Randalph's heart fell into hibernation as the plane took off. Randalph left the airstrip, saddened to the core, in abject misery and heartache.

And then magic happened. The next week, still by himself at his base, he strolled along the coarse gravel road up to the airstrip to wait for the plane, hoping, as the volunteers always did, for mail from home. From where he was standing in the shade of the airstrip terminal building – a wooden hut with a flag, a windsock and an officer sitting cross-legged on the ground – he watched the plane taxi to a halt, cut its engines, and lower the stairs from the door under the wing.

He was about to walk over to greet the pilot and pick up any mail when his heart stopped. The first person to alight from the plane was Juliette, who had seemingly spotted Randalph during the landing. All smiles and sunshine, she waved and walked confidently over to him. Her first words in her thick French accent were "I want to make babies with you". Randalph had been hit on the head by a thunderbolt. He was struck dumb. The best he could do was to sink to the ground and look up in disbelief.

For the past week, Juliette had been learning English and had mustered up just enough vocabulary to communicate to Randalph that she was in love with him. Still under the shock, Randalph stood up, slung her bag onto his back, took her hand, forgot the mail, and headed with her to the lakeside, where he rented a rowing boat and paddled out to the middle of the lake. The setting was romance in its essence. The sun was high in the sky. The mountain skyline to the north was glimmering like a Christmas tree and reflected on the mirror-like surface of the lake. The two lovebirds were beaming like they had been lit up. Life, Randalph understood, had just begun.

After a blissful week spent together roaming the foothills, camping in secluded fields, and smiling at each other as if they had invented the gesture, it was time for Juliette to go back to Paris and her studies at the Sorbonne. They would write to each other. Yes. Every day. Twice a day. And soon they would be united forever. It sounded like the trailer for one of those dark movies where you have that nagging intuition from the outset that something unforeseen and evil is going to happen. Something horribly bad and terribly cruel.

During the next weeks they rained letters on each other. The plane's mail box was full of blue airmail envelopes for Randalph, whose bulging envelope of letters for abroad was filled with mail for Juliette. But after a month or so, the monsoon of letters waned, the air-mail storm began to lose its intensity and the continuous downpour was reduced to intermittent showers. Desperate, Randalph increased the frequency of mail from his side, writing letter after letter, sometimes three in the same day, but the French monsoon was over.

At just about the same moment when he had resolved to pack his bags and fly to Paris, the letter he had been dreading arrived. Juliette, who was back in the swing of life in the French capital, had met up again with her old boyfriend, Samuel. Samuel was studying medicine and would soon be graduating. Her family liked him and her mother loved him. She was so sorry. It was so difficult for her to tell this to Randalph. In a nutshell, the dream was over.

Twenty-five years later, after the death of Randalph's mother, Randalph, now married, was driving back to his home in Switzerland through Brittany, the *département* Juliette was from. He decided to try to find her. He had to find out what had happened and hear the full story from the horse's mouth. Armed with bags of coins, he stopped at almost every telephone booth on his route and dialled the next number in the long list of entries under her family name. Introducing himself in French – which he had by then adopted as his everyday language – he explained that he was Randalph from Nepal, an old friend of Juliette's, with whom he had lost contact.

After dozens of attempts, he found her.

"Randalph from Nepal?" The lady at the other end of the line spoke as if with disbelief. "I'm her mother. Juliette spoke so often about you."

After his initial heart attack, all his indicators in the red and shooting off the end of the scale, Randalph listened as her mother told him that Juliette was happily married to a lovely doctor, with whom they had four fine children. Randalph guessed it was the lucky Samuel, offered some small talk, thanked her mother for the news, and wished them all a happy life. He knew it. A doctor. Now probably a rich man. Randalph had nothing that could compete with Samuel's status and bank book. Who would be so crazy to have entrusted their life into the hands of this reckless scoundrel?

A few weeks later, back home in Switzerland, the phone rang. Randalph's wife picked it up and thrust the receiver furiously into Randalph's hand, saying, "There's a Juliette that wants to speak with you". They talked for an hour, happy at last to have the opportunity to come full circle. It had been a long wait, during which they both had suffered. Freed from their guilt and pain, they wished each other well. Randalph felt relief. Their dream had come full circle. Some things are simply not meant to be.

GOODBYE NEPAL

When Randalph stepped off the plane at Heathrow on his way home from Nepal in the autumn of 1981, his teeth were chattering. He was wearing a red mountaineering jacket, heavy trousers and climbing boots. On his back was his trusty travel-battered washed-out lilac-coloured Karrimor 35-litre rucksack. In Delhi when he had taken off eight hours previously the temperature had been 46°C, but in London it was 15°C. Impatient to get on with life and frustrated at the little he had been able to achieve in a year and a half in the field, he had cut short his stay in the Himalayan mountain kingdom of the green-eyed yellow idol and headed home, hoping to find a job with more hands-on action.

In the arrivals lounge at Heathrow, he stopped to gaze at a kid holding a cube with nine smaller coloured cubes on each side. The smaller cubes seemed to be connected in such a way that they could be moved around in groups of nine. It looked like some sort of 3D mechanical puzzle. The kid, who was totally absorbed in turning the plateaux of cubes from one side and then to the other, suddenly looked up and noticed Randalph staring at him. "What is it?" asked Randalph. "It's a Rubik's Cube," replied the kid, "Everybody's got one. Where are you from?" He spoke in a disapproving tone that suggested that Randalph had just beamed down from outer space.

Apart from the arrival of Rubik's Cubes, nothing else had changed. Heathrow was crowded. The underground was packed. Taxis were still black. Buses were still double-deckers. Traffic was still driving on the left. The streets were still lined with litter. The lack of change and new things disappointed Randalph, who had hoped to step back into a world bustling with innovation and modernisation.

In a pub he stopped off at for a bar lunch and a pint of beer he struck up a conversation with a fellow traveller wearing a colourful Indian-style tunic, long hair and round John Lennon-style glasses. He had just arrived home after spending six months wandering around in India. Sensing Randalph's shared lack of enthusiasm at finding himself back in cold grey Britain, he looked around himself, as if making an inventory of who was in the pub, and proclaimed to Randalph, "The problem with London is that God doesn't live here. He doesn't even come on visits. You'll never see him in the streets and he'll never buy you a drink. Victoria sent him packing when she built the empire".

That statement rummaged around in Randalph's mind for years, like a zen koan you never find an answer to. It certainly felt like God's presence had been so much more tangible in the friendly, open, welcoming faces of the Nepalese than it was in the closed-down frowns of the millions of commuters scurrying to get to wherever they were going in busy London.

By mid-afternoon, Randalph had made his way to his organisation's headquarters and was shaking hands with the desk officers and senior staff. In less than an hour they had gone over the essentials of his short, hand-written report and were asking Randalph about what he would like to do next. Randalph had no idea. Another mission as a volunteer was out of the question. He needed to earn some money and didn't have the patience for the slow-moving pace of development aid.

"How about an emergency relief assignment?" asked one of the debriefing team, putting in Randalph's hand a one-page flyer explaining the need for engineers in humanitarian emergencies. The flyer presented a chap called Peter Guthrie who had been working in a refugee camp during the Vietnamese Boat People crisis and, realizing there was no real system in place to deploy engineers to respond to humanitarian crises, had formed an organisation the previous year to provide engineers to front-line humanitarian agencies.

This was more like it. Action, thought Randalph. His organisation put him in touch with the newly created roster of engineers and the next day before travelling home to Scotland he was able to have a meeting with an endearing old gentleman by the name of Jack Muggeridge, the brother of the famous journalist and broadcaster Malcolm Muggeridge. Jack had spent six months the previous year in Malaysia with Oxfam supervising the maintenance and improvement of refugee camps set up to care for the so-called Vietnamese Boat People and emphasised for Randalph the desperate need elsewhere around the world for engineers with the expertise necessary for laying on basic services, such as clean drinking water and sanitation.

Randalph was excited as he took the train back to his childhood home in Ayrshire. A quick 'hi' to mum, then off on a humanitarian mission, he thought. The 'hi' lasted longer than Randalph had hoped, and it was three months later before Jack called him. Meanwhile, Randalph had found a part-time job of sorts distributing leaflets around north-east Scotland for his good friend Simon's father, who was hoping to sell ready-made garages to homeowners. By now it was late November. In Scotland winter had already arrived and Randalph's mood was deteriorating, as he contemplated the dark days ahead with no sign of light at the end of his tunnel.

Then, one day towards the end of the month, the phone rang. "Are you still interested in working with us?" asked Jack, after a minimum of civilities. Of course he was. "It's rather urgent, I'm afraid," continued Jack, "Could you come to London tomorrow?" Of course he could. "I could take the night train down and be at your office for morning coffee," said Randalph. "Good," replied Jack, "You'll be flying out the same day to the UN in Geneva, where you'll be briefed about the next steps. They need you in Malaysia."

Here we go, smiled Randalph to himself. Your time has come…

PART 3

The fun's over
Close calls in the big bad world

CHAPTER 10

UN Passport

The UN? Malaysia? Urgent needs? Randalph was already floating three feet above the ground as he hastily packed his bag, said goodbye to brother Jack and Helma, waived to the neighbours, walked down to the bus stop on the main street in his village, took the first bus to Kilmarnock, walked up to the railway station, and bought a one-way ticket for the night-train to London.

The meeting the next morning with London Jack was short, sweet and to the point. Randalph was to report to the UNHCR head office in Geneva the next day, where he would leave his UK passport and be given a United Nations Laissez-Passer, which Jack explained, reading out loud from the document he was holding in his hand, was "a diplomatic travel document issued by the United Nations under the provisions of Article VII of the 1946 Convention on the Privileges and Immunities of United Nations personnel around the world".

Wow, thought Randalph, how did they know I was

coming? He has never forgotten the feeling of elation at hearing those magical words. Special agent Randalph felt important and needed. This was more like it. But where was Geneva, he wondered? Randalph's knowledge of the world in his early twenties was still not universal. He remembered the railway station in Genoa, Italy, and thought it couldn't be there. He had heard about Geneva as a place where important meetings are held, but had no idea it was in Switzerland.

After the briefing, which only lasted an hour and a cup of tea, he and another more senior engineer called Dave, who would be Randalph's team leader in the refugee camp in Malasia, headed down into the underground to catch a plane at Heathrow to fly out together to wherever Geneva was.

Having cleared Swiss customs and paid for a horrendously expensive taxi ride to Geneva city centre, the two engineers checked into their chic hotel on Route de Lausanne overlooking Lake Geneva, then went out for a walk. It was early evening, a biting cold wind was blowing from the East across the lake and into the city, which was lit up like a fairy-tale setting, with the signs of famous watch brands and banks glowing on the rooftops of the elegant six-storey facades facing them on the other side of the lake.

After crossing the Pont du Mont Blanc road bridge that connected the city's Rive Droit, on the west side of the lake, to the Rive Gauche on the east, they headed up the small hill with the church spire on top that they discovered was the centre of the old part of the city. Gazing at shop windows as they passed, both were amazed at the display of expensive jewellery, watches and fur coats, with price tags often into six figures. Neither had ever seen such wealth. Randalph was baffled and hovering between awe and disgust. He couldn't imagine that anyone would pay hundreds of thousands for a piece of metal studded with precious stones or whatever to hang around their wrist just to tell the time.

In the show cases of the many chic jewellery and clock shops he could see up close the same watches that figured on the huge posters in the tunnels connecting the airport's arrival hubs to the terminal building, all brandishing a smart slogan, telling the potential buyer of the lifestyle benefits he or she would reap by owning one of these hand-crafted masterpieces. But they were only watches, thought Randalph. Wasn't a cheap Timex good enough to tell the time?

As the two gazed on in bewilderment at the opulence on display, playing the game of who could spot the most expensive watch or necklace, both were struck dumb at this display of decadence in the extreme. They were heading to a refugee setting where they had been told the people possessed only the clothes they stood up in. They formed an opinion of mutual disgust, to somehow hide their envy, sneering critically at those who had so much money to spend on the superficialities of life.

Back at the hotel, with their hands and feet frozen and scanning the menu for something to eat, they changed their game to spotting the cheapest prices – everything on the menu was so expensive.

The next morning, at their briefing at the UNHCR offices, just a five-minute walk along the lakeside from their hotel towards the city-centre, things got serious. Randalph and Dave were passed around from desk to desk and handshake to handshake. There were forms to fill in, emergency telephone numbers and contact addresses to register, basic health checks to endure, stern warnings about conduct to take seriously, and a chilling pep talk about what to do in the event of witnessing death, murder, abduction, rape or torture.

Randalph and Dave were informed that they were heading to an island refugee camp inside a military restricted zone under military law, where the military commander, Major T, had the last word. "Cross him, and you might not come home. Do what he says and we'll see you again in six months," were the cautionary words of the South-East Asia Desk officer, the last person the two were to see on their briefing tour.

The warning was loud and clear. The cloud-nine feeling Randalph had enjoyed until then suddenly shrunk in size to ground zero. Finally, armed with their sky-blue UN passports, the new saviours of humanity were released, directed to the in-house travel agency to pick up their tickets, and left free to grab another expensive taxi to take them to Geneva Cointrin and their flight, in business class, to Kuala Lumpur.

CHAPTER 11

Boat People

The Vietnamese Boat People were the millions of souls who fled by sea the economic devastation, infrastructure destruction, societal disruption and political persecution of their devastated homeland during the aftermath of the Vietnam War. Records show that out of the two million people who attempted to flee Vietnam by boat, roughly 800,000 were successful in finding new homes outside the

Small boat overloaded with refugees heading to one of the many Vietnamese refugee camps in and around the South China Sea
(Image downloaded from Wikipedia)

country. Somewhere between 200,000 and 400,000 are estimated to have died trying to escape the country by sea in fishing boats or in other small vessels.

Their journey was often incredibly dangerous and hazardous. The Boat People faced numerous obstacles on their voyage including piracy, extreme weather conditions, limited resources, and the risk of being turned away by recipient countries. Even after reaching a foreign port, they were often left stranded in refugee camps with no immediate solutions for resettlement. If the boat travellers were lucky enough to make it to a nearby country, they would often have to resort to living in refugee camps until their requests for resettlement were processed.

Back then in 1981, UNHCR reported a total of some 19.2 million asylum seekers, returnees, stateless people and a portion of the world's internally displaced. Today, in 2024, for the first time in recorded history, the number of people forcibly displaced is now over 110 million, with over 36.4 million refugees worldwide.

The humanitarian crisis was so dire that eventually significant international intervention and cooperation were allocated to alleviate the situation, with the result that many of the boat people who were successful in their journeys ended up in countries all across the world including Canada, Australia, France, Germany, and the United States. In a few rare cases, some even made permanent homes in the refugee camps they were initially placed in.

Proudly presenting their UN identities, Randalph and Dave passed unchecked through customs and past the Kuala Lumpur airport border police. In the early 1980s, there was still a commonly held belief that UN, NGO and Red Cross personnel were on a mission to do good. The kidnappings, killings and persecution of aid workers in the 1990s and thereafter had not yet begun.

Cleared and in, the two were picked up by a Landcruiser, driven to the UN mission for more briefing and in-country admin requirements, then taken back to the airport and put on a plane to Kuala Terengganu on the east coast, where they boarded the *Blue Dart*, a powerful motor launch that would take them to their tropical refugee island destination in the land of Major T.

Although on an island in Malaysian territorial waters in the South China Sea, to all intents and purposes Randalph and the dozen or so other ex-pats on the island could well have been living in Vietnam. Until a few months previously, the island had been the temporary home of some 40,000 survivors of the crossing by boat from Vietnam over the deadly waters of that sea. In an effort to reduce the numbers in this camp, and other similar camps in the region, the governments of the US, France and many other nations had stepped up their vetting procedures and were allowing the Boat People to flock to their countries of adoption in their thousands. When Randalph landed on the island, there were still about 10,000 waiting their turn to relocate to their new home.

Travelling to the island on the *Blue Dart*, which was used for carrying supplies and aid workers back and forth to the island, Randalph forgot for an hour the purpose of his being there. He had found a spot out on deck under the sun, where the spray and the wind caressed his face and he could watch the white crests of the waves carved by the raised bow of the vessel as they splayed out in a gentle corrugated curve towards the horizon on either side of the boat. He was loving every minute of the trip.

As they approached the island, at a distance Randalph could initially only make out coconut palms covering a small dome-shaped outcrop in the sea. A few minutes later he could distinguish the colourful roofing of low-level structures among the trees and hordes of people on the beach. As they got closer, between the greenery he could see densely packed makeshift shelters and skimpy bamboo structures covered in corrugated-iron sheeting that seemed to cover the entire forest floor. There were also tall poles every twenty or so metres with megaphones attached to them, which gave him his first introduction to the Vietnamese language and numbers – the megaphones made an incessant din and, as he was soon to understand, were used primarily to call the occupants of a particular boat to proceed to registration.

It was only when he stepped down from the boat onto the quay that he had his first close-up glimpse of the Boat People. They looked just as they had in the documents and pictures he had seen of them at the UN. His first thought was how ample and comfortable the tunics and wide pants worn by both the men and the women appeared to be, and how well the conical bamboo hats protected them from the sun. He was struck also by the warm smile he got from anyone whose eyes he met. Despite the squalor and precariousness of the context, young Randalph told himself he would make the best of his time here.

Pulao Bidong Vietnamese Refugee Camp one year prior to Randalph's arrival, at the time when it was home to some 40,000 refugees (Images downloaded from UN media)

Randalph and Dave were greeted by a young engineer called Brian of about Randalph's age and from the same organisation. Brian had been recruited earlier and had already been there for some weeks. Getting straight into the business at hand, he suggested that they should leave their bags on his veranda while they made a tour of the camp. On their tour, the three concluded that while the scenes of squalor, desperation and inhumanity witnessed by Jack a year previously had visibly diminished, there was still cause for concern. Not least of all because social disorder was brewing and security incidents were becoming more frequent, with the growing number of Boat People that had not been accepted for adoption beginning to show their miscontent.

In addition, drinking water, which was the engineers' prime concern, still needed to be transported by barge, and rotting vegetables and the remains of fish and meat lay everywhere. To add to the mess, raw sewage ran along channels criss-crossing the camp and the rat population was estimated at twenty times that of the humans. The engineers' mission was to sort out the mess. But where to start?

Before jumping into the nitty gritty of their assignment, the new arrivals were introduced to the rest of the team of ex-pats living on the island, each of whom had a wooden hut on stilts in a small compound by the island's northern beach, separated from the rest of the camp by a dense row of coconut palm trees.

The team was a haphazard assortment of aid workers, each with a specific task, each with his or her own idea of what was important and what needed to be done first. There was a Canadian couple who saw the camp through the lens of social protection and injustice, a Dutch doctor who would have spent the entire six months of his assignment diving along the island's coral reef if it weren't for refugees plaguing him with requests for help, a Scandinavian dentist who would have extracted the teeth of everyone to be able to enjoy cocktails on his veranda uninterrupted in the evenings, and a confrontational New York American Jew who walked around with bare feet, ate fish raw from the sea and stamped admin papers all day long at a desk. Another New York American Jew, this time an elderly lady, argued with him every evening about the finer points of their beliefs. An endearing Australian nurse was followed around all day by hordes of orphan kids looking for attention, and there was a young dark-haired French beauty who teamed up with the Australian, Captain John, a permanently drunk American Vietnam veteran who had lost his entire platoon in an ambush in the jungle and fell into a sort of trance every evening after a bottle of whisky when he told his terrifying story to anyone who was listening, or simply to himself.

To complete the team, there was also a highly-strung terribly-posh English administrator lady called Pippa who strutted around aggressively, tossing her long blond hair to the side and screaming at the refugees to get in line. An overweight and horribly hirsute Scandinavian lady teamed up with Pippa against the dentist who, as well as wanting to enjoy cocktails undisturbed on his veranda, also held the point of view that we were all down here on earth to fuck around as much as we could. He fleshed out his arguments with so much intimate detail that listening to him was like watching porn.

Then there was the UN rep, a descendant of Romanian royalty who spoke English with the most theatrical French accent, a middle-aged English engineer called Dan, with a thick accent that no one understood, who had been hired by an independent charity and strutted around with a clipboard measuring up the camp to make a map, which he kept to himself, and Brian, who, unlike the rest of the aid worker clique, was just a normal guy, like Randalph himself. The team was completed by Dave, who had flown in with Randalph and enjoyed pestering the mapmaker about his progress, and a young French-speaking medical laboratory technician who arrived a few weeks after Randalph and became his lady friend. This young lady, who was called Annette, had taken with her a dozen cassettes of French singer-songwriters whom Randalph had never heard of, and Randalph had taken with him a cassette player, with no cassettes. Destiny, thought Randalph, brings together people in the strangest ways. In all, less than twenty do-gooder idealists were assigned to improve the living conditions of this camp of 10,000 escapees from war-torn Vietnam.

The aid workers were not alone in running the camp. Serving under the unbending will, fierce determination and all-pervading inquisitiveness of the much-feared Major T was a platoon of Malaysian military, who saw to it that the Major's rule of law in the camp was strictly enforced.

After being briefed about the aid workers and having met a few, Brian took Randalph and Dave to meet Major T, who had been informed of their arrival and had prepared his welcoming warning. Greetings were not his thing. "This camp is my camp," were his first words, spoken defiantly as he shifted his stern, suspicious eyes between Randalph's and Dave's. "These men," pointing to his soldiers, "are my men. The refugees are my concern and only my concern. You are here to do a job in my camp. Do your job well and there will be peace. Do your job badly and there will be war. Interfere with the refugees or bring drugs to the island and you will never see your homeland again. Understood?" The two nodded. "Dismissed!" growled the Major as he turned on his heel and strode back into his office. It looked like what they had been told about him in Geneva was in no way exaggerated.

The next briefing was about the Vietnamese themselves. Brian explained to Randalph and Dave how the Boat People had organised themselves into sectors, each with its own chief, each with its own task, and all reporting to a certain Commander Nguyen, their undisputed leader. The formidable Commander Nguyen was the silent type. He spoke little of himself or of his past. He didn't need to. Among the Vietnamese he was a walking legend whose authority crept deep into every crack in the camp's social fibre. Nothing could be achieved or changed in the camp without his involvement and consent. If you wanted something done, you made friends with the Commander. Even Major T understood that he was dealing with a persona that commanded automatic respect.

With the first day's briefings over and done with, the three returned to Brian's veranda, where Randalph and Dave, the new team leader, picked up their bags, were shown to their huts and spent the rest of the evening enjoying cool beers, getting to know each other, telling stories and cracking jokes. With their feet resting on the horizontal beam screwed to the bottom of the wooden struts that served as railings for their verandas, they gazed out over the big blue sea beyond. They had arrived.

The next day, on Randalph's first day of work, as he walked around with Dan the Map, as the engineers came to call him, he spotted Commander Nguyen barking orders at a gang of refugee workers busy shovelling dead leaves and twigs out of a ditch. Commander Nguyen looked frightening. He had the eyes of an eagle and the jaw of a hyena. He talked quickly, moved fast and pointed at people's faces, his other hand clenched in a fist. He commanded total, non-negotiable obedience.

Randalph instantly observed that no one joked with the Commander. No one looked for privileges, they just nodded. When the Commander questioned someone, you could feel nature go cold, as he stuck his face directly in theirs, his eyes drilling into their mind, beyond the lies, deep into the truth, all the truth, and nothing but the truth, which his piercing presence would squeeze out of them.

The aid workers never learned about what happened to anyone who stood up to the Commander, or if there even were such people in the camp. He was the only person that Major T spoke to politely. The few refugees in the camp who spoke English talked of him with reverence and fear. None of them ever dared to question his authority or criticise his decisions. Some even said he was the incarnation of the God of Fire. Whatever he was and whatever he represented, he sent shivers down Randalph's spine. To do his job, Randalph would need to befriend him. How do you befriend a stalking tiger, he thought?

Commander Nguyen was not an easy man to approach. You either had to have a good reason to do so or something he needed. Randalph found out from some of the Vietnamese who worked under him that he was looking for empty sandbags to line the banks of a channel his people were digging for draining storm water to the sea. On this assignment, unlike during his time in Nepal, Randalph had buying power and could easily procure building materials from the mainland through the UN office in the capital. He asked the Commander's men for the size and number of bags he would need, and duly set the wheels of procurement in motion. In those glorious days before the world was strangled by cumbersome administrative procedures, a hand-written note with a signature sent in an airmail envelope was enough to order a boatload of bags, planks, tools, cement, food, drink or whatever.

A few days later, only hours after the bags were delivered, the Commander approached Randalph to thank him. Randalph said it was nothing and offered his help in procuring any other materials he might need. The Commander said he would make a list. The list reached Randalph that same evening in the hands of one of the Commander's workers, who turned up at Randalph's veranda with his outstretched left hand holding a folded sheet of paper. With his right hand he saluted Randalph and said in a staccato voice, his eyes looking respectfully away and upwards from Randalph's, "From the Commander", then disappeared between the trees back into the camp.

The Commander's list was long but detailed and precise enough for Randalph to simply pass it on to his HQ, who duly organised the three boatloads necessary to transport all of the materials and tools on it to the island. When Randalph was summoned to the quay by Major T's men to answer questions about the cargo of supplies, he simply said it was for the Commander. It was like a password, and it had the same effect as when Luke Skywalker ordered the barbarian guards with the big tusks to stand down in *Star Wars*. Anything regarding the Commander was beyond question. Could it be that he was a Jedi knight? By and by Randalph gained the Commander's trust, and even got from him a smile. It was now his turn to ask for a favour.

To elevate the base of the communal toilet facilities so that rats could no longer bite the bottoms of the people squatting there, especially the bottoms of the children, who were terrified of them, and to rid the camp of the rats and the many piles of festering organic waste altogether, would require a lot of manpower, coordination and materials. Randalph did not command a workforce and had no authority for coordinating work gangs in the camps, but the commander did. Randalph showed him what he thought could be done to improve the deplorable hygiene conditions and how they could exterminate the rats. The Commander, who spoke excellent English with a hint of an American accent, added his thoughts and observations. In a matter of hours, they had drawn up a basic plan and set to work, with Randalph ordering materials and the Commander ordering over two hundred people to volunteer on around-the-clock work crews.

Who was this man, Randalph wondered, who had the authority to order fellow countrymen to volunteer in a context where they were all stripped of their previous status and branded wholesale as asylum seekers in this shared temporary existence on an island, far away from home, in the middle of the sea?

Whoever he was, it worked. As if in preparation for an invasion, as soon as the needed tools and supplies had arrived, gullies were being dug in just about every direction connecting with main ditches lined with sandbags that drained away to the sea. As the weeks rolled by, the ground-level toilet and shower block were raised on stilts, and bamboo canes were strapped together to form waterways from the island's jetty to the header tanks on the perimeter of the camp. The Commander just had to snap his fingers and as if by magic things got done. It was as if Mary Poppins was in town.

With the camp infrastructure and facilities substantially improved, the next item of concern was the extermination of the rats. How do you get rid of rats, Randalph wondered? Maybe someone at head office would know. In one of his calls to the mainland for materials, he asked if anyone knew if there was an expert in rat extermination in the country. There was, and after negotiating a contract with him, the honourable Mr. Ratcatcher duly made the trip to the island, turning up at the quay one day carrying a briefcase bursting with documents, books, diagrams and pictures of rats and how to get rid of them.

The rat catcher was one of those colonial types who still wore the broad-brimmed bush hat that many of the British wear whenever they find themselves south of the English Channel. In his theatrical introduction, Randalph learned that his name was Rodney. Eliminating rodents was his trade. Reward was his weapon. Randalph was surprised that he didn't blurt out *God Save the Queen*. Rodney's argument was that if Randalph could find a way of rewarding the camp's kids, for example with a tin of sweetened milk for every ten rats killed, he could oversee the construction of half a dozen furnaces to incinerate them in.

Randalph did the maths. With theoretically twenty rats for every refugee, an estimated two hundred thousand would need to be eliminated. Twenty thousand tins of sweetened milk would need to be ordered. Easy. Randalph revelled in the absence of red tape tying him and his procedures up. He called HQ on the island's radio.

"Hi Pete, could you send twenty thousand tins of sweetened milk to the camp on the next boat?" Pete was the dispatch officer at the UN warehouse.

"You having a party?" came the reply.

"Big party", smiled Randalph, "We're doing a gig with the island's rats."

"You're sure they like milk?" laughed Pete. "Ok for next Tuesday?"

"Perfect" replied Randalph. No forms, no signatures, no emails, no fax, no telex, no fuss. Just trust. If you had the job you were trusted to get on with it.

Randalph reflected resentfully on how, three decades after a career of sorts in Switzerland, when he returned to humanitarian aid work to dedicate the last five years of his working life to the plight of displaced people and refugees, humanitarian aid had become one of the most admin-polluted and sluggish industries on the planet.

Randalph couldn't believe the change. Instead of guys like himself hired to find and implement solutions on the ground, aid organisations had transformed themselves into remote offices with rows of desks lined with computer screens, as often as not manned by young graduates with no or very little practical experience or aptitude, and with absolutely no nerve for bending the rules to get things done. The world of humanitarian aid, where things had to move fast, had become a world of compliance, procedures, lengthy reports, endless meetings, flag flying and cowardly indecision. Things moved slowly, if they moved at all. It disgusted Randalph to the point where, in the middle of 2021, at the age of 63, he quit his last assignment early, before the end of his contract, wanting nothing more to do with it.

Randalph's favourite recollections of life on the island were the delicious Vietnamese food, swimming every day after work in the crystal-clear waters of the South China sea on the landward side of the coral reef, diving for colourful shells among the abundant sea life, and spending carefree evenings on his veranda with a cool beer in his hands overlooking the northern horizon through tropical palm trees, their high branches swaying gently in the wind.

Among these wonders from the natural world, Randalph was also amazed to see 10-year old Vietnamese kids on the beach dragging behind them huge manta rays they had killed with their bare hands and a knife during a free dive – it was not uncommon for the kids to hold their breath for three or more minutes underwater – and watching other kids scale 15-metre tall palm trees with their bare hands and feet, a saw slung over their shoulders to cut off coconuts, and a rope to tie them up and lower them to the ground.

Randalph often reflected at the dexterity and skill of these kids, who had the ability to feed themselves and their families at such a young age with whatever food nature provided high in the trees or at the bottom of the sea. He wondered why, back in the West, kids' movements were so restricted. "Don't do this – it's not good for you." "Don't do that – it's dangerous." "Don't climb trees – you'll fall." "Wear your helmet – you'll hurt yourself." How was it possible that Western society had clamped down so severely on the freedom and need for experimentation of kids? What had we become afraid of?

While those were some of Randalph's favourite moments on the island, there were others that galvanised him to the core of his being and haunted him with terrifying nightmares for decades.

Some of the survivors of the perilous crossing landed on the shores of smaller islands close to Pulao Bidong but further out at sea. One of them was called Shark Island. Randalph had not signed a contract specifying a specific scope of tasks, authority or limits of autonomy. It was expected of him to help as best he could in whichever way presented itself to him. One of his off-the-task-list jobs was occasionally to join the crew of the coast guard's motor-torpedo patrol boat that scanned the outlying islands looking for shipwrecks and survivors when ship movements had been spotted on their radar. It was a sobering mission that those who had completed more than once usually didn't want to ever do again.

Approaching Shark Island, the crew drew their breath and went deathly silent, their eyes scanning the horizon, hoping not to find what they had found the last time. The memory of scenes of indescribable horror on previous missions was all too vivid in their minds. On one of those previous missions that Randalph had volunteered for, they had found the remains of shipwrecked bodies, some ripped apart by sharks, others raped and hacked to death by pirates, and yet others – usually the men, or at least bits of them – chopped up by the propellors of the pirate boats. It was not a sight for the human eye.

On that previous mission, when they had landed the patrol boat's skiff on the island's beach, the stench of death and the horror of the dismembered bodies left a scar and a cry for vengeance deep in the souls of everyone on board. On some missions, rarely, some Boat People had been found still alive, dehydrating under the sun, the scars of their trauma engraved forever in their terrified eyes. They had witnessed the young girls being savagely abducted and dragged off to wherever the pirates kept them and seen the men executed.

On this particular trip, Randalph and Captain John had volunteered to join the crew of the patrol boat and fill in the gaps left by those crew members who had seen too much and refused to make another trip. On approaching the island, the hull of the vessel spotted on the coastguard's radar the night before was visible, lying on its side in the sand. As on previous sorties, the pirates had got there before the patrol, leaving the dismembered remains of their bloody rampage rotting on the beach under a buzzing cloud of black flies.

The sight was sickly, and horrible beyond description. Cutting through the skin like rusted scalpels, through the rib cage, deep into the heart. How could human beings do this?

Captain John snapped. He was on his knees in the sand, raging with despair, tearing at his hair, tears streaming down his face like fresh blood. The rest of the crew were huddled together, sharing what comfort they could in the proximity of each other. No one spoke. No one moved. They would have to bury what was left of the lifeless, mutilated corpses. The helmsman was handing out spades from over the handrail in the prow of the boat, which he had anchored bow-first near the beach. When John eventually stood up to take a spade, there was a look of death in his eyes, the sort of look that actors try to emulate in thriller movies but never quite achieve. John was going to kill. It was written all over him.

The events of the next few days overturned the peaceful coexistence of the various populations in the camp like a tidal wave toppling and breaking up flimsy beach huts in its path. That night, back on the island, Captain John was silent as a tomb. The aid workers had never seen him like this. The next day he had disappeared. So had the coastguard's patrol boat. Speculation was rife. Had he stolen it? Had he attacked pirate ships out at sea? Had he headed back to Vietnam for revenge? Had he killed himself? Nobody knew. Nobody would ever know.

To punish whatever it was that John had done, Major T was out for blood and had sparked up a witch hunt for potential sympathisers or complotters. The aid workers were called in one by one to appear before the Major, who questioned them about the captain. What did they know about him? Who was the last to see him? What had he said to them? How much had he drunk last night? Were you his friend? Did you help him? It was a scary encounter. Major T didn't have time for niceties.

Mike, the Canadian, was the first to be punished for whatever crime John had committed. Mike's wife heard later that he had said something to the Major that he didn't like about human rights. The last anyone saw of Mike was when he was led handcuffed to the Blue Dart and whisked away to the mainland. On arrival he was released. No charges were pressed, but he was ordered to leave the country. This was just a warning to the rest of the ex-pats, whom the authorities now wanted off the island.

Only two weeks before the end of his assignment, Randalph was next in line for sanctioning. Before John's disappearance, any of the aid workers who went to the mainland would come back with a boatload of alcohol ordered by the other aid workers, as well as by Major T's men. Everyone did it. As on previous trips, Randalph had duly loaded up the boat with the usual crates of beer and some harder drinks purchased on the mainland. This was to be his last trip there before his departure. On this occasion, however, waiting for him on the quay when he returned to the island were two of the Major's men, who promptly arrested him and took him to the Major's office. The Major was sitting behind his desk.

When Randalph was hustled in, he looked up at him and, without any preliminaries, promptly began with his indictment, prosecution and judgment all rolled into one: "You are aware that alcohol is not allowed on this island. You have purposefully broken the law. You are a criminal, and an enemy of the state. For this crime you will be severely punished." Addressing his men without taking his eyes off of Randalph he finished with "Take him away". Randalph was reminded of the Major's welcoming speech on the day of his arrival. Today was his goodbye speech.

Randalph remembered the icy shiver creeping down his spine as the blood drained from his face. Enemy of the state? All he had done was to bring some alcohol to the island in broad daylight, with the benediction and complicity of all. When had the rules changed, he wondered? From the Major's office he was promptly handcuffed and marched onto the boat. He was not allowed to go to his hut to pick up his stuff or even to say goodbye to his colleagues. From the passenger compartment of the boat where he sat between his guards, he watched the island getting smaller and the mainland approaching. He was scared. What was going to happen to him? What had John done?

On the mainland he was bundled into a police car that was waiting at the pier and driven to a local police station, where he was brought before the officer in charge, a slightly built sinister looking man wearing an unbuttoned police jacket with one collar sitting higher than the other and spectacles too big for his face that dwarfed his hair-line moustache. He reminded Randalph of the inquisitor in Kafka's The Trial. The officer sat behind an over-sized dark wooden colonial-style desk in the centre of a dank, unwelcoming room with bare light bulbs hanging from the ceiling.

"Does this belong to you?" the officer was pointing to a spear gun, a long diver's knife with barbs on one of the edges and the sawn-off point of a harpoon lying on his desk. They did belong to Randalph, who used them for fishing when he went diving on the island's coral reef. "You are a terrorist," the officer barked. "You are under arrest for conspiracy against the state. He added a string of insults and bad language, his out-stretched finger pointing menacingly at Randalph. He could have been the Major's twin brother. "Take him away!" he yelled.

The next moment, Randalph was marched to the basement and locked in a cell with a wooden bed and a squat toilet with a water tap above it. Thank God it was hot, Randalph thought, as a memory flashed up across his mind of a film he had seen where the 'terrorist' was thrown into a cell somewhere in the freezing wilderness of Siberia. Randalph had never felt so alone and vulnerable in his life. What was going to happen to him?

When his cell door swung open some hours later and the officer from behind the desk strutted in, he almost fainted. "You are guilty of conspiracy against the state. The penalty is death." With this, the inquisitor spun around, strutted back out, the door slammed shut, Randalph's knees folded up and dropped him on the edge of the bed, where he sat in silence, not even daring to breathe.

Randalph couldn't focus on anything. In desperation, in his mind he went over and over the officer's statement. He had not said Randalph was going to die; he had only said the penalty was death. It was the only straw he could clutch, as he sank ever deeper into his fear. The minutes seemed like hours, the hours like days. The day eventually passed and became night. Then night became the next day. Randalph hadn't slept a minute, sitting on the edge of his bed staring ahead of himself at emptiness.

Breakfast arrived along with a cup of water. Randalph's mind was racing. He had neither been tortured nor beaten; surely this was a sign that he was going to live?

On Randalph's previous trip to the mainland three weeks earlier he had flown to the capital, where he had stayed with Ryan, a high-ranking diplomat based in Kuala Lumpur he had met and befriended at some meeting at the UN. Ryan was the security attaché at a friendly embassy and lived in a penthouse suite somewhere near the city centre. Inside his sumptuous living quarters, he had a fridge so full of tins of beer all of the same brand and so neatly stacked in rows that it could have been used for a TV commercial. In his living room, which looked more like the reception hall of a grand hotel and overlooked the lights of the capital through floor-to-ceiling sliding windows, he had a powerful VHS projector that made a whirring sound just like at the movies, a 3-metre-wide drop-down screen and a vast collection of blockbuster movie cassettes. On his last visit, the two had both passed out watching an apocalyptic film about the end of the world on his enormous sofa, which could easily accommodate half a dozen guests.

While Randalph sat in his cell, word had reached Ryan about his arrest.

Even back then in the early 1980s, when the UN was still credible as an organisation, the individual agencies did not have the clout to influence domestic affairs of state, and especially not matters of domestic security. Randalph learned later that when the UN had tried unsuccessfully to have him released, someone at the UN office who knew about Randalph's camaraderie with Ryan had contacted him to ask for help. Ryan had passed the message on to his ambassador, as only an ambassador would have the connections and leverage that could open an arrested foreign citizen's cell door and set him free.

The entire next day Randalph sat quaking in his cell, terrified about his outcome. Another night passed slowly by, one minute after the other, one heartbeat at a time, desperation and hope competing for attention.

In the early morning of his third day, his cell door swung open and two tall stern-looking gentlemen in perfectly tailored black suits draped over white shirts and ties stepped inside and instructed Randalph to follow them. He was sure he was being taken to the gallows. With every step of his walk up the stairs from the basement, along the corridor, across the inner courtyard, and back to the officer's room with the desk in the centre, he was convinced he was going to die.

The Kafka officer was the first to speak. "You are lucky, young terrorist. You have powerful friends. Get out of here and never come back to my country. Go, son of the bitch!" he barked, pointing to the door. Randalph's thoughts were racing around like flies in a jar. What the hell was happening?

Once outside, the man in black was the next to speak. "You're free young man, but you have to leave the country. We're taking you to the airport," he said, handing Randalph his UN Laissez-Passer, a handful of cash and a one-way ticket to Thailand. "When you get to Bangkok, buy a ticket and get the fuck out of south-east Asia. When you get back to Geneva, you'll have thirty days to get this money back to our embassy. Your UK passport will be held by the UN until you've returned the money. Oh, and by the way, this never happened. You were never arrested. You never met us. Is that absolutely clear?"

Randalph had no idea about what was clear and what wasn't. All he knew was that he was alive and free.

On the ride to Kuala Lumpur airport, he sat in the back of the Men-in-Black's matching black limousine, feeling angry and unhappy at not being able to say goodbye to the guys on the island and to the many Vietnamese he had befriended. He would also have loved to shake hands with the Commander, to whom he would gladly have given his address if he asked, imagining meeting up with him again someday in America or wherever. He looked out at the countryside as they drove south to Kuantan, then at the jungle and the rubber plantations as they crossed the country from east to west. In his gut he felt the emptiness of saying goodbye forever.

Once at the airport, he headed straight for the ticket counter. There was no way he was going straight back to Geneva. He thought of Thailand or Singapore but remembered that the Men in Black had advised him to get out of south-east Asia. He settled for Nepal. There he could lick his wounded pride in familiar surroundings and forget about the stress and fear of the last week.

It was summer. The monsoon would be in full swing. His favourite walks would be impossible, and even the lake in

Pokhara would be brown with storm-water runoff from the mountains. So what, thought Randalph, he didn't care. He had thirty days of freedom in front of him.

CHAPTER 12

Beirut

When Randalph eventually got back to Geneva for his debriefing, everyone had heard about his arrest and wanted to know what was happening on the island. He gave them the story and his understanding of the events that had led up to it. In parallel, he arranged with the accounts department to pay back the cash and ticket expenses to the Embassy of the Men in Black. Once the cheque had been signed and cleared, he handed in his UN Laissez-Passer, took back his UK passport and booked a flight to London.

Malaysia and the island already seemed so far away that it might as well have all been a dream. London was as busy and as familiar as before. No one had won the rat race.

At the roster organisation that had sent him he met up with good old Jack and gave him an account of his six months on the island. "Don't worry", said Jack with a friendly smile, clapping Randalph on the back, "It's not the end of the world. By the way, the other day I heard that the Red Cross is looking for someone like yourself to deploy to

Lebanon. Should I tell them you're interested?"

It was mid-June. Even London looked pretty. Of course he was interested in going to Lebanon but he had no idea about what was happening there. While he was in Malaysia, all the news and the talk had been about the Falkland Islands war. Having spent some time in the Air Training Corps as a kid Randalph had even received a letter stating that depending on the outcome of the 'hostilities' – the conflict was never declared as a war – he may need to be called up. The thought had terrorised him.

As Jack had mentioned that the Lebanon job could be imminent, Randalph took the train that same night back home to Scotland. It was summer there too, and for once not raining as he crossed the border in bright morning sunshine, enjoying the view of the rolling countryside as the train climbed steadily into Scotland's southern uplands and south Lanarkshire to Beattock Summit, the highest point of the West Coast Main Line railway. Randalph was feeling good. He was a free man, with the perspective of a new adventure on the horizon.

He had only been home for a few days when the phone rang. It was the Red Cross in London. Good old Jack had let them know about Randalph's availability. The call was short and sweet. If Randalph was interested, they would like to meet him the next day in London. "Tomorrow?" asked Randalph, "Is it so urgent?" It was.

In anticipation of the call, Randalph had not yet unpacked. He once more said a quick goodbye to his mother and brother, waved to the neighbours and took the bus to the railway station and the night sleeper to Kings Cross, turning up at the Red Cross office for morning coffee. As a precaution, having by then heard that the situation was not good in Lebanon, he told his mother he was heading to the Seychelles and would be back for Christmas.

A day later, Randalph was again in Geneva, this time for a briefing at the Red Cross. By then, his third visit to the city, he already knew his way around part of the Rive Droite, where the international agencies and organisations are located, and easily found the building of the Red Cross. He was proud of himself, feeling as enthusiastic and self-confident as a seasoned traveller.

The briefing, however, stopped him dead in his tracks. Lebanon wasn't going to be like Nepal or Malaysia. There was a civil war on. From north to south, warring factions were shelling each other from one mountain range to the other. Beirut was being pounded by fighter jets every day from morning till night. The number of casualties was high, and growing by the day. Randalph would be in the thick of it.

His first glimpse of Lebanon was on TV in a hotel room in Rome opposite the Colosseum. His onward flight from London with Alitalia, changing in Rome for Damascus, had been overbooked in Rome, where he found himself stranded between flights for two days. Randalph looked on numbed as he watched the bombing and the fighting. His gut had that uncomfortable feeling you get when you know you're trapped or have been found out. It was too late. There was no turning back. Besides, Randalph was consoling himself with the thought that the mission to Lebanon was worth four months' pay and another headline on his CV.

After two lonely days walking the streets of Rome, too preoccupied by his destination to be interested in any of the sights, Randalph was finally rerouted on Syrian Arab Airlines via Aleppo to Damascus. The Red Cross were notified about his late arrival and had arranged for him to be picked up in Damascus and driven overland straight to Lebanon.

En route, as they changed planes in Aleppo, he observed that he was the only foreigner flying onwards to Damascus. In the free-for-all on the tarmac, when the other passengers ran towards the plane, jostling each other to get on first, he also realised that he was one of the few passengers not carrying a weapon. In this crowd of flowing robes, long moustaches, bushy beards, head bands, daggers and the odd machine gun strapped over the back, all heading as fast as they could to the plane, it could have been a set for a modern version of *Lawrence of Arabia*. All that was missing was a caravan of camels grazing beside the runway.

In the front of the plane's passenger compartment, Syrian Arab Airlines had sacrificed two rows of seats to stash guns and other weapons during the flight in a pallet-sized crate made of meshed steel. The passengers were allowed to keep their knives but had to deposit their guns. Randalph sat next to a window behind the starboard wing, looking all the time out of the window and trying not to be noticed, hoping nobody would ask him anything or want to spark up a conversation.

The plane had hardly begun to taxi when some of Lawrence's men stood up and walked up the aisle in their flowing elegance. The poor stewardess was brushed aside like dust, looking on concerned but not daring to speak out as the men entered the galley, pulled the food trays out from their storage racks and began to pass them down the plane, over the heads of the passengers. Randalph took his tray and nodded a timid "shukran". Totally oblivious to danger and bent on doing only what they wanted, when they wanted, one of the men produced a kerosene pressure burner from a shoulder bag, placed it on the gangway floor, pumped up the pressure, lit the stove's blackened ring with a match and started to boil water in a kettle someone else had found in the galley.

As the old 727 tore down the runway, Randalph's blood ran cold. The unspoken hero deep inside him was screaming out to put this right. He imagined pulling out his shining sabre, forcing the men back to their seats at knife point and lecturing them on their ignorance, stupidity and total disregard for safety and for the poor stewardess who, by that time, had taken refuge in the cockpit. Instead, he just looked straight ahead into the safety brochure on the back of the seat in front of him and asked himself where the hell he was going.

During his first weeks in Lebanon, Randalph was based in the north, where war was raging between the factions to the east and the west of the Bekaa valley. His mission was to look out for opportunities to provide aid in the area of water supply. To get around safely, Randalph had a local driver called Mustafa assigned to him by the local field office in Baalbek. Although it was strictly forbidden and potentially dangerous – there was a war on – Mustafa carried a gun in the car. In the cities' chaotic daily traffic jams, as well as peeping the horn he would sometimes shoot into the sky, hurling angry abuse at anyone blocking his way.

On one particular day, Mustafa got so angry at the traffic that was going nowhere that he shot out the traffic lights. This scared Randalph, but he was afraid of confronting the brazen, trigger-happy, highly emotional Mustafa and didn't know what to do about it. Instead of confronting him and risking a conflict – and perhaps a bullet in the head – Randalph played safe and contented himself with complaining to his team about Mustafa behind his back, hoping that he would somehow get the message.

In that part of the world, however, you don't talk behind people's backs. If you want things done or to pass a message, you speak straight to the face of the other person or not at all. Word eventually got to Mustafa that Randalph had been talking about him behind his back.

At their delegation office in Baalbek, the chief insisted on having a daily debriefing meeting in the early evening when the teams had returned from the field, where everyone present would say a few words about their day. Randalph hated the meetings and felt they were a total waste of time. Instead of everyone making a succinct report to the chief who could then sum up the day and inform the team about the essentials, everyone had to sit around in a circle and listen to each other's news of the day. Invariably, the meeting dragged on for nearly two hours, leaving the participants frustrated, edgy and hungry.

On the day that Mustafa had learned about Randalph's cowardice and talking behind his back he turned up at the evening meeting with a buddy who was armed with a Kalashnikov and a full belt of cartridges strapped over his shoulder like a cowboy. As they strutted in, ordering everyone to shut up, his buddy menacing them with his machine gun, Randolph knew instantly that they had come for him. Turning to Randolph, Mustafa spoke clearly, with anger in his voice and total disrespect in his eyes. "So you don't like me, Mr Randolph? You talk shit about me? You tell people I am bad? Is it true?" Getting no reply from Randolph, who had only shrugged and looked sheepish, Mustafa stepped forward, commanded Randolph to get to his feet, and with his face almost squashed against Randolph's shrieked "Is it true?"

Mustafa's buddy then joined in the action. Pushing Mustafa aside, he stuck the barrel of the Kalashnikov in Randolph's mouth and screamed out "Answer, piece of shit!" Mustafa came in next with, "Say it, you bastard, say it! I am not good? I am bad driver? I am crazy? Say it, piece of shit, or we blow your head off". Mustafa's buddy pulled the barrel from out of his mouth, then with one hand holding the butt and trigger fired half a dozen rounds upwards into the ceiling. "Say it!" "Say it!" By then the two were livid. Someone in the team screamed.

Mustafa lunged forwards, pushing Randolph backwards with his fists on his chest, his eyes glaring into Randolph's with the rage of a rabid dog, the droplets of spittle smacking Randolph's cheeks. As if knowing he was going to die, Randolph spoke up: "I'm sorry Mustafa for speaking behind your back". "Say it, you fucking bastard!" retorted Mustafa even more enraged. "Say it!"

And so Randolph said it. "Yes, it's true. You know it's

true. I talk behind your back. I hate you. I hate everything about you." The room fell deadly silent, like when someone pulls the pin out of a grenade in a film and you wait for the imminent blast. "You hate me?" "Yes," blurted out Randalph, "I fucking hate you. It's you that's the piece of shit." Randalph had no idea where the words were coming from, but they were coming and he couldn't stop them. "Who the fuck do you think you are? You drive around like a cowboy with your gun. You think that makes you big? It just shows how fucking small you are!"

Randalph felt like he was on a stage. Any minute now there would be the sound of automatic fire. He didn't care. He was going out with a bang. From injury to condemnation, Randalph spat his words out at him, insulting his parents, his country, his name, and even his God for having created him. The more he insulted Mustafa, the more the words flowed, and the more Mustafa's eyes opened wide. For Randalph it was like a dam bursting. He spat the words out. Twenty years of pent-up range and revolt were exploding from his mouth in swearing, cursing, hatred for Mustafa, the world, and everyone that had ever put him down. Later, the team said that Randalph even lunged at Mustafa, pointing at him, threatening him. Everyone was shitting themselves.

They say that when you're shot at close range you don't hear the gun going off. The ball was in Mustafa's court. Nobody moved. Stalemate. The room was as silent as the inside of a coffin buried six feet underground. One of the girls in the team was whimpering.

Mustafa stepped back, grabbed the gun, held it in one hand, finger on the trigger, aimed it at Randalph, then turned it upwards and shot a dozen or more rounds at the ceiling, this time bringing down plaster, dust and cobwebs.

"So you think I'm an asshole?" he shouted. "Allah, this piece of shit thinks I'm an asshole. Maybe he's right. Maybe I am an asshole?" he had turned and was asking his buddy. "Kbeeri asshole. A fucking asshole. An asshole just like you?" His arms shot up in the air like he was about to give a speech and exclaimed: "Me, Mustafa, much bigger asshole than you can ever be! Me, big boss of assholes!"

Mustafa and his buddy burst out laughing. Randolph had no idea what was going to happen next. "Come" said the buddy, pointing at Randolph. "You come with us." Still convinced they were going to crucify him, Randolph tried to resist. "You come with us!" he shouted at Randolph, aiming his gun at him.

Then, out of the blue, Mustafa's buddy produced a bottle of whisky from a black plastic bag he was carrying in a sling over his shoulder. "Assholes drink with assholes," he said. They grabbed Randolph by the arm and led him out. Behind him, he could hear crying and dismay.

In the room next door, they sat Randolph down, stuffed the bottle of whisky in his hand and forced him to drink from it as it passed round the trio, from one mouth to another. The three of them drank themselves to oblivion, with the bottle emptied in a matter of minutes. In spite of the lingering fear, the uncertainty of what would happen next, his head and guts reeling from a third of a bottle of whisky on an empty stomach, and the odds strongly against him, for the first time in his life Randolph had beaten his fear and been able to speak out. It had saved his life.

For the rest of the evening, Randalph felt like a hero, and for the remainder of his time in the north, Randalph got on well with Mustafa, who no longer carried a gun in the car, at least none that Randalph could see. Both had earned the respect of the other.

News from the south was troubling. In a sombre voice, the chief informed the team that Beirut was under daily bombardment from the sky and being pounded by artillery from every direction. Reports, he said, talked about dead bodies lying strewn like discarded garbage everywhere. The possibility of an epidemic and total public health breakdown was looming. Something had to be done.

Turning to Randalph, he said that the head of delegation in Beirut had sent a dispatch ordering him to get ready to travel to Beirut at the next ceasefire. He was to report to the Lebanese Army, who would organise his safe passage.

In peace time, driving to Beirut would have taken a little less than three hours. In June 1982, because of the numerous checkpoints and outbreaks of fighting along the way, it could take two days or more. Under the protection of the Lebanese army, transport was organised in two steps, with a stopover at Zahle, where Randalph could spend the night at the Red Cross sub office.

The next ceasefire came sooner than Randalph had hoped for. As soon as it was broadcast, he set off, passing from checkpoint to checkpoint, quaking in the back of the Jeep that was carrying him as it made its way to Zahle. When they arrived it was already early evening and the Scandinavian medical team working there had gathered to review the day in the office, which was within the walls of the local hospital where they worked. Randalph wondered if these evening pow-wow sessions were standard practice across the organisation.

Simultaneously, as if to welcome Randalph, heavy street fighting suddenly broke out nearby, with stray bullets pinging against the walls. The medics knew the drill off by heart and waved energetically at Randalph to follow them down to the morgue in the basement. The morgue, they explained, was the safest place in the hospital.

As the evening drew on and night fell there was no sign of a let up in the fighting. In the basement and behind closed doors, intense gunfire and muffled explosions could still be heard and the occasional trembling of the ground felt, with slivers of masonry and dust falling from the ceiling. The medics were mumbling among themselves, apparently trying to reach a decision about what to do.

Having reached a verdict, they explained to Randalph that their lodgings were a street away, but in the direction of the fire, and they thought it best to spend the night here. "In the morgue?" asked Randalph. "Yes, when it gets bad, we sometimes sleep here," replied a nurse. "It's not so bad, the mortuary cabinet freezers are off." She giggled.

"What do you mean?" asked Randalph horrified, "You sleep in the corpse drawers?"

"Yes," she replied again, "and tonight you'll sleep there too." The medics laughed.

Randalph jumped up with "Are you fucking kidding? Is there nowhere else?"

"Nowhere else, unless you want to sleep on the floor."

The experience sent the creepy-crawlies up Randalph's

spine. To climb into his cabinet Randalph needed a short ladder, which was then taken away and used for the next one to climb in. While the cabinet was wide enough for his body with his arms lain by his side, it was not wide enough for him to lie in the foetus position he slept best in. To add some comfort, the medics had placed blankets on the bottom of the cabinets to provide a layer of cushioning from the metal base, which slid inwards as Randalph slithered in, creating an uneven surface beneath him.

Randalph spent the night wrestling with the blanket, turning and tossing as far as he could from left to right, and all the while staying alert to any noises in the morgue that would warn of approaching danger. As soon as he had grasped the morbid reality that he would be sleeping in one of the drawers, he had instantly developed a phobia about being locked in.

By the time the night was over and the team had crawled out of their holes in the wall, the fighting had stopped. The medical team's mission was to treat any injured civilians as well as fighters from both sides, regardless of who they were, and that morning there were many. Randalph had never been in a medical environment and was horrified by the injuries of the people brought to the hospital upstairs. Many had gunshot wounds and were peppered by shrapnel, while others had had their hands, arms, feet or legs blown off.

What was it all about, thought Randalph; why all this violence? In the wake of the scenes of barbarity he had witnessed in Malaysia and the aftermath of the violence he was now witnessing in Lebanon, he was struggling to remain an idealist. Inside him the battle raged between thoughts of anger at the stupidity of all this and thoughts of hope that there was some way these people could talk to each other and live in peace.

After breakfast, an army Jeep turned up to collect Randalph and take him to Hamra, in the heart of Beirut, where he was dropped off late in the afternoon at the Red Cross country delegation. The delegation was a dozen-man operation made up of a handful of delegates whose job it was to visit prisoners in an effort to reunite them with their families, a war-zone doctor in charge of all things medical, a radio operator, some admin staff, security personnel, a munitions specialist, two drivers, the head of delegation who had privileged contacts to the various armed factions, the authorities and the international community, and Randalph.

The delegation offices were on the fifth floor of an empty apartment building plastered on all sides with Red Cross posters written in English and in Arabic. A massive Red Cross flag was draped across the roof and permanently lit with spotlights. Previously, the offices had been on lower floors, closer to the basement where the staff could run to quickly during bombing raids, until a spate of car bombs going off in the surrounding streets chased them upstairs.

After the initial car-bomb blasts some weeks previously, the delegation staff had positioned their desks behind the building's concrete pillars and stair walls to at least save themselves and any vital equipment in the event of another blast. Shortly after Randalph's arrival, two car bombs had indeed gone off one day after another, shattering the remainder of the glass in the building and sending doors, chairs, tables and paperwork flying.

Randalph remembered the feeling of the high-pressure blast of dust-filled air that picked up and threw his typewriter onto the floor, and the flying glass that cut his forearm and shoulder. During the next weeks, three more bombs went off. Everyone in the delegation had developed an acute, uncontrollable fear of parked cars. "Car" was the word used to warn the others that a parked car had been spotted near the building. The word sent everyone scurrying like blind mice escaping from prowling cats.

The delegation was the only inhabited apartment left in that part of the city, where the surrounding streets had been for the most part reduced to rubble. It was also the only building that was allowed to be lit at night when all around was pitch-black darkness. In the oppressive blackness, people could sometimes be heard scampering from one side of a street to the other. The only continual sound was the mechanical din of the oversized 40 kVA generator in the basement that supplied power to the building. Frequently, sustained bursts of automatic fire and exchanges of RPGs erupted like firework displays, muffling even the noise of the generator. In daytime, the ground shook every time fighter jets pulverised buildings in the vicinity.

Supplies could not easily reach the delegation, which was stranded like a desert island in the centre of a disputed quarter of the town, which frequently changed hands from one warring faction to another. It was, however, close to a shopping area, where stores had either been boarded up and survived, locked away behind thick metal struts, sheeting and heavy industrial padlocks, or lay open like looted tombs, their broken shelves, upturned tills and smashed displays piled up on the floor.

To get supplies to the delegation had become an urgent necessity, but a dangerous business. The solution adopted to keep supplies coming in was for delegation staff members to go out and loot whatever they could lay their hands on. The chances of being shot were high.

Experienced as they were in diplomatic stuff, the delegates had no idea about how to move around in relative safety under live fire. They needed to learn fast. "Let's ask the Lebanese Army for training," someone suggested. The Lebanese Army, who were friendly to the Red Cross cause, were duly contacted by the head of delegation and sent in an expert in urban warfare who, in training the delegates how to avoid being shot, probably saved their lives.

In a matter of days of gruelling training in mock scenarios in the protected courtyard to the rear of the building, the delegates' survival skills were upgraded from 'zero' to 'good to go'. The idea was for everyone to take their turn at pillaging whatever they could find, but on a volunteer basis. In spite of the training, not all the delegates wanted to take the risk and only a few volunteered.

When it was Randalph's turn to go out, he slid his white Red Cross vest over the bullet-proof waistcoat the army had provided, buckled his white Red Cross helmet under his chin, slipped on the shrapnel gloves the army had also lent them, went down to the front entrance, and froze. His heart was beating like a snare drum. He was shitting himself. He could neither focus on nor remember what the trainer had painstakingly trained them to do.

Adrenaline was pumping through his head like a fire hose. He was sweating like he had just come out of a sauna. 'Fuck it,', he said to himself eventually, looking left, then right, inching his head out from behind the entrance pillars. *What was it he said?* thought Randalph, a last time, then aimed his body at the sheltered entrance across the street, put his head down as instructed, and leapt, zigzagging as they had been trained to do to the other side. In a bag strapped to his back he was carrying an axe, a crowbar and a heavy set of wire cutters, and in his waistcoat pocket his VHF radio.

The shops he was aiming for lined the street just around the corner. The colleagues who had volunteered some days before him talked about at least half a dozen that looked like shored-up mini markets. His luck was in. At that moment nobody was shooting. Randalph zigzagged up the street until he came to one shop whose shutters looked like they had been ripped away by one of the car bombs. The store was his for the taking.

Although it also looked like he was not the first looter to pass by, enough tins of conserves were still left behind scattered around on the floor to feed the delegation for a few days. He packed what he could carry into his shoulder bag and set off, zigzagging again back to the delegation. Randalph had never been more frightened in his life, and at the same time never as focused.

When the fighting eventually moved away from the part of the city where the delegation was based, Randalph could at last get to work. The doctor delegate in charge of medical things had set him up with a van and a team of young volunteers from one of the refugee camps. Their job would be to drive to the scene of the air raids and ground fighting and spray chemicals on dead bodies and human remains to stop the potential spread of disease.

Out on their first sortie, Randalph was appalled at the destruction they witnessed and the blood-soaked, lifeless corpses and body parts that so often covered the ground in the aftermath of bombings or battle. On several occasions, he retched up his guts in the middle of the street. His team did likewise.

Back at the delegation, word had gotten around about the horrendous conditions this gang of young men were exposed to, and the delegates – all of whom were twenty years older than young Randalph – began to show him respect and offer him the perks, like a glass of whisky and the occasional bar of chocolate, they had stowed away for their personal consumption. By and by, Randalph's team became the delegation's eyes on the ground, allowed by the warring factions to pass freely through checkpoints, and checked on every day by the regular army.

By the time their supplies of chemicals ran out, the soldiers of the international peace-keeping force had arrived and were anchored off the coast. They flew new supplies to them in a helicopter in which the same soldiers also packed a crate of chocolates and other goodies for the team. Randalph and his boys were doing a job that nobody else wanted to do and were being recognised for it. Whenever they passed a gang of armed militia they would exchange salutes. On the notorious Green Line during ceasefires, both sides stood down when they moved in to pick up remains.

One night at the delegation, after a particularly gruesome day in the field, Randalph remembered remarking to one of his colleagues that he had made the acquaintance of more people in Lebanon in two months than during the whole of the rest of his life, and that he felt safer in war-ravaged Beirut than back in his hometown in Scotland. Personal safety, he realised, was all about the people you knew and could rely on.

Even so, in the bomb-cratered streets and the crumbling, burning neighbourhoods through which Randalph's team passed, there lurked dangers that no training could ever prepare them for. Driving home one day in early September from a mission to disinfect the bodies of kids in the playground of a school that had been decimated on the other side of town, Randalph's team got caught up in a queue of cars waiting to cross a new checkpoint that had sprung up, apparently overnight. The masked gunmen who manned the checkpoint were only letting some cars through and turning others back. Randalph's colleagues didn't know why.

After a wait of half an hour or so, it was the turn of a VW Beetle that was in front of the team's van. The gunman stopped it, looked in through the open windows, ordered the four occupants to hang their hands out of the windows, then waved it through, signalling to the driver to drive slowly. Once the Beetle was about 20m clear of the checkpoint a gunman appeared from behind the sand-filled petrol drums with a rocket launcher and fired an RPG at the car, which erupted in a ball of flame. Randalph and his team were speechless, stunned by the sudden violence, numbed by the atrocity before their eyes.

That day Randalph was driving. He was now in pole position for crossing. It was his turn next. The gunman who had checked the Beetle now approached the van, again ordering the occupants to place their hands outside the windows. He then opened the back doors of the van and asked what the drums of chemicals were. One of the team explained. Without any further comment he waved Randalph through.

Randalph remembers how difficult it was for him to press the accelerator and lift the clutch pedal. His feet wouldn't obey. It was only when the gunman shot some rounds off in the air shouting "Yalla!" that Randalph found the courage to drive forward. He neither looked at the mangled Beetle burning by the side of the road nor in the mirror, not wanting to give any suspicious signs to the gunmen behind him. 10 m (32 ft), 20, 30, 40, 50… It looked like they were clear. Nobody spoke for the remainder of the ride back to the delegation.

A few days later, the team was called out to clean up the remains of an ambush that had happened at the entrance of one of the big refugee camps to the south of Beirut. The team usually didn't venture so far out of the city centre, and definitely not in the direction of the airport and the camps in the south. The green light for their mission, however, was given by the Lebanese Army, who said they were not expecting any trouble along the way.

Once parked at the entrance of the camp, Randalph

noticed that petrol drums had been stacked at the top of a stairwell leading underground. When he asked via one of his colleagues where the stairs led to, he couldn't believe the answer: "It's an underground hospital."

"They stockpile petrol drums at the top of stairs leading to an underground hospital? Are they out of their fucking minds?" Randalph was furious. Furious at life. Furious at the needless death and destruction he was witnessing every day. Furious at just how stupid people can be.

"Who's in charge here?" he cried out. By then some people had gathered, all wanting to know why Randalph had lost his rag. A massive militiaman, as wide as he was tall, with a thick black beard, broad cheeks, an oversized nose, beady black eyes, a belt of grenades slung round his waist and the usual Kalashnikov slung over his shoulder, stepped forward and announced that he was in charge and asked what the problem was. Despite the anger that had taken control of him, Randalph realised that he should be careful with what he said.

Trying the rational approach, Randalph asked Blackbeard if he knew what would happen if these drums caught fire. "You telling me how to do my job?" barked Blackbeard in surprisingly good English, shaking the barrel of his gun towards him. Randalph was triggered and barked back: "I'm telling you that if these drums catch fire and everyone in the basement is burnt to death it'll be your fault."

Oops, he shouldn't have said that. Too late. Blackbeard grabbed Randalph by the biceps and marched him off into the camp and almost threw him through the open door of a tent. Someone wearing the traditional keffiyeh of a tribal leader beckoned with his hand to Blackbeard to speak. "This foreign bastard thinks he knows better than us," spat out Blackbeard, who obviously didn't think much of Randalph's interference. He went on, apparently, to explain in Arabic what the fuss was all about.

The leader looked at Randalph, and with the reflex of a true diplomat thanked him for helping his people. Then with the theatrical gesture of a Roman centurion dismissing an argument, waved towards the door of the tent, in simple body language that Randalph correctly understood to mean the audience was over. When he got back to the team who were waiting by the van and told them what had happened, they grabbed him, thrust him into the back of the van, and sped off.

"Do you know who you were talking with?" they asked. Randalph didn't. They never told him.

CHAPTER 13

Sabra and Shatila

The following week, on the evening of September 16th, Randalph and the rest of the delegates were summoned late to the desk of the Head of Delegation, who informed them that they were getting reports of a massacre that had occurred in the camps in the south. Everyone was to remain in the delegation. All movements were blocked until they got more information. The next day, hundreds of refugees arrived screaming and distraught at the delegation asking for shelter and were allowed to go down into the basement, where the Head of Delegation told them, translated into Arabic, that they would be protected by the Red Cross ensign and the Geneva conventions.

All of that day, September 17th, allegations of a spine-chilling massacre that had been perpetrated in the Sabra and Shatila refugee camps reached the delegation. By the next day it was clear that hundreds had been murdered in a bloody rampage that was still going on. In the early morning of September 19th, Randalph was summoned by the Head of Delegation, who explained to him that the responsibility for cleaning up the horrific mess fell squarely on Randalph's shoulders as he was the delegation's only 'sanitation guy'. He instructed him and his sanitation team to do everything in their power to "ensure a dignified end to the lives of the victims".

By then, Randalph had become accustomed to seeing death sprawled out in pieces. His team had learned how to deal with it, and how to get over it. But the sight that met their eyes as they reported for duty at the northern gate of the first camp drained the blood from their veins. In all directions, hundreds of bodies lay rotting under the sun, some with their stomachs burst open, others maimed with hatchets, most with maggots crawling out of their eyes. When people are blown to pieces by bombs dropped from the sky or disintegrated with artillery shells there is a sense of distance and detachment in the killing, observed Randalph later to a TV crew. But the horrors they witnessed

Sabra and Shatila massacre.
Photo downloaded from https://prc.org.uk

that day were inflicted close up with knives and guns, and drawn out, intended to inflict pain.

The Lebanese authorities had been asked to assist Randalph's team with manpower and equipment. They would need to dig trenches, photograph the dead, organise safe access for relatives to identify the corpses, and provide de-mining support when removing bodies that had been boobytrapped. The few diplomatic missions that had not left the capital sent delegations to the scene. The thousands of bereaved were screaming their grief and their anger at the top of their voices. It was a nightmare. A bloody nightmare.

The press was everywhere, cameras wanting closeups, reporters wanting interviews, news agencies wanting exclusive stories. A reporter even scaled the three-storey façade of the building where Randalph had set up office, suddenly appearing at the window and wanting "insider information". Randalph's chief had instructed him to talk only to the BBC, who, in the early 1980s, were widely believed to be the least biased of the dozen other agencies who were milling around, looking for scraps of news that others may not yet have covered. "Were there signs of torture?" "Were members cut off?" "Can you confirm that people were decapitated?" "Was there rape?" The questions they asked Randalph disgusted him. Could they not see that the situation was horrible enough without inventing additional gory details?

Randalph had arrived on the scene a few hours after Robert Fisk, the influential British war correspondent, who in 2019 captured the scene in a Canadian documentary film titled 'This Is Not a Movie', which Randalph recommends everyone to watch. In 2018, Randalph's path again crossed that of Robert Fisk as they walked through the empty streets of Homs in Syria, asking each other where the population had fled to and wondering what it is in human nature that apparently condones death and destruction on such a massive scale.

Of all the many videos and reports available on the internet explaining the troubles of that time and their origin, all asking the same questions: what's Israel's role in Sabra and Shatila? Is it a Holy war? What about the PLO in 1964? Whose war is this? The Arab war? The Lebanese war? Randalph, who had been there, found Fisk's version to be closest to the facts, and also frighteningly realistic in terms of warning us all of what was coming.

That afternoon, Randalph gave an exclusive interview to John Simpson of the BBC, relating as factually as possible what he had seen. Unbeknown to Randalph, the interview was broadcast that same day back home on the evening news, which his mother was watching. Before leaving for Lebanon, he had told her he was going on a mission to the Seychelles, where there was no mail delivery, but that he would be back by Christmas.

Randalph's mother was the worrying type, always fretting about something to be careful about. But this… According to the neighbours, she ran from house to house to tell them Randalph was on the news, complaining bitterly that he hadn't told her the truth about where he was going and asking what to do. There was nothing to do. The local press did it for her.

The next morning, she was besieged by reporters who

had identified "their boy" and wanted the inside story. "Why is your son in Lebanon?" "What is he doing there?" "Is he safe?" "Have you heard from him?" "When is he coming back?" The poor lady couldn't handle it and appeared the next day in a number of national newspaper articles all talking about a mother's anguish over her son's appearance in "death city".

In August 1982, before the massacre, the governments of the United States, France, Italy and Great Britain had deployed a multinational peacekeeping force – the MNF – to Lebanon in an effort to stabilize the country and stop the fighting between Syria, the Palestine Liberation Organization (PLO), and Israel.

To quote Wikipedia:

"The MNF was created following a 1981 U.S.-brokered ceasefire between the PLO and Israel to end their involvement in the conflict between Lebanon's pro-government and pro-Syrian factions. The ceasefire held until June 3, 1982, the date of the attempted assassination of Israel's ambassador to London. Israel blamed the PLO and three days later invaded Lebanon.

West Beirut was besieged for seven weeks before the PLO accepted a new agreement for their withdrawal, involving the deployment of the MNF to assist the Lebanese Armed Forces in evacuating the PLO, Syrian forces and other foreign combatants involved in Lebanon's civil war.

The four-nation MNF was created as an interposition force meant to oversee the peaceful withdrawal of the PLO. The participants included the U.S. Multinational Force (USMNF), which consisted of four different Marine

Amphibious Units (MAUs), British 1st Queens Dragoon Guards armoured reconnaissance regiment, the 1st inter-arm Foreign and French Brigade, 4 Foreign Legion Regiments, 28 French Armed Forces regiments including French and Foreign paratroopers, units of the National Gendarmerie, Italian paratroopers from the Folgore Brigade, infantry units from the Bersaglieri regiments and Marines of the San Marco Regiment.

The relatively benign environment at the beginning of the mission gave way to chaos as the civil war re-escalated following the assassination of President-elect Bashir Gemayel in September 1982. The MNF ended its presence mission in Beirut and went offshore before completely leaving Lebanon in July of the next year in the aftermath of the October 1983 barracks bombing that killed 241 U.S. and 58 French servicemen. It was replaced by the United Nations Interim Force in Lebanon (UNIFIL) already present in Lebanon since 1978."

In the aftermath of the massacres, what was left of hope of peace and a way out of the besieged city for the delegation members had dwindled away to nothing. The tension in the streets was bristling like high tensile steel ropes about to snap. The threat of more violence was very real. All perks and fun and games like going out to raid stores were instantly outlawed. The curfew that followed was brutally imposed. A shadow on a wall would be obliterated by a rocket. The sound of footsteps in the street would be shot at by snipers. Would Randalph ever get out of West Beirut to answer to his mother's anger at having lied to her?

August rolled into September and the massacres went

on, September into October, and October into November. Despite the presence onshore of the MNF during the last quarter of 1982 to help the new Lebanese Government to establish its control, the effort failed. By then, in the approaching winter of 1982 Randalph's delegation was the only international aid organisation still open for business in the city. The mood in the delegation was suicidal. Most of the delegates reckoned that if a car bomb didn't get them, a stray bullet would.

The only way out was an organised ceasefire between half a dozen warring factions, most of whom were the sworn enemies of the others. Getting Randalph and his colleagues out would require a safe passage by road to the airport, braving a rigorously enforced, no-movement curfew, clearance from at least three governments for an aircraft to pick up the delegates, the threat of heavy military exchanges in the event of a breach of ceasefire, and an airlift to outside of Lebanese airspace before some trigger-happy commando fired a missile at them.

It seemed like months since anyone in the delegation had spoken optimistically about the chances of getting back to Europe alive. For weeks, they had been sleeping fully dressed, boots on, bags packed beside them, first-aid kits at the ready, behind an improvised wall of sandbags in their 5th floor prison. Each night was like the last. Every explosion sent them ducking under their pillows, breath held tight, heart beating uncontrollably, praying.

And then one night, early in December, chaos broke out on the street. Vehicles had pulled up. Randalph could tell by the sound of the engines that it was armoured troop carriers. Someone was shouting. The shouting had reached the stairs and was climbing upwards. Awake, alert and terrified, the delegation team crouched low behind the sandbags. The shouting reached their landing. Lights went on. "Yalla umo, badna n'ruh al matar! – up up up, yalla airport!" The men shouting wore Lebanese insignias. The army had come for them.

This was it. They were going home. No time for last-minute panics. No time for looking back. Bundled into the backs of two armoured troop carriers in a convoy led by a heavy gun and followed by two more, the frightened delegates were ordered to sit tight and cover their ears. The convoy thundered off into the black of night with no lights, like a ghost train in a tunnel, waiting for vampires with staring black eyes and long knives to jump out from the darkness and decapitate them.

The route to the airport led under the flyover to the south of the centre and then straight through the southern suburbs, past the camps, and into the occupied zone around the airport. No checkpoints. No stops. No tricks. It seemed unreal, like in a fairytale. Surely, the ugly head of bad surprises was about to spring up in front of them and slash their hopes in a blinding flash of artillery fire.

The airport gate was guarded by four tanks pointing directly at the convoy and following it as it turned, first left as if heading to the terminal building, then right down the maintenance slip road to the runway. The heavy security barrier had been lifted, and as they drove past Randalph could see the helmets of soldiers dug in around the perimeter. It looked like everyone who had a gun was pointing it at them. Clear of the gate and the fortifications, the convoy slowed. They were on the runway.

When the 15-year-long Lebanese Civil War began in April 1975 the airport lost its status as one of the premier hubs of the Middle East and lost virtually all of its airline services with the exception of two Lebanese carriers, Middle East Airlines (MEA) and Trans Mediterranean Airways. That night, the airport lay in ruins and was closed, having been badly damaged by shelling during the September 1982 invasion. Previously in June, an MEA Boeing 720 had been destroyed. Four days later, three 720s and one 707 were also destroyed. In August, a 14-hour non-stop bombing raid on Beirut had destroyed yet another Boeing 720.

Later, in 1983, the airport was the site of the Beirut barracks bombing, in which the 241 American and 58 French servicemen mentioned earlier were killed. Unknown to the delegation, the airport's runways had been renovated after the invasion and made operational again. In spite of the total black-out, as they drove out along the taxiway Randalph could make out 18/36 painted in giant letters on the tarmac and then at the other end 03/21. As they drove towards the end of the runway Randalph spotted the silvery silhouette of a passenger jet painted against the night sky, motionless and silent like an owl hiding among dark branches, bearing the emblematic cedar of Lebanon on its tail. Miraculously, despite its losses, MEA had managed to save at least one aircraft. This was their plane, their way out, their ticket home.

The plane was empty. They were the only passengers. With no lights to guide them they fumbled to find seats in the front rows. The tension was unbearable. An officer from the convoy made a summary head count, where each had to call out his name. The doors closed. The moment of truth had arrived.

After a few moments the co-pilot appeared and explained that the take-off was imminent; they were waiting for final clearance. In true Lebanese style, impeccably dressed in his elegant uniform, his hat held under his armpit as if on parade, the co-pilot instructed the passengers to fasten their seat belts tight, and warned them that they would need to make a very tight and uncomfortable turn out to sea at the end of the runway, as soon as they were airborne. He insisted heavily that under no circumstances were they to put on individual cabin lighting or press the assistance bell. The plane would be taking off in the dark, on a blacked-out runway, with no landing, wing or taillights, and it needed to fly low and remain invisible under the radar until it had cleared Lebanese airspace. Then, as an afterthought, he added, "If Allah the merciful wishes, you will soon be home. You should all pray".

Randalph had grabbed the aisle seat of the first row in the first-class compartment immediately behind the cockpit. Its door was open, and he could hear the chatter of the pilots. The waiting was painful, wrong, unbearable. The minutes felt like hours. Randalph imagined what it must be like to have your head on the chopping block in your last minutes, waiting for the guillotine to drop.

Someone spoke over the radio. The co-pilot raised his hand in a furtive thumbs-up gesture to the passengers. The silence was broken by the port engines of the 707 running up, then the starboard. The plane was already parked in take-off position on the runway threshold markings. The pilots were hastily going through their pre-flight check. They had obviously no time for the prestart, startup and before-taxi checklists and jumped straight into the take-off sequence. As they released the brakes Randalph watched the co-pilot slam his left hand down over the captain's right hand as they both simultaneously thrust the engine throttles forward with such determination that it looked as if they were going to push-start the plane.

The four jet engines leapt through the revs, thrusting the passengers back in their seat. Randalph imagined them flying into space. The pilots were going through the take-off list: "V1, check… Vr, rotate… V2, 150…" The nose lifted… "Gear up"… They were in the air…

"Flaps full retract", ordered the captain. The plane lunged downwards, as if it was about to dive into the sea. You could see the glimmer of the waves in the starlight. You could feel the plane gaining speed fast, engines screaming. The pilots kept their firm grip on the throttles, as if they were holding the reins of a wild horse preparing to jump a high fence.

God only knows what speed they had already reached, but at that low altitude it felt like they were in a rocket. Suddenly, and without any warning the plane heaved upwards, throwing everyone even more heavily back into their seats. If you were going into space, thought Randalph, his sweating hands gripping the underside of his seat, this is what it would feel like. The climb seemed to go on forever. Through the left window, Randalph could make out the lights of southern Lebanon. On the right-hand side, darkness.

The plane levelled off, trimmed, turned gently to the right, then just like in a fairy tale the first rays of the morning sunshine lit up the winter sky. The co-pilot appeared again. He looked relaxed, confident, and grateful to be alive. Randalph remembered how his dark eyes and striking features, like those of the Arabian kings of old, had intrigued him.

What happened next, in its every detail, would never be erased from Randalph's memory.

The co-pilot raised his hands to draw everyone's attention and spoke: "It looks like Allah heard our prayers. A few minutes ago, we exited Lebanese airspace. Ladies and gentlemen, you're going home." And in a brilliant twist of Lebanese humour, he added "The Captain and myself would like to thank you for choosing Middle East Airways". Pointing to a container in the galley, he concluded: "The bar is now open. Compliments of MEA. Please help yourselves." While Randalph and the rest of the delegation were all big boys and girls that had come through tricky times together, none had developed the necessary self-control to hold back the waves of tears that flooded and filled their eyes, running unashamedly down their faces.

When the plane finally landed at GVA (Geneva), only the captain and the co-pilot could walk in a straight line. The police escort that climbed on board had apparently been warned by the crew about what to expect and just smiled.

CHAPTER 14

No man's land

Randalph was deeply disappointed by the unceremonious nature of the greeting the delegation received back at the Red Cross headquarters in Geneva. He had hoped for a cocktail reception with claps on the back and speeches and press cameras. Instead, there were forms to fill out, questions to answer about their achievements, suggestions for improvements, and a coffee with your desk officer.

International administration in all its glory, thought Randalph – bureaucrats, desk people, procedure people, paper pushers, conformists. Randalph had a deep dislike for them all. He would have loved to put them on a plane to Beirut and let them explore for themselves their suggestions for improvements. Discharged from his contract, all papers signed, non-disclosure promises made, he was free to leave. His flight back to London had been booked for the following afternoon.

What at the time was still referred to by many as shell shock, but today falls under the de-personalised designation of post-traumatic stress disorder (PTSD), hit Randalph as he walked down the stairs in front of the Red Cross building onto the pavement along the Route de Pregny, past the UN Geneva headquarters, down Avenue de la Paix and arriving at the Place des Nations, where he intended to catch a tram to the railway station. As well as being full of bureaucrats, Geneva was also full of parked cars. In Randalph's recently gained understanding of life, parked cars exploded and killed people.

Anyone watching Randalph on his walk through Geneva would have concluded that he was either mentally and emotionally unstable or up to something. Randalph's tactic and sole focus was to stay as far away as he possibly could from parked cars. If there was one parked on his side of the road he would cross to the other. If there was also one there, he would walk down the white line in the middle of the road. When the road got narrower and there was no way of putting between himself and the parked cars a safe distance he made a detour through the wooded grounds of the UN.

In the tram his phobia persisted. He first took a seat on the left, away from the road kerb and the cars parked there, then moved around from side to side depending on how close the tram got to other parked cars. A ticket inspector who had spotted his antics asked him if everything was all right. Randalph, who didn't speak a word of French and hadn't realised that his phobia had got complete control of him, replied something about 'les voîtures'. "What about les voîtures?", asked the inspector in fairly good English.

Randalph, who was suddenly aware of his phobia-induced behaviour and realised what was happening, replied that he had just arrived from Beirut where parked cars sometime explode and he was afraid of them. "Pas de problème, Monsieur," the inspector chuckled, "Here, ze cars do not go boom." How could he be so sure, Randalph wondered? Life can be full of surprises, even in Geneva.

The next day, back at the UK Red Cross head office in London, Randalph shared his story with a room full of captivated listeners. At least in London his experience was given credit. One of them, Charles, himself a civil engineer, asked Randalph if he would be going to the talk that evening at the Institute of Civil Engineers in the City. Randalph knew nothing of the talk but answered, why not? The two men agreed to meet in the lobby at around five in the evening at the Institute's offices on N°1, Great George Street. Agreeing to come to a meeting at the institute of the very engineering body that Randalph had wanted to distance himself from felt like either the past was catching up with him or the future was laying a trap.

Unbeknown to Randalph, Charles had called the institute in the afternoon and slipped Randalph's name onto the agenda for the evening. Halfway into the proceedings, someone in charge of the event started telling the audience about the experience of one of their young members in Lebanon and asked Randalph to come up to the microphone. Randalph, who wasn't a member, and even if he had been one was in no way prepared for this, stood up to a round of applause as he walked to the front. What to say? He had done nothing in the line of engineering in Lebanon. No roads. No bridges. No piers. No airports.

No buildings. No water. No sewage. All he had done was disinfect dead bodies, channel funding from the EU to rehabilitate war-damaged water pumping stations in Beirut and learn about survival in an urban war zone.

As he stumbled his way along the thorny path of unprepared speeches, trying to sound credible and intelligent, the above was precisely what he told the audience, adding for drama that perhaps some people in the room had had similar experiences – that'll shut them up he thought. The crowd were polite and clapped again as he sat down, but Randalph wasn't fooled. The speech had been a bummer.

In the early morning of the next day, Randalph chose the option of the day train ride from London Euston back to Scotland instead of a flight. He loved travelling by train and was looking forward to enjoying to the full the 400-mile ride through the rolling scenery of Northwest England, between the Yorkshire Dales and the Lake District National Parks, and then the southern highlands of Scotland. It was a way of reuniting himself with his childhood and teenage days. He was reminded of the pleasure he used to get ticking off the names of the stations when he used to travel the route on his way to or from his summer holidays in Germany – Watford Junction, Milton Keynes, Rugby, Stafford, Crewe, Warrington, Wigan, Preston, Lancaster, Penrith, Carlisle...

The pleasure ended as they crossed the border into Scotland, when wind-driven rain and sleet began to pound the train's windows, forming rivulets of water and mushy-white snow clusters streaming downwards diagonally across the glass. Did it ever stop raining in Scotland, Randalph wondered? The gloomy grey of the skies and the sudden disappearance of the landscape behind the rain left him feeling melancholic. He could feel the cold through the glass which, within only a few minutes, had steamed up, revealing the traces of previous hands and fingers that had tried to rub the steam away. No man's land, he thought. Wherever he would be heading for next, it was definitely not northwards to home.

By then it was mid-December and biting cold. Randalph felt lost. For anyone who would listen, his mother kept the story alive about him telling her he was flying to the Seychelles. His good friend Simon from university days had settled in London. Nathan was now living in the Highlands. He had lost contact with the others. The friends of his parents were still talking about the same kind of stuff as when he last saw them and had become too much for him to put up with.

Göta from Sweden flew over to spend Christmas and New Year with him to try to rekindle the flame of their relationship, but it was too late. Randalph's heart had closed. On the last day of her visit, as they sat in the bus to Glasgow Airport, Randalph knew it was over. This would be their last goodbye. She turned round and waved as she cleared customs and the security desk, just before turning the corner towards the departure gates. Randalph felt miserable, alone, with nothing ahead to look forward to, and no one in his heart.

As if clinging to the memories inside this place where

they had said goodbye, Randalph wandered into the airport bookshop, browsing aimlessly along the shelves, not looking for anything in particular. Destiny, however, was hiding in the shelves, waiting for him. In the past, Randalph had already experienced how destiny's hand can reach out to you at the most unexpected moment and turn your life upside down. This was one of those moments.

On one of the shelves, he spotted Louis Fischer's *The Life of Mahatma Gandhi* and picked it up. As he read the preface, his mind wandered back to India and Nepal. He felt nostalgic, almost homesick. He remembered the colours, the smells, the rituals, the simplicity and the feeling of freedom he had known there before his path had led him into the big bad world.

Randalph bought the book, and already on the bus home he began to plough his way through the pages. All through January he couldn't put the book down. *The Life of Mahatma Gandhi* was a treasure chest of references to many of the books that had inspired Gandhi. Randalph had heard of only a few of them but knew he should read them all. He made a list of the more accessible titles, starting with George Orwell, Huxley's *Perennial Philosophy* and *The Doors of Perception* and *Heaven and Hell*, Dickens' *Tale of Two Cities*, *How Green was My Valley* – Randalph had seen the film – John Ruskin's *Unto This Last* and Thoreau's *Walden* and *Civil Disobedience*. He then added Tolstoy's *The Kingdom of God Is Within You*, the works of Ralph Waldo Emerson and Dostoevsky's *Crime and Punishment* and *The Idiot*. He made a list of the less accessible titles – for a rainy day, he thought – T*he Bhagavad-Gita*, *The Bible*, *The Tibetan Book of the Dead*, *The Quran*, and many more. He would buy them all, he decided. Wherever he was going to next, they would go with him.

CHAPTER 15

Goodbye Sudan

'Next' turned out to be South Sudan. Good old Jack at the roster of engineers for humanitarian emergencies in London, who had sent Randalph to Malaysia a year ago and pointed him in the direction of Lebanon, had given his name to a charity organisation in England that was recruiting a team of engineers to dig water wells in refugee camps on the Ugandan border in South Sudan.

Around mid-January, the organisation called him to ask if he was available for an assignment to Africa. If he was interested, he would be flying to Khartoum in two or three weeks and from there with a hired pilot in a four-seater single-engine aircraft to Juba. In Juba he would be met by the charity's rep, who would drive them by road to Yei, where the camps were. Randalph had nothing else to do, nowhere he particularly wanted to go, and nothing in the pipeline work wise. Of course he was interested. Africa here we come!

From his briefing a few days later at the organisation's

offices in Oxford, Randalph learned that this assignment would be very much a hands-on mission. He would need to personally be able to cast concrete, make bricks, dig hand-dug wells, rig pulley systems, capture surface springs and, above all, find water. Feeling elated and useful, Randalph loaded up with the relevant books and documentation that would teach him the various skills he would need to put into practice on the ground.

With two weeks to go, he had just enough time to spend some days in Switzerland with Annette from the island refugee camp in Malaysia, whom he hadn't seen since he was arrested and taken off the island, and talked her into him staying with her at her parents' house for a few days.

Annette's family lived in a small village in rural Switzerland nestled at the bottom of a steep valley beside a picturesque river a few miles from the French border, where the sun shone for a few hours only in winter. They were hard-working people of the land, living in a world as remote from Randalph's as a metro station in New York is from a ranch in Wyoming.

The village was tiny, with a hundred or so inhabitants living a rural life on the outer rim of civilisation. The villagers observed him with the same precaution and suspicion as wild animals do when they detect an alien presence. They were wary of outsiders. After some weeks, once they had got used to him, a woman from the village asked Annette why Randalph was so white, suggesting that people from Corsica had brown skin. She had confused Ecosse (Scotland) with La Corse (Corsica). Few people in the village had ventured out beyond the district market town on the other side of the hill, and Scotland might as well have been an island in the Indonesian archipelago, or a crater on Mars.

Switzerland at that time was still very much an island in the middle of Europe with its own rules, local-only economy, banking secrets, patrolled borders, and the belief that you needed to be ready at all times for the enemy, who would one day come from the East.

The fear of the East was very real at the time. Citizens were obliged by law to construct nuclear bomb shelters in the basement of their houses. Young men who refused military service went to prison. Those who accepted increased their chances of a career in the thriving banking, insurance, watch-making or pharmaceutical industries.

Throughout the country, trains, buses, boats and trams ran like clockwork, were kept spotlessly clean and followed timetables to the second. Turning up five minutes late for a meeting could result in sanctions. Switzerland was then – and still is now – a country of precision, fiercely independent, politically different from the rest of the world, functionally democratic, and a place where a young Scotsman like Randalph with an engineering degree under his belt and no relevant experience some years later was able to settle, be accepted into the community, raise a family and thrive. It was a country where what you did and how you did it was more important than your credentials. It was also a country that was immensely proud of its military, and especially of its air force and the world famous Patrouille Suisse acrobatic team.

It was Friday. Maman, Annette's mother, had prepared a juicy rabbit stew which lay steaming in a Pyrex dish in the middle of the table. Randalph sat on a wooden bench, his back to the wall. To his left, at the head of the table, was his future father-in-law. Opposite, with her back to the oven, was his future mother-in-law, and to his right his future wife.

On that particular Friday, a Swiss Airforce jet was flying low, screeching down the valley towards the village, approaching fast. This was a rare event. In Switzerland in the 1980s the standing joke was that 'the enemy' could invade the country during the rigidly observed 9 o'clock morning coffee breaks, lunch times, and weekends off. People worked a 45-hour week. No one worked overtime. Unemployment was at 1%. And except for highly exceptional circumstances, military planes never flew outside working hours.

Randalph had the sneaky feeling that something suspiciously wrong was going on. He felt fear rising, his reflexes twitching, adrenaline flooding his reason. Suddenly, like a frightened cat he dived for cover, flinging his arm around Annette and launching her and himself under the table. The juicy rabbit, which had been minding its own business in the dish in the middle of the table, went flying to the floor as the table tilted up, landing on its side in a puddle of gravy by the feet of Maman.

On his desperate scramble to safety Randalph noticed his future father-in-law's bewildered expression as he looked towards Maman, who was blurting out something incomprehensible in her native Alsace dialect. Papa put his finger to his temple and turned it in a corkscrew motion with his hand in the way people do when they point out that someone is nuts. They were right. In many respects,

Randalph was nuts. It would take him two decades to get control of this and subsequent war-related traumas.

Back in London after those few hilariously disastrous days in Switzerland, Randalph travelled once more to Oxford for a final briefing for Sudan, then again by train back to Scotland to pack his bags. When the time came to leave, he met up at Heathrow with Graham and Paul, the two other engineers also recruited for the mission and flew with them from London via Paris to Khartoum.

Influenced by what he had read so far about the ascetic life of Gandhi, in mid-flight from Paris to Khartoum, once the meals had already been served, Randalph took the life-changing decision to exclude meat, fish and poultry from his diet, and asked the stewardess if he could exchange his meal for a vegetarian dish. Not only had Randalph decided on the spur of the moment to become vegetarian, but he was also about to become a total pain in the ass for his two colleagues.

The teachings and example of the life of Gandhi had so inspired Randalph that he was bent on copying him. Years before in Glasgow, Nathan, his Australian flatmate had been a vegetarian. Randalph remembered how he had tried to trick him into eating meat, and how Nathan, not in the least perturbed by young Randalph's stupidity, had said to him "One day you'll understand". The question of meat or no meat had nagged Randalph in India and Nepal, where the majority of people didn't eat it.

In the plane from Paris to Khartoum, Randalph's mind was finally made up: If it had eyes and a nose and moved around independently, he wouldn't eat it. Randalph's argument was that since you could strike up some sort of a relationship with almost any animal, they must have some form of intelligence. Randalph would give them the benefit of the doubt and let them live.

While not eating meat, fish or poultry is an easy choice in Europe, where there is an abundance of fruit, vegetables, cereals, and stores full of plant-based factory-food, he soon found out that in South Sudan, where the staple diet is meat with some rice or other cereal, the choice is not so easy to live with. It was not Randalph's problem; he would find a way round it.

To add substance to his newly inspired meatless lifestyle, and again inspired by the Mahatma, he also decided to fast on Sundays. Randalph's life-style changes so far were acceptable to his colleagues, who said "fair enough, it's your choice", but when he added to the changes an attempt to stop them swearing, or at least to persuade them to swear less, he met with a brick wall of resistance marked by a significant increase in the swearing exchanged between them in the one-roomed, four-bed hut that served as their temporary home from home. Their message was clear: "Don't you fucking tell us to stop fucking swearing".

Looking back years later, when he had mellowed and was less adamant about being right, Randalph often thought about what an asshole he had been at the time trying to get others to accept his new habits and way of thinking. Thirty years later, when he was delivering training in time management, organisation and communication skills to managers and employees at in-house workshops in big business enterprises in Switzerland, and some other countries in Europe, as well as in the USA, he used this experience as an example to show how cautiously we need to approach behaviour change, and how easy misunderstandings can arise when someone in a group decides to change their habits.

Back in early 1983, when Randalph and his team landed in Juba, the city had a population of 85,000. Forty years later in 2023 it was estimated at around 450,000. 1983 was also the year that fighting broke out again between North and South Sudan. The second Sudanese Civil War, which lasted

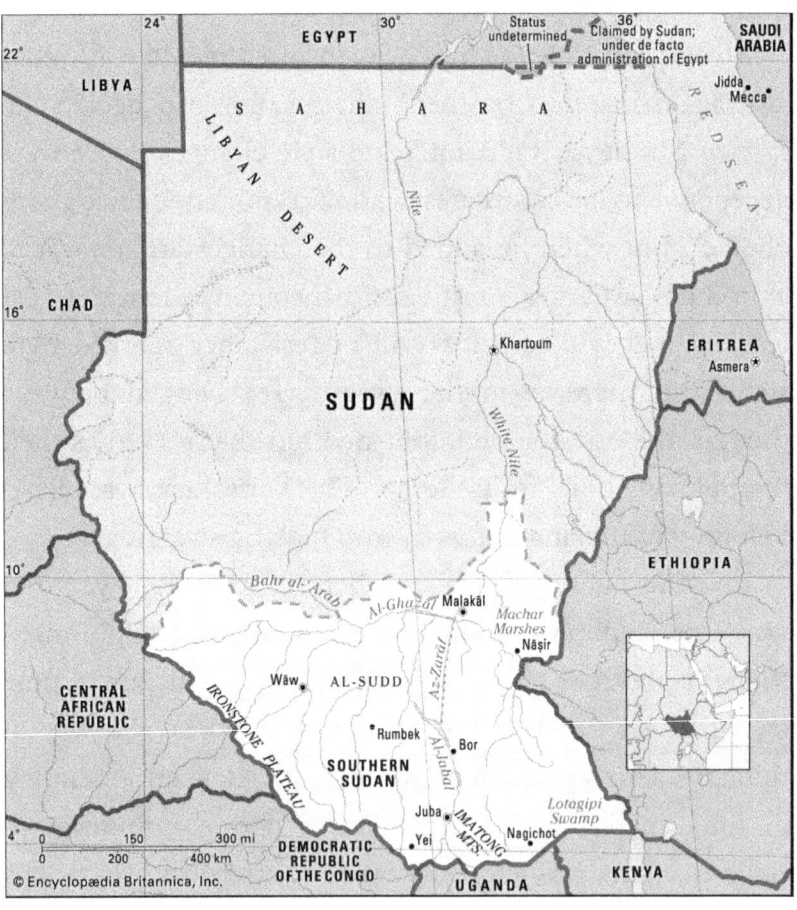

Map of Sudan. Photo downloaded from Encyclopaedia Brittanica

from 1983 to 2005, began there when the then Sudanese president, Gaafar Nimeiry, declared the country an Islamic state and revoked the autonomy of the majority-Christian South Sudan Autonomous Region (SSAR) that had existed from 1972 to 1983. After more than two decades of conflict, the number of casualties exceeded 2.5 million.

Randalph was happy to have seen Juba in the days before the population explosion and the civil war, when movement was unrestricted and the vast plains, savannah and hill lands of South Sudan could be explored. He was happy also that his and his team's mission could be carried out in safety. Their focus was the southern border, where refugees from Uganda had fled to Sudan due to political turmoil and persecution under the oppressive regimes of Idi Amin Dada and Apollo Milton Obote, where they faced violence, starvation, and illness. Some of the refugees were also targeted as supporters of the Amin government and feared execution if they stayed in their country.

In all, around 200,000 Ugandan refugees sought refuge in Sudan, with many crossing the border close to the town of Yei in Western Equatoria (the west bank of the Nile) and others spread along the border in fourteen planned settlements provided by Sudan and supported by the United Nations High Commissioner for Refugees (UNHCR), who put the figure at 160,000.

The conditions in the camps were dire. Refugees faced poor health, malnutrition, and inadequate shelter. Many lived in poorly constructed huts and slept either on bare ground or in makeshift beds. The camps were overcrowded, food was scarce, and there were cases of illness and starvation among the newly arrived refugees. Additionally, there were social tensions, distrust, dishonesty, and occasional violence within the settlements, making the situation challenging for both the refugees and the aid workers.

Randalph's job was to find water and establish water points. While in Switzerland in January, he had met with a friend of his lady friend, Annette, who had shown him how to use divining rods – a little trick that was soon going to elevate Randalph to the rank of saviour, but would brand him as a sorcerer.

When Randalph first set foot in the first of the camps that he would be working in it was dry, sandy and desolate. Although trees and bushes grew abundantly on the perimeter of the camp, there was no surface water to be seen. Armed with two thin twigs of flexible wood that looked similar to willow – the water diviner's magic wand – Randalph set to work marking out the areas where he would start prospecting. Walking purposefully and slowly along the lines of the grid he had drawn on the ground, sticks held loosely in each hand, making sure to scuff his feet on the sandy earth and not lift them, he wandered up and down the lines for hours until, at one point, the sticks bent inwards and across his forearms. Not at all sure about the accuracy of the indication, Randalph repeated the procedure from different angles and at different speeds, and sure enough, at almost the same point, the twigs moved again. Randalph had no idea if there really would be water there, and if so, how deep beneath the surface. The only way to find out was to dig, and the only way to dig was to persuade the refugees to take up spades and get to work.

From a book he had read, he remembered that the best way to get people to do something was to do it yourself, proving to them that you're up to the task, and invite them to help you. It was midday, hot and parched dry. The sun was high and the temperature was hovering around 40°C. To provide some shade, Randalph had covered his head and shoulders with his shirt before picking up a spade and beginning to dig. Very soon he was sweating and out of breath. This was not a climate for his pale skin and not an activity that his out-of-shape body was happy with. Around him, hundreds of refugees were looking on, some with inquisitive, serious expressions on their faces, some laughing. For most of them, Randalph realised, this was the first time they had ever seen a white man working manually. That being as it may, no one was showing any signs of wanting to help.

After a few hours, Randalph put down his spade. He was exhausted. The hole he had begun was only a few inches deep and there was no sign of any water. Unsatisfied with the result, he approached the UN representative who was in charge of the camp explaining the situation and asking for advice. At first the rep just laughed at Randalph's witchcraft, but finally he gave him the benefit of the doubt, explaining that if he needed a gang of refugee workers to help him, even if the water was for them, he would need to give them something in return, adding that the best and only commodity available there for bartering was extra food.

The only food available for hundreds of kilometres in all directions was fresh mangoes and sacks of flour. Randalph's team had a budget and enough available cash and agreed to buy a truckload of each. No one had come up with an alternative idea. A few days later when the truck arrived, mayhem broke loose. Randalph hadn't thought about how he was going to make a crowd of hundreds of near-starving refugees accept that only those who helped him would get food. It took the crowd only a few minutes to pillage the entire truck, leaving Randalph with nothing to barter with.

If any progress was to be made with the well digging, Randalph would need to learn from his mistakes. Before ordering a second truckload he set up a committee of committed diggers who agreed to defend the truck and distribute the food only amongst themselves. Imagine for a moment the scenario. At a random spot near the centre of a makeshift camp housing ten thousand hungry refugees, a truck is to be unloaded by a hundred or so able-bodied men at a spot where a young white guy with a big bushy beard and two diving rods had proclaimed there would be water under the ground. The hundred or so are to get the food if they help the white witch doctor to dig until they find water.

After the first day, the diggers had dug down about one metre (three feet) without finding a drop. As the soil was sandy, Randalph realised that if they had to dig much deeper, there would be a risk of the sides of the hole collapsing and engulfing the diggers. He would need to find a way to secure the sides. Digging stopped for a few days while Randalph and his team grappled for a solution. The surest way would be to line the well with caissons (concrete rings). To ensure that the sides didn't collapse, they would need to sink caissons into the hole as they dug. To make the caissons they would need moulds, preferably of at least two metres in diameter to allow room for the workers to continue digging as the rings descended.

An alternative could be drilling tube wells. Tube wells drilled in that part of the world were drilled by mobile drilling rigs mounted on the back of trucks and equipped with handpumps. Randalph and his team found out, however, that due mainly to the distance from where the nearest drilling crew were operating, as well as the cost of transporting a rig to the camps, this option had been dropped by both the camp authorities and the UN since the outset of the refugee influx. It would have to be caissons.

Finding two-metre diameter steel moulds for casting rings in the vast expanses of South Sudan was not quite as challenging as finding a needle in a haystack, but almost. As this is not the sort of equipment that people have lying around in their yards or depots, Randalph and his colleagues began asking around for any clues that might lead them to the magic moulds.

Fortunately, the expatriate community of Yei in the early 1980s was tiny and easy to approach, and as luck had it one of its members – a middle-aged German with a cowboy hat and a saggy boiler suit draped over a checkered shirt with rolled-up sleeves – had heard about moulds used on an experimental site somewhere to the west. How far to the west he was unsure, but it was definitely to the west and neither to the east nor to the north. German precision.

Later that evening the German, who introduced himself with a firm handshake as Müller, turned up at the team's hut. Müller, who the team later got to know as Heinrich, worked on a long-term development project and had been in Yei for years, and had meanwhile remembered that he had seen the moulds in a town called Wau.

The next day, Randalph's two colleagues set out across the bumpy dust roads in the team's Land Rover towards the town of Wau, half a day's drive north-west from Yei, in search of the moulds. Some days good luck is lurking behind the bushes along the sides of life's road, waiting to jump out and surprise someone with its blessing. This was one of these days. Not only did Randalph's colleagues come back late that evening with news of the moulds, but they had also found an abandoned tank transporter whose owner agreed to let them hire it to transport the moulds back to Yei.

The agreed deal was that the owner would load the moulds on to the transporter, Randalph's colleagues would come back the next day with Randalph, pay the hiring price in cash, and Randalph would then accompany the owner and the moulds to Yei while the colleagues headed south towards the border area to visit another camp the UN had heard about.

The road to Wau had become corrugated, with troughs and crests about half a metre apart as it wound its way across the vast dusty savannah and through the many scattered one-street villages of central Africa. To drive comfortably in the Land Rover, it was necessary to maintain a speed of around 50 mph (80 km/h), leaving the passengers with the feeling that they were being tortured with a hammer drill. Arriving shattered and covered in red dust, Randalph was dropped off in Wau and introduced to the tank transporter's owner, this time a Belgian by the name of Guillaume, which none of the three Brits could pronounce properly, who had also been in the country for years. Unlike Heinrich, however, who spoke German and good English, Guillaume spoke only French, and very little English.

As it was already late in the day when they arrived in Wau, the team thought it wise to spend the night there and head off early the next morning to their respective destinations – the two colleagues south to scout for the new camps, and Randalph back to Yei with the moulds. To drive comfortably in the tank transporter was impossible. The transporter, an M19 US Tank Transporter used in WWII which had somehow found its way to the middle of Africa had a four-speed main and three-speed auxiliary transmission. The main transmission had a 'low' first gear and three road gears, fourth being direct. The auxiliary had low, direct, and overdrive gears. The low setting enabled several very low gears for extreme off-road use. The direct and overdrive allowed the three road gears to be split, making six road gears in all.

In simple language, once the transporter had reached, let's call it its 'cruising speed', it required a circus juggling act to go down through the gears to reduce speed, for example to avoid an obstacle or negotiate a particularly corrugated stretch of road, and another high-wire hands-and-feet performance to bring it back up to speed. Guillaume explained to Randalph that he liked the old transporter very much but drove it very little, because of the pressure needed to release the clutch when changing gears. He had a bad knee that would swell if he drove it for too long.

With that introduction, after less than two hours on the road, Guillaume began to complain about pain in his left knee and asked if Randalph wouldn't mind taking the wheel. Randalph loved driving and remembered his experience in Sweden some years previously, driving an articulated asphalt truck totally illegally through the busy streets of Stockholm. Of course he wouldn't mind – he would do it with pleasure – but first he would need Guillaume to explain the gearbox to him.

Randalph wished that he had had a camera with him. He would have loved to have a photo of himself at the wheel of this heavy-weight iron-clad survivor of the Second World War.

Arriving late in the evening in Yei, Randalph parked the transporter along the street in front of their hut, organised a place for Guillaume to sleep for the night, and apologized for the basicness of his humble dwelling.

Close to where Randalph and the team were living there were no shops with fridges. No cold beers. No ice cream. No ice cubes. No supplies of anything below 35°C. The best Randalph could offer was a glass of lukewarm filtered water, as many mangoes as he could eat, and some biscuits from Juba. They were lucky to have stopped along the road at one of the many one-street villages to fill up with something substantial to eat before they arrived.

Although both Randalph and Guillaume were covered in a layer of red dust propelled upwards in a thick cloud from the massive front wheels of the transporter's drive unit, they would need to wait until the next morning before they could wash the dust off. There was no shower at the team's hut and no running water. To have a wash, they would need to go to the well down the road to fetch water in buckets. They were too tired. As well as no water, there was no electricity and only a rudimentary outside toilet. However, Randalph did have a brush that they could use in turn to get at least some of the dust off of them. That night he would have paid in gold for a hot shower.

Before turning in for the night, Guillaume and Randalph sat on the flimsy wooden stools at either side of the hut's door discussing and joking about how to unload the moulds from the transporter. The sky was ablaze with stars, the full moon cast razor-sharp shadows of some nearby trees on the façade of their little house. In the distance they could hear the plinky-plonky electric guitar sounds of local pop music played on battery-powered radios, a sound that was impossible to escape from. If you could accept it as a background noise that replaced the eternal chatter of the insects and the haunting howling of the night, you would agree with Randalph that there was something magical about being in Africa.

The next morning, Randalph and Guillaume drove down to the camp in the team's Land Rover, which Graham and Paul had returned in during the early hours to check if their ideas from the previous evening were pertinent. Each mould was a quarter circle in shape, about 60 cm high, comprising an outside and inside lining, and with an outside diameter of around 3 metres. Guillaume had used a crane at his depot to load them, but in the camp there was no crane. They would have to use ropes and a makeshift pulley system. Randalph remembered a store selling reels of rope in Yei.

What was great in those days was that the two gentlemen could turn up at the store, choose the rope they needed, negotiate the price, and pay cash. No need for a procurement procedure, no need for offers from other bidders, just cash and a little bit of common sense. If there was only one rope wholesaler in the town you could get a good deal by bargaining the price down. If there were two or more, he would probably give you a competitive price anyway. If you were crooked, you could mark up the invoice, in the very same way that crooked people mark up invoices and entire vetting procedures today. The difference then was that you got your merchandise over the counter when you needed it, not delivered six weeks later by some unknown courier who had purchased it in some unknown country far away. Randalph definitely preferred the simplicity of the world back in the early 1980s.

Now that they had rope, they would need to build some sort of wooden structure to sling the ropes over to lift the moulds, and later also the concrete rings. Their next call was at a timber yard, where they were able to purchase a few sturdy wooden beams strong enough to support the moulds and the caissons and long enough to extend far enough on each side of the hole being dug. They augmented their purchase at the wood yard with four wooden poles to lash each beam on to – two at each end – and half a dozen heavy-duty planks to slide the caissons over once they had set and could be moved.

The next job was to assemble the wooden structure,

firstly fitting it above the transporter, so that they could lift the moulds individually and hoist them using a pulley system and a cantilevered beam to carry them from the transporter's deck and place them on the ground. Back home in Scotland, when Randalph was packing his bags, he had slipped in a small pocket-sized book of knots and lashings he had picked up somewhere along the way to complete his collection of technical literature on how to dig hand-dug wells, capture surface springs and make bricks. The book of knots proved to be the most valuable resource the team had. They used it for lashing the poles to the beams, lashing the beams to each other, fixing the ropes to the moulds and to the rings, and improvising a rope and pulley system using multiple strands of rope, as pulley wheels were nowhere to be found.

The last ingredients were steel reinforcing bars, reinforcing mesh, wire, sand, gravel, cement and water. How easy back home, thought Randalph, where you take your wish list to the local hardware store or building yard and a few hours later the items are delivered to wherever your site was. How difficult out here in the middle of nowhere, where you needed to cut the steel yourself, bind the mesh, sift the sand, grade the gravel, and transport individual bags of cement in your vehicle. Even the water could be a challenge. To make good concrete you need clean water, with no bacteriological or carbon-based pollutants. And all of this in the middle of a refugee camp under the sweltering sun, surrounded by hundreds of curious faces and the spectre of failure. What happens if you dig for days, cast concrete caissons, laboriously lower them into the ground one on top of the other, and at the end of the day find no water?

Randalph's memory of the day the first caissons were ready for lowering into the well was vivid. The diggers had levelled the bottom of the well at a depth of about 2 metres. The wooden structure and the pulley system had been erected. The caissons had cured for ten days on planks, ready to be pushed by wooden poles acting as levers and pulled by ropes onto other planks straddling the well. Once in position above the well they were to be attached to the rope and pulley system, lifted a few centimetres so that the planks could be removed, then lowered ever so gently into the hole. Once the first caisson was in place the others followed suit. Once all four were in place, the diggers could continue in safety, with no fear of the walls caving in. The next step was for them to dig deeper, creating a hole of a slightly smaller diameter, until they hit water.

That day, the gods must have been looking on benevolently at all the work and effort being put into finding water for that parched population of homeless migrants. At a depth of around 3 metres the bottom of the well began to get damp. By 3.5 metres a puddle had formed. By 4 metres you could legitimately call the hole a water well. What's more, they had found water in abundance. No matter how many pails they filled and hauled out, the water level in the bottom of the well didn't change. To the refugees gazing on and to the queue with plastic buckets and pails that had instantly formed, a miracle had happened. The idea had worked. Luck – lots of luck – had been on Randalph's side.

From start to finish, this first well had taken around

four weeks to complete. In the remainder of his time in the camps, Randalph supervised the construction of three more. Wells, Randalph discovered, were not the only source of water available. As he wandered around with his rods in the bushland surrounding the camps, he also came across water sources just under the surface that could be captured as spring catchments. To capture the springs, however, he would need to excavate the area around them and build small dams to hold the water. This could best be done using bricks and cement. As mud bricks would simply wash away, the bricks would need to be made of fired clay. While sand and cement were available, fired clay bricks in that remote part of the world were nowhere to be found.

Among the other reference books the team had brought with them was a book on how to make bricks. As they turned the pages, they were sceptical. There were many easier things to make in the bush than fired clay bricks. They estimated that in order to construct half a dozen spring catchments they would need around a thousand bricks. Now that Randalph the enchanter had demonstrated that his divining rods were a magical force to be reckoned with, it was easier to persuade the refugee population to provide labour for capturing the springs. Once the negotiations had concluded how much each worker would be paid in mangoes and flour, the work gang set about gathering in a pile of around 3 cubic metres of malleable clay.

According to their bible on brick manufacturing in the bush, the team would also need about 0.5 cubic metres (17 cu ft) of water stored in drums, wooden brick moulds, sand for lining the moulds and preventing the wet clay from sticking to the sides, and some 3 cubic metres (106 cu ft) of firewood. Randalph was learning painfully that to produce good quality bricks, he and the team would need to supervise every single step of the process from start to finish.

First, the clay would need to be 'tempered' in a tempering pit of about 3 cubic metres. This involved first digging the pit, then adding water and allowing the soaked clay to stand undisturbed for a few days before mixing, in order to soften the clay and break down the lumps. To make a smooth, soft, homogenous mixture with no stones or lumps, the tempered clay would need to be mixed and kneaded. The suggested method was to trample it underfoot on a flat piece of ground. As Randalph imagined the scenario, his mind flashed back to the story his father used to tell of how, as an apprentice baker in a small town in south-west Scotland in the four years between leaving school and the beginning of WWII, he and the bakers used to sit around a deep, wide cauldron and trample the dough for the day's bread with their bare feet.

The next step would be the trickiest, requiring half a dozen wooden moulds to be built. The brick bible's authors recommended not to employ the traditional method of 'slop moulding' used in the bush to make mud bricks, in which the clay is sometimes so wet that it easily deforms under its own weight, but rather to go for 'sand moulding', using a drier, stiffer clay mixture. Rudimentary as this sounded to the apprentice brickmakers, it proved to be necessary to do several trial-and-error runs before the workers got the knack of filling the moulds, releasing them and carrying the wet bricks to the drying area where they were stacked. The initial drying process took about a week, after which the bricks were turned and stacked for another week.

The real challenge, they learned, came when the bricks were to be stacked to make a kiln. To fire them correctly they needed to be stacked in layers, creating a sort of pyramid, like a miniature Inca burial mound, with narrow tunnels in the lower part of the kiln between the piles of stacked bricks and open at each end. This was where the fuel for the fire – the wood – would be introduced. Once the kiln had been built, it also needed to be insulated with a layer of mud and broken bricks on the outside, to maintain its temperature. To keep the fire burning, piles of easily accessible firewood cut in approximately one-metre lengths needed to be prepared.

Next would be the moment of truth – the firing itself. The book went on to explain in detail about the various chemical reactions that happen as the temperature rises, emphasising that the temperature should rise to well above 900°C to produce well-fired bricks. So much for theory, but how were Randalph and his crew going to be able to monitor and control the process? Nobody had a clue. Thermometers that can read up to 1000°C are not the sort of instruments people carried around with them in the prairies of South Sudan.

In addition to the technical challenges of building and firing up the kiln, crews of workers needed to be put together and trained. The challenge was double, as the crews would need to tend the fires around the clock for one to two weeks with at least one person checking the fires and feeding wood to each tunnel 24/7.

If nothing else, thought Randalph, the experience was a once-in-a-lifetime episode with so much to learn and put straight into practice. With the preparations done, the kiln constructed, firewood stockpiled and everyone trying to reassure themselves and the others that they had followed the book's instructions as meticulously as possible, the fires were eventually lit one day just after sunrise.

There was something ceremonial about the lighting, as if some great sacrifice were about to be made to the gods. Hundreds of refugees from inside the camp were joined by curious farmers and cattle herders from the villages around to witness the offering. For a moment, Randalph had the uncomfortable thought that if it did turn into a sacrifice, he might be the one laid on top of the funeral pyre.

To make sure there was always someone tending to the fires in the tunnels, Randalph and the team agreed on supervising the operation in shifts. Randalph took the night shift while Graham and Paul split the day between them, starting at dawn and finishing at midnight. The first night was new and somehow exciting, although in reality not much happened. The next nights dragged on, with impatience digging its teeth into Randalph after a week. Eventually, after nine days the fires were no longer fed and allowed to simmer out. It took another two full days for the kiln to cool down enough to start removing the bricks. The moment when all would be revealed had arrived.

Gingerly, the outer layer of insulation was scraped off and the first bricks lifted carefully from the top of the kiln. To everyone's amazement, the process had been successful. The bricks were hard, strong and baked red-black.

Hallelujah, thought Randalph, as his smile mirrored the happy smiling faces of all around. Randalph the sorcerer had graduated to Randalph the maker of bricks.

In what developed into a career spanning more than forty years, with work experiences in twenty different countries and as many different contexts, this would remain Randalph's crowning moment. Wells had been dug and were producing water where the earth was dry. Surface catchment dams were constructed using only the materials available in the bush, along with a box of imported matches. Very soon, precious water would be flowing – perhaps even abundantly – in this parched land, where for many long, dry months children and adults had been dying of dehydration. At no time in his working life had Randalph felt such a sense of achievement, elation, pride and satisfaction, until he retired forty years later, settling on an island in Greece where he landscaped a derelict plot of land, planted an orchard with dozens of different fruit trees and occasionally fed his neighbour's flock of sheep in the field next door.

The joy, sadly, was short lived and came to an abrupt end for Randalph and the team when an urgent message from Khartoum warned them of the advance of an army from the north, imploring them to get out of South Sudan by any means possible. The situation was serious. Other agencies working in the area had received similar instructions. Within a few hours they had packed up their gear and belongings. To split up in case of the worst, Randalph and the original member of the team would catch a flight from Juba to Nairobi. Graham and Paul, who had flown with him from London, would drive overland into northern Kenya by

Land Rover. They would meet at the embassy in Nairobi, hopefully two or three days later.

As Randalph and his other colleague took off, spiralling upwards above the airstrip to remain out of reach of possible anti-aircraft fire, he could see out of his window a line of fires stretching to the horizon. The wave of death and destruction had already arrived. He thought about the people in the camps that had been his comrades until the day previously, the smiling faces of the kids, the competition among the workers, the celebrations when they had found water. He would never see them again. He would never know what happened to them. All swallowed up by the blind uncompromising violence of the big bad world.

After a mere four months in the country, Randalph and his team escaped only hours ahead of the northern invasion, which was to destroy in an instant all traces of the infrastructure they had helped to build.

In Nairobi, Randalph and his colleague were taken to the house of a diplomat, who let them stay in his guest rooms until Graham and Paul arrived. The house, obviously in some suburb for the wealthy whites, was opulent and had a garden full of luxurious trees with a trimmed lawn and a swimming pool, but it also had a high wall thickly studded with pieces of broken glass and crowned with coils of barbed wire. Spotlights had been installed at each of the four corners of the property. Randalph could feel the insecurity, the danger in the streets. Who would want to live like this, he wondered?

Danger also lurked inside the house, as Randalph found out when he locked himself into the bathroom for a long-overdue wash. This was the first time in four months that he could shower with warm water and shower gel, and he rubbed it joyfully all over himself. The more he used the gel the soapier the bathtub became, and the more he enjoyed his new-found cleanliness – until, when he reached for a towel to wipe the soap from his eyes, he slipped, landing with an audible crack on the rim of the tub. The fall had fractured four of his ribs.

A few days later Randalph left Kenya, scared of laughing or coughing, his ribcage wrapped in tight bandages. He was feeling sad and bitter about the abrupt end to their mission and angry at the invaders from the north, but trying nevertheless to find some solace in the fact that he had stuck to his resolve not to eat any meat, fish or poultry.

He was also wondering if in the grand scheme of things, it mattered at all. Animals die, he reflected. People die. Dreams die. Trust dies. Team spirit dies. And friendships die. He left South Sudan disillusioned and feeling distant, satisfied with his effort and motivation but unsatisfied and confused about the disastrous end to his work, and about the way he had handled himself inside the team. What was the point, he pondered? He had distanced himself from his team. The results of four months of hard work were now being burnt down. Tens of thousands of people who had fled their country were now running back to it. Innocent people were being slaughtered in their hundreds. The news from Yei was unbearable.

At his debriefing back in England, their desk officer gave Randalph some sound advice: after his narrow escapes in Malaysia and in Lebanon and now this last-minute forced departure from Sudan, he should consider taking a break from the field. Randalph felt it too. It was time for a change.

CHAPTER 16

French in, English out

While Randalph was in Sudan, he had exchanged letters once or twice a week with Annette, who had rented for them a ground-floor studio in Geneva. They lived there together when he came back from Africa, with the idea that he would stay there until the wind of destiny blew him to wherever he was going to next.

With Annette working on weekdays and Randalph not having much to do in the city of Calvin, he decided to learn French. Knowing nothing of the language, he enrolled in a four-week long summer school for total beginners in Lausanne, to which he commuted by train. Randalph loved Lausanne, and every day during the long lunch break set off on foot to explore a different part of the city centre, taking photos as he went. In the public gardens below the Canton of Vaud district court he was surprised to see a statue of William Tell erected on a stone pedestal. Although he had already travelled to some far-off places, he knew so little of the world that he thought William Tell was an English folk hero and therefore couldn't understand why there should be a statue of him in a public park in Switzerland.

A quick browse through Google, which didn't exist then, would have bridged his general knowledge gap, but in those days to learn more about a subject it was necessary to buy a book on it. Inspired to kill two birds with one stone, he bought a book on the history of Switzerland in French, with a picture of Mr Tell on the front cover. Armed with his dictionary, he waded through the pages and picture captions, discovering that William was the founder and hero of Switzerland. Why did he not know that, he wondered? Why did he think William Tell was an English folk hero? What had they told him at school?

By the end of the four-week beginner's course Randalph had acquired a taste for French and was enthusiastic about continuing to learn the language. By then, however, in the sweltering heat of June 1983, he had had enough of commuting by train every day between Geneva and Lausanne, which not only was costly but took an hour and half each way door-to-door. Instead, he enrolled in the Geneva University summer school, which besides offering a higher and more rigorous level of instruction, was also free. From day one, the teacher there set the bar high: no talking or interaction except in French. No dictionaries. No chit-chat with your neighbour. If you had a question, you asked Madame. Serious stuff, thought Randalph. This was more like it.

For the duration of the nine weeks spanning July and August, Randalph attended the three-hour morning and afternoon sessions and diligently did the abundant homework assigned to them every evening. It was a tough course, but he was rapidly gaining a grasp of the language. The teacher was a genius. Instead of dragging the class through grammar lessons from some textbook she taught the language via music and literature. By the end of week one the class was singing some golden oldies by Edith Piaf and Jacques Brel, and by the beginning of week three they were dissecting *La Peste* (*The Plague*) by Albert Camus.

Randalph was so thrilled with his progress after only one month at the Geneva summer school that he decided one day to speak only French throughout the five months left until Christmas. The only exception would be for telephone calls to his mother or brother. While this propelled his ability to use the language forwards in leaps and bounds, it was a nightmare for Annette and a chore for her family, who had to put up with his stubborn obsession with looking up words he didn't know or couldn't remember in a French dictionary. Every word he looked up would inevitably lead to a dozen others he didn't know. He wanted explanations about verb endings, the subjunctive case, the past, the imperfect, when nouns take on a plural, why in French it's not good to repeat words in the same sentence or paragraph, or even in the same page. He found this French obsession about not repeating words totally illogical and would argue the point forever. It took him the best part of twenty years to finally accept that in French 'On ne se répète jamais!'

Once the summer school came to an end Randalph had time on his hands and a city to explore. He bought a map of Geneva and decided he would walk every street – it was the sort of thing he did. He made no specific plan but would set off most mornings heading in whichever direction his whim took him, scoring off the streets as he went. One morning, while he was still in Champel, the chic inner-city suburb they were staying in, he stopped off at a local supermarket to get some juice, or probably chocolate, for the day's walk and noticed someone sticking an advert on a notice board at the entrance to the store. This was not any old notice board but a Swiss notice board, with every advert written on the same standard light-green-coloured A6-sized paper form. He approached the notice board and started reading the adverts from left to right, and from row to row.

Among all the imaginable services people were offering and the bits and pieces of household stuff they wanted to get rid of either for free or for a price, someone had inserted an advert for teaching French to foreigners. Randalph thought about it, then had an idea: He would teach conversational English to locals. Why not?

He looked around and saw that blank advertising forms were available at the information desk and picked up a dozen. That night he conjured up a text in French, driving Annette mad with his questions about syntax, grammar, and what price to ask, then duplicated it onto the dozen slips. He settled for a rate of 25 Swiss Francs an hour, which was sufficiently under what he observed was the going rate to be attractive but didn't sound so cheap as to be worthless. The next day he went on a supermarket tour, sticking his adverts in half a dozen stores. Then he waited.

As 1983 was before the advent of mobile phones and they didn't have a phone at the studio, the advertisement had to be specific about what time to call. Randalph had given the number of a phone booth nearby where he would wait in the evenings between 6 and 7 pm. To his great surprise it worked, and within the first week Randalph had been contacted by three locals who wanted regular sessions of chit chat in English.

His private conversational English lessons, along with learning French and walking Geneva's streets, went on into November, by which time it was getting cold and Randalph began itching to get back into the field again. Not necessarily wanting to charge off on another emergency relief mission, he had taken up contact with a number of the UN agencies and the many international NGOs head-quartered in Geneva, none of whom offered him an opportunity to join a project or get involved in some ongoing mission. Then on the billboard of one of the organisations he spotted a flyer advertising a talk by the French author Dominique Lapierre, about a project he was supporting in Calcutta.

Dominique Lapierre? A year or two previously Randalph had read *Is Paris Burning?* and *Freedom at Midnight*, both of which were co-authored by Lapierre and Larry Collins, and decided to go along to the talk. At the presentation, which was in the foyer of one of the Geneva-based NGOs not far from the Red Cross building, Monsieur Lapierre told the audience about a project he was sponsoring in Calcutta that focused on helping destitute kids from leper families. He explained that he was currently working on a book about titled *The City of Joy*. As an anecdote, he mentioned that he was looking for volunteers to help manage the project, and if anyone in the audience knew of someone who might be interested, they were to contact him.

Monsieur Lapierre had spoken the magic words. While some people ponder over decisions for days, weeks, months, years, decades or even a lifetime, Randalph was the sort of person who jumped straight into things, leaving the worrying about whether it was a good or bad decision for later. Sometimes it brought him luck, but more often than not it led him into a dead end which, in theory, should by then have taught him a lesson. But Randalph was a slow learner when it came to putting logic and common sense before the thrill of embarking on a new adventure.

At the end of the talk, Randalph approached Monsieur Lapierre, who explained his ideas, outlining the goals and challenges of the project. After some questions and answers, although he was not yet fully convinced, especially as this was a volunteer position again and this time with no pay at all, Randalph took the plunge and decided this was for him. What the hell. He was off again, heedless of the details, oblivious to the risks, unconscious of the context, and deaf to any argument to the contrary or point of view that could make him change his mind. Randalph was back on the road. His next mission would be in Calcutta. For better or for worse, he was heading for India. Maybe he could even join forces there with Mother Teresa…

Just before buying tickets for the flight, Randalph played his joker and proposed to Annette, who accepted, became his fiancée and agreed, albeit reluctantly, to accompany him to India on his next adventure.

CHAPTER 17

Calcutta

The cheapest flights Randalph could find to Calcutta were via Moscow with Aeroflot, and the cheapest date he could find for the flight was in the first week of that New Year of 1984. Moscow would be cold then. Very cold. Moreover, at that time the Cold War was still on and East-West relations were just as icy as the outside temperature.

When they stepped off the flight from Zurich at Moscow's new Sheremetyevo-2 Airport, which had been built for the 1980 Moscow Olympics, passports were checked firstly on disembarkation, then between gates inside the terminal, and again when boarding the ongoing flight to Calcutta. In the queue in front of Randalph was a young Sri Lankan whose passport photo had become slightly unstuck. At the desk the officer scrutinizing the photo asked in poor English "This is you?" pointing to the photo. The Sri Lankan, who was probably Randalph's age, nodded. "Why not stick photo?" asked the officer in a sinister tone. "But...", the Sri Lankan guy was about to reply when the officer called over a guard, who escorted him out of the queue. Randalph had no idea what happened to him, but witnessing the encounter sent shivers down his spine.

Next was Randalph's turn. On UK passports at the time, if your face had changed significantly, for example by growing a beard, it was possible to have two photos – one before, one after, which was the case for Randalph, who had an original photo when he was around eighteen and a photo of him with a beard in his early twenties. "Who is second person?" asked the same officer. "It's me," said Randalph, who was about to explain when the officer called a guard for him too. He was promptly marched off to a room in which one wall had been covered in a floor-to-ceiling mirror with another mirror running horizontally from corner to corner at the top of the wall in the angle between the wall and the ceiling and positioned at about 45° to the vertical. Facing the mirrored wall was a long high desk with two bulky screens each manned by an officer wearing a broad-brimmed hat slanting slightly backwards with a prominent red hammer-and-cycle emblem staring at you from above the officer's brow, as if to impress on you that you were in the Soyuz Sovetskikh Sotsialisticheskikh Respublik (CCCP), far away from the safety of the Geneva conventions.

In a sergeant-major type tone, as if about to shout out 'quick march', the officer on the left of the desk facing Randalph ordered him to strip to the waist and lean his back against the mirrored wall. the same officer then barked questions at him in broken English with a thick accent about his parents and grandparents, where he lived, which school he had gone to, where he worked, where he was travelling to, why he was travelling there, what his religion was, what his political beliefs were and what he was doing in Russia.

Why the question about what he was doing in Russia, wondered Randalph, wasn't it obvious? And how to answer the question about political beliefs? Randalph didn't really have any but said he believed in socialism, hoping that would please them.

He answered the others as accurately and as level as he could, given the discomfort of his back pressed up against the cold mirror and the fear blocking his mind. The officers made neither signs of acceptance nor of rejection. All Randalph could hear was the impact of their fingers as they typed whatever it was they were typing on their keyboards.

The 'hearing' lasted only about twenty minutes, after which Randalph was released, escorted back out of the room and taken to his flight gate. He would have loved to know if he had truly been investigated or if this was just a pantomime conjured up to intimidate foreign travellers.

He was relieved when their plane landed in Calcutta, but would have wished that their luggage had arrived there too. Wearing big boots, thermal trousers, heavy woollen pullovers and thick outdoor jackets, they were perfectly well equipped for the climate in Zurich, where it had been -10°C when they took off, but not for Calcutta, which, although it was winter, reached a very pleasant 25°C in the middle of the day.

The two hung around the airport, filling in lost baggage forms and hoping their bags would turn up by magic on one of the other conveyor belts, but it was not to be. After clearing customs, where they had absolutely nothing to declare, they were met by Peter, an English clergyman who oversaw Lapierre's project and who was to introduce Randalph to it. At first sight, Peter was as English as they come in clothes that could have fallen straight off of any shelf at Marks and Spencer. While Randalph was expounding about how happy he was to be back in the smells, sounds and tastes of India, Peter was quick to point that he didn't like Indian food, nor the way the Indians drink their tea, and insisted on an English menu for breakfast, lunch and dinner.

Randalph was instantly resentful and critical of how someone who had lived for so long in India had remained so distant from the local culture. It reminded him of the posh dignitaries who filled the room in Kathmandu, where he removed the chair from under the pompous old windbag sitting next to him when the guests stood up for the toast to the Queen. What was it with the English, he puzzled, that they were so reserved about opening up to other cultures?

Randalph and Annette were temporarily accommodated in a noisy high-rise apartment block surrounded by other equally noisy high-rise blocks somewhere in one of the central districts of Calcutta, near Bara Bazar. In the evening, it seemed that each apartment was competing with its neighbour to see who had the loudest radio or television. The cacophony was unbearable, and even with the windows closed the noise got inside and went on until late into the night. It was impossible to sleep, especially the first night when all they had were the clothes they were standing up in. To add to the discomfort, Peter had bought the couple two single steel-framed military-barracks styled beds with a steel spring base on which, no matter how still you lay, every movement was amplified in a creaking sound that would wake the dead, and certainly Randalph, who was a light sleeper. When he raised the issue with the beds, Peter said he had bought the two single beds as he didn't know if the couple slept together. Ask and ye shall be told, thought Randalph cynically.

Before they could go to the village where Lapierre's children's project was, they would need to find clothes. On hindsight, Randalph was secretly happy that their bags hadn't arrived, as this meant they would have to buy local clothes. He remembered how comfortable he had felt some years previously when he had worked in Nepal, wearing the loosely hanging traditional tunics he had had made for him in Pokhara, and how much the locals enjoyed seeing him wear them.

Over the next two days, which started with Randalph and Annette heading out to explore the local shops, Randalph bought some Indian-style loosely-fitted cotton slacks, shirts and another tunic, while Annette kitted herself out with Punjabi-style trousers and the tunic dresses that ladies traditionally wore over them, as an alternative to saris. Looking back, Randalph thought the two must have looked grand as they stepped out onto the busy crowded streets of Calcutta. To add to their flair, the local look acted like a protective shield that kept the beggars away. They were in and loving it. All they needed now to complete the disguise was some saffron-tainted stains on their cuffs from eating delicious, spicy local street food with their fingers.

Clad in their new outfits and at last ready to travel to the village, Peter had set up a convoy with him and his Indian wife, Aaradhya, in the lead in a taxi and Randalph and his fiancée to follow on a motorbike he had purchased for the two to make the daily trip from their apartment in Calcutta to the village. The bike was an ageing second-hand Royal Enfield Bullet 350, a model which on its first appearance in India in 1955 instantly became a legend, enjoying cult status as a recognizable symbol on Indian roads. Much as he was seduced later by the many bystanders at the side of the road who cheered them on as they rode past on their mythical two-wheels, Randalph, who would have been satisfied with a second-hand scooter, nevertheless wondered why Peter had gone to such an unnecessary expense.

Apparently, it hadn't occurred to Peter, who wasn't a very practical man, that riding an unfamiliar bike for the first time with a passenger on the back on unfamiliar roads behind a taxi, with no helmets, through the chaotic traffic of India's second-biggest city might be a little dangerous, and they would have to take it slowly. To his credit, however, Peter's less practical bent was largely compensated for by his big heart. Years previously he had come to Calcutta as a volunteer to work on a school feeding program, which fed up to ten thousand children six times a week. In 1970, during his time there as a volunteer, he was asked by a child protection organization to open a home in Calcutta for its most neglected children. He met Mother Teresa to seek her advice, and together they identified children of leprosy sufferers as being the most neglected and in need of support, due to the stigma around their incurable disease.

That same year he took a first bunch of children from leper families to a building he had rented near Calcutta, which became the home for the rehabilitation of leprosy sufferers' children where Randalph and Annette later volunteered to help.

Back on the road, it turned out to Randalph's relief that slowly was the only way forward for their taxi as it squeezed through the traffic, inching its way north along the Hooghly River on the old highway, through Barangar, Kamarhati, then Titagarh, before turning right to cross the railway line and heading east to Barrackpore. Eventually, four hours later they arrived at the village totally exhausted by the sunshine, the traffic and the concentration needed to negotiate it.

The village where the children rescued from their leper parents lived was set at the end of a forest path in a patch of cleared grassy ground surrounded by banana and mango trees, close by the sprawling suburban town of Barrackpore. The village consisted of four recently constructed, two level brick houses with vertical metal bars in all the windows. The houses were laid out in a straight line with dormitory accommodation on both floors for half a dozen kids aged three to twelve. Each house had two outside squat toilet cubicles and a shower on the ground floor, next to the entrance.

The fifty or so kids ate two meals a day sitting on the concrete floor or on the outside steps of a communal kitchen, close to the path, constructed at a right angle to the row of houses. Opposite the houses stood a one-level utility building full of rudimentary tools and the remains of construction materials. Between the row and the utility building, in the middle of the square, if you could call it that, stood a brick-built hut with one window, a red-painted wooden door and a corrugated tin roof.

In theory, Randalph and Annette's mission was to support Peter in running the place. In practice, they ran it themselves. Except for occasional visits, Peter remained in Calcutta with his wife, where he looked after the administrative and financial aspects of the village and his little congregation of the faithful. To look after the kids and give them some basic education, Peter had hired Gopal, a local teacher, Prasad, his assistant, and two caretakers to maintain the surroundings and the buildings. The village was wholly financed by donations from private individuals in France.

After that first trip riding slowly behind Peter's taxi, Randalph would have to find the road by himself. Once out of Calcutta centre, the road to the village was relatively simple to find, as long as you remembered the turnoff for Barrackpore. Coming back to the city at the end of the day was more challenging, as they had to find their way to their building through the densely packed city centre with its many look-alike streets lined with high-rise buildings and roads choc-a-bloc with traffic.

The first few trips took around three hours in each direction, which Randalph was later able to reduce to two, once he had become familiar with the route and had found his bearings, and as long as he was not stuck behind the barriers of the railway crossing at the turn for Barrackpore.

At least twice a week, the barriers were down and could stay down for an hour or more while waiting for a train to pass. While this stole from the precious little daytime available for them to spend in the village, Randalph didn't mind because nearby the barriers in the shade of a massive peepul tree was a stall selling West Bengal's delicious *mishti doi*, a sweet yogurt made with milk, curd culture and sugar set in small earthenware cups, giving the yoghurt an earthy and unique flavour. Randalph could easily eat five or more at a time. Some days, the stall also sold *shrikhand*, a thick creamy, and delicious Indian dessert made with strained yogurt, powdered sugar, cardamoms and sometimes saffron and nuts. When it was available, Randalph used to buy a small box full that the vendor wrapped up for them to take home for the evening. He blamed the lack of coordination between the train timetables and the barriers for the weight he visibly gained every time he stopped at the stall to fill up with the mouth-watering sweets.

Almost every trip on the motorbike was an adventure and frequently more dangerous than avoiding bullets in Beirut. Trucks would pass the bike – which Randalph never dared to ride at more than 40 mph (64 km/h) on the chaotic Indian roads – and suddenly swerve to the right or to the left to avoid an obstacle on the road in front of them, which could be a cow, a dog, a vendor selling betel nut, fallen hay bales, an accident, or any combination of improbable movements of the rest of the traffic.

The biggest vehicles had right of way and drove where they wanted – on their side of the road, in the middle or on the side of the oncoming traffic. Motor bikes, bicycles and pedestrians were at the bottom of the list of precedence. Cows were at the top. During the five months that Randalph spent there he witnessed more than a dozen accidents, which ranged from bicycles carrying crates of chickens stacked six high toppling over to the wooden superstructures of dangerously-fast-moving, grossly-overloaded trucks disintegrating under their load and smashing into anything and everything in their way.

Travelling to the village early one morning while the day was still fresh, the sun not yet high in the sky, and for once the traffic moving smoothly, Randalph was enjoying the sultry air, the aromatic smells and the omnipresent sounds of India when a richly-decorated, hugely-overloaded bog-standard Tata truck overtook him, horn blaring, black smoke pouring out of the exhaust pipe, its cabin crammed full of at least a dozen people all of whom were trying to get a look out of the passenger window at the two foreigners on a motorbike. Suddenly the truck began wobbling like a top-heavy table jelly quivering on a plate.

Kolkata street scene, with heavily overloaded truck. Photo downloaded from Reddit.com, as Randalph's camera and spools were stolen in the armed robbery recounted later in the chapter.

Randalph could hear the driver shouting and saw him lunging at the steering wheel to stop the swaying, visibly oversteering from left to right and right to left, making the load on the truck sway even more, and pushing it out towards the side of the road – Randalph's side – where the camber got steeper towards the edge. On its last outward swing, as if at the end of its improvised dance routine, the truck struck the high embankment with its front left wheel and toppled over on itself to the sound of screaming, cracking wood and a roaring engine as it perfectly executed one and a half somersaults, landing on its roof.

As the truck was going down, Randalph had braked hard, swerved to the right to avoid it, realigned the bike with the side of the road and stopped a few metres further on to witness the scene of carnage. He felt totally helpless, being unable to do anything about it. This was India. In only a few minutes a crowd of hundreds had descended from the multitude of other vehicles by now also stopped on the road and were carting off the driver. If any of the passengers had died, they might kill him.

On another occasion, on a similar section of road with a steep camber on either side, constructed at the top of a high embankment leading down to wide ditches, Randalph found himself facing a truck hurtling towards him in the middle of the road. With its triple horn blaring and a hundred different decoration lights flashing, Randalph spotted it a mile off. Aware of what could happen if the truck lost control, Randalph slowed down and stopped at the top of the embankment. If he needed to get out of the truck's way, there was no way he could ride the heavy bike down the slippery slope. In the worst-case scenario, he could jump off and run out of the way of the truck.

His intuition paid off. At the moment he stopped, another truck going just as fast in the direction Randalph was travelling in passed him, heading towards the truck coming towards him. One would have to give way. It was the name of the game. At the last moment, both did, but only the truck coming towards him kept control, proudly taking its place again as king of the road. As the other truck tried to swerve back into the middle of the road after its sharp-left, sharp-right avoidance manoeuvre, the front left wheel spun off, the rear of the truck skidded round to the left and the truck fell over, blocking most of the road.

By the time Randalph had started up again and reached the scene, the usual crowd had gathered and a hundred distraught individuals in their multi-coloured glory were pointing, shouting, arguing, pushing forwards to get a better view, and thus obstructing anyone from the outside, like a doctor, who might be able to lend real assistance to any injured. Again, there was nothing Randalph could do to help except get out of the way and let the crowd sort it out.

At the village, as Randalph's tasks were only vaguely defined, he could more or less do anything he wanted within his shoestring budget to maintain or improve the conditions for the kids. As Annette was a laboratory technician trained in tropical medicine, and as many of the kids suffered from all sorts of stomach disorders ranging from worms to dysentery, they decided to set up a basic laboratory to analyse the kids' stools and check for water-borne diseases. Based on the findings of the lab, they decided to try to improve the health of the kids through hygiene education and medicine, if necessary, and if they could afford it. The challenge was how to set up a laboratory with next to no cash.

They shared the idea with Peter, who supported it and would get in touch, via Monsieur Lapierre, with a wealthy Indian pharmacist he had contact with who owned a medical laboratory in Calcutta city centre. A week or so later, Peter dropped by with the good news that they were invited the following week to lunch with the pharmacist, who had some equipment and materials she would be happy to donate to the village.

In the meantime, using pieces of scrap wood found in the utility building, Randalph had already got to work to make a workbench for the laboratory. With an all-purpose pocketknife that included a fold-out saw blade and a rusty hammer with a fractured shaft as his only tools, he shaped the best pieces of wood into short planks using the saw blade of the knife and laid them on trestles made of other scraps of wood. The end result was a 60 inch (150 cm) long table, about 30 inches (75 cm) wide, standing by the wall below one of the windows looking into the open space between the buildings.

On the day scheduled the next week for lunch with the pharmacist, Randalph and Annette rode to the address given to them and were surprised to find themselves parked in front of a tree-lined driveway leading to an old and fabulously elegant, colonial-styled building set in pristine gardens. They were expected, and ushered in by an impeccably dressed gatekeeper wearing a bright red turban, a white double-breasted tunic with shiny brass buttons, white gloves and parallel trousers with a red-and-black line on the outside. The gatekeeper showed them to a stylish round table set under the lush branches of a tree with big red flowers surrounded with six ample wickerwork armchairs where sat Peter and his wife, an elderly lady with gold-rimmed spectacles wearing a luxurious turquoise sari – Randalph presumed she was the pharmacist – and another lady, equally well dressed.

It turned out that the other lady was a press agent who was going to take some photographs of the meeting and write a few words about it in the local newspaper. In such a luxurious and visibly expensive setting, Randalph's expectations of the donation they were about to receive had gone far beyond the microscope they had talked about. As they sipped their tea and enjoyed strawberry tarts served by waiters with elbow-length white gloves and bright turbans, all the while smiling and joining in the small talk to please the dear old lady, Randalph had imagined they were going to receive a cartload of expensive laboratory equipment and instruments, donated in a ceremony attended by the Prime Minister.

Once the tea, tarts and chit chat had come to an end and everyone had said 'cheese' to the camera, Randalph was to drop by the laboratory on his way back to the village and sort out the transport of the laboratory equipment. Navigating using a paper map of the city centre read by Annette on the back of their bike, he eventually found the laboratory, whose staff had been notified about their visit and were waiting with the booty which, to Randalph's utter surprise and total disappointment, amounted to a rusty old microscope with no electrical cable and a battered wooden table with three legs.

Randalph and Annette were horrified. What sort of a donation was this? Whether they liked it or not, this was it, the be all and the end all of it. To crown their disappointment, it was up to Randalph to organise the donation's transport to the village. They would have to pay for a taxi to follow them to the village with their own money. Desperately trying to let some gratitude shine through his anger, Randalph asked the laboratory staff if this was all. Yes, they replied visibly embarrassed, this was all.

That night, back at their apartment in Calcutta, exhausted after riding around the city centre with a map then back and forth to the village, Randalph reminisced about a very wealthy-looking and arrogantly behaved Indian 'gentleman' he had witnessed four years previously stepping out of a first-class carriage in Delhi central station and spitting on beggars. He remembered some lines describing similar scenes that had struck him in one of V.S. Naipaul's books on India and others he had read in Louis Fischer's biography of Gandhi regarding the gulf existing in India between rich and poor, and the immense disregard for the poor and the needy in this land where so many were so rich.

Back in the village, with the aid of some tools and de-rusting compounds he found in a car-repair garage, Randalph eventually managed to restore the microscope enough to enable the lenses to travel vertically along the central shaft and was able to fix makeshift stage clips –

which he had to buy – onto the flat platform where the specimens could be viewed.

The next job was to collect samples from the kids and analyse them. With the help of Gopal and Prasad, who explained the needs to the children, samples were collected and a profile of their health was drawn up. Out of fifty kids, only a handful did not have worms and most of them had some form of mild dysentery.

Again, with the help of the two teachers, the next step was to impart to the kids some notions about basic hygiene, like washing hands thoroughly before meals, cleaning their toilets, not playing in the nearby garbage dumps, and regularly taking anti-worm medicine. In an ideal world, it would also have been possible to construct a basic water filter to pass their drinking water through, but their little village nestling among some trees and bushes close by the neglected semi-suburbia of West Bengal was not the ideal world, and so the idea was dropped.

Although it was necessary to constantly remind the kids of their new habits and to get the teachers to help them to make drawings of these new activities, within a month the number of worm infections and dysentery cases had dropped.

After a month and a half of trundling back and forth to the village on the motorbike, Randalph asked Peter if they could move to the village and stay in the little hut in the open space. It would be so much easier for them and bring them closer to the kids. Peter agreed reluctantly, explaining that he had bought the motorbike specifically for them to commute back and forth to Calcutta. "At least," he ventured, "we can transport the beds from the apartment and won't have to buy new ones." Luckily for Randalph and Annette, the two bed frames side by side wouldn't fit into the hut, and only the mattresses could get through the door.

Living in the hut was much closer to what Randalph had imagined his stay in India would be like: Simple, basic, discreet, and not creating a visible contrast with the living conditions of the local population. During the first weeks in the hut the couple enjoyed their close-to-the-people existence, fetching water from the nearby tap stand, washing clothes on a wooden scrubbing board in the open air, eating with the kids, and enjoying tea in the early morning mist with the teachers and the caretakers. Randalph could relax there, safe from the daily ordeal of four hours on the bike.

As Randalph didn't have a lot to do during the day, he offered to help Peter with some of the administrative work. Peter was only too willing to pass the paperwork on to Randalph, who by and by got his nose into the accounts. On the surface everything looked fine, but between the lines Randalph became suspicious that a lot of money was flowing out in repairs and material investments, of which he could not find evidence in the village. He broached the subject with Peter and discovered that lump sums were being allocated on a trust basis to the caretakers, who were supposed to spend it for the benefit of the village and the kids.

To get a better grip of the finances, Randalph suggested he should take control of the spending, requiring the caretakers to make proposals to him and to give out money on the basis of proposals backed up by quotes. Randalph had expected that this would be an unpopular move and wasn't surprised when the caretakers, along with the teachers, turned up to argue the point. Their claim was that if Randalph didn't let them decide how the money was spent it meant that he didn't trust them and was basically calling them liars.

The storm blew over, but there was more bad weather to come. A few days later, the caretakers demanded another meeting at which the subject of contention would be the motorbike. They wanted to know why Randalph, a total foreigner and newcomer, had the privilege of riding around on an expensive motorbike paid for by village funds while they, dedicated long-term employees, were no longer trusted to spend petty amounts of cash. The meeting this time was louder and longer, ending with the caretakers stomping off and warning Randalph that this was not the end of the matter. Gopal and Prasad, who had stayed behind with Randalph and Annette, told them not to worry, they were only making a lot of noise to frighten them. Randalph, who had grown up in an environment where threats were not to be taken lightly, was not convinced and sensed that trouble was on its way.

The first wave of trouble came while the two were enjoying an early-morning walk in the lanes and footpaths surrounding the village. Suddenly, the caretakers and a gang of around a dozen local guys turned up and surrounded them, shouting at them and pushing them towards a derelict building. The gang packed itself densely around Randalph and Annette and hustled them into the building's damp and gloomy unlit basement, where it kept them for the rest of the day. The shouting and jostling went on without end. As far as Randalph could understand, they would let them go if Randalph gave them the motorbike. It was Gopal and Prasad, who hadn't seen the two all day, who discovered what had happened and came to their rescue. The scene resembled two defence lawyers pleading with an angry jury to repeal a unanimous verdict of guilty.

The abduction, although lasting only the better part of a day, had shaken the young idealists, who now felt less secure and safe in the village and became suspicious of anybody coming in and out that they didn't recognise. One night, their worst fears materialised. In the middle of the night, they heard a knock at the door and the voice of an old man asking for water: "Paanee sa'ab. Mujhe paanee do". Randalph and Annette woke up and looked at each other. In their guts they knew it was a trap. Randalph still in his pyjamas picked up a hammer and went to the door, asking who was there. The old man repeated his request, adding sorrow and plight to his voice.

Fear has a tendency to blot out the mind's logical thought pattern. If Randalph had been able to think instead of imagining the worst, he would have remembered that there was a tap stand in the village, and therefore no need for anyone to beg for water, and he would have raised the alarm by shouting towards the dormitories to alert the kids and the staff. As it was, fear was in command. Unsure of what to do or not to do, Randalph unlocked the door, which was instantly pushed open by a gang in dark clothes wearing handkerchiefs over their faces, red headscarves around their foreheads tied in a knot on one side of their heads and brandishing two sawn-off shotguns and many long machetes. Within seconds, there were around a dozen of them inside the hut, gesticulating to be quiet and demanding money. One put his shotgun in Randalph's mouth and pushed him against a wall. Another was holding his machete over Annette's hand, threatening to cut it off. Randalph was terrified, but nevertheless he was still in control of himself enough to plead with the machete man in hand signs not to chop Annette's hand off and point to a box on a shelf. The box contained their passports, their return air tickets, some dollars and a handful of Indian rupees, all of which the gang took, along with their cameras, then disappeared into the night.

The kids and the teachers had been wakened by the commotion and came running over to the hut, where they found Randalph and Annette in shock, but alive and unscathed. They said it would be better for them to sleep in the dormitories with the kids, where they would be safe. The feeling of safety, however, never returned. Whoever it was that had abducted them and robbed them knew they were scared and began putting on the pressure to get them out.

The next night and the night thereafter, from inside the kids' houses they could hear people shuffling around outside. The two caretakers were very obviously on the side of the aggressors and were running around outside with lit wooden torches, telling everyone there was going to be an attack. No matter how much the teachers tried to explain that this was only intimidation and that nothing more would happen, Randalph and Annette became scared.

After a week of sleepless nights and fear, Randalph fired up the motorbike and, with Annette on the back, headed to the police station in nearby Barrackpore. The scene there was horrific. The previous night there had been a riot or a gang fight and some dead bodies still lay on the street. One had been stuffed into a road drain, from which his lifeless legs were sticking out. The talk on the street was that prisoners at the local jail were being interrogated about something and some had had their eyes burnt out. The riots were in protest at the jailers' barbarity. It was impossible to know if this was true, but the thought of it haunted Randalph for years to come.

At the police station they were told that as they were foreigners they should go to the Commissioner's office in Calcutta – in Barrackpore they dealt only with local matters, like the mess in the streets. Naively believing that the Commissioner could help them, the couple drove to the impressive colonial-style redbrick police headquarters in the city centre, parked their motorbike outside, and asked at the reception desk if they could see the Commissioner.

Who did Randalph think he was? Did he have an appointment, the officer at the desk asked? Randalph tried to explain briefly what had happened but was cut off by the officer, who told Randalph the Commissioner was busy. Pointing to a row of chairs by the entrance, he told him to take a seat and wait. It was around midday.

In the early evening, an officer stepped out of one of the many doors leading onto the spacious entrance hall and beckoned to Randalph to approach him. He led him down a corridor into a busy room, where it was just about impossible to have a conversation above the ambient noise and chatter of the many police and civilians all talking at the same time. Having sat Randalph down at an empty desk he started to take note of his plight.

When Randalph had finished his recital of the two events, the officer explained that according to the Indian Penal Code the first gang's acts were tantamount to criminal intimidation and the second to armed robbery. While the first was punishable with up to two years imprisonment, the second was sanctioned by the death penalty. He asked if Randalph wanted to press charges.

Randalph just wanted to feel safe in the village and get their passports and money back. He didn't want to get involved in criminal proceedings that could end up with people being hanged, so he declined to press charges. Without charges pressed, the officer explained, the police could do nothing. Randalph had guessed right; this was precisely the outcome the officer had wanted to lead him to. He settled for a paper signed by the police saying their passports had been stolen, which the officer explained they could hand over to their Embassies, who would issue them with new ones.

Armed with their chitty with the police station stamp on it, the couple set off to their individual embassies to explain their predicament and ask for new passports. They also needed money to buy new tickets home, which the Swiss Embassy was willing to lend subject to a written promise by Annette of reimbursement within ten days of their return to Switzerland. The UK Embassy, on the other hand, was not so willing to lend money, explaining that there were many has-been hippies roaming the country who sold their passports on the black market for cash or drugs, and that to provide cash for Randalph's case would set a precedent. But how would he get home, Randalph asked? "I'm sure your organisation will be able to help," came the reply, which Randalph understood to be a polite, diplomatic way of saying 'Fuck you'.

With the passport dilemma in the process of being sorted out and cash found for the road home, Randalph's thoughts turned back to the village. By now, he had developed a phobia about men dressed in dark clothes and wearing red headbands, which was most of the male population of West Bengal. Everyone he saw wearing one, whether they were taxi drivers, farmers, coolies, shop owners or waiters, reminded him of the armed robbery and the intense, dark, violent eyes of his assailants threatening him with their guns and knives.

Too afraid to spend another night in the village, Randalph and Annette decided to move back to their apartment in the city centre and begin again to commute backwards and forwards on the motorbike, spending only a few hours a day in the village. The psychological damage, however, had been done, and neither of them felt safe enough to even spend an afternoon there. Things had changed since they had pulled back to Calcutta to solve their passport and cash issues. Word had it that gangs were roaming the area and there was even talk that there was a risk that they would kidnap some kids and hold them to ransom. Randalph knew that sadly, this was common practice in some city suburbs, where kids could be lifted off the street on their way to or back from school and sold back to their parents. He had also heard that when ransoms were not paid, or to encourage parents to pay, the more desperate kidnappers would even resort to cutting off a finger or an ear and sending it to the parents.

There was no way that Randalph could live with the thought that their presence in the village, or even in the country, could lead to violence of any sort against the kids, so he decided to pack up and leave as soon as they had received their new passports. In the meanwhile, they would take a train south and lie low and relax for some days by a beach on the sandy eastern coast of the Bay of Bengal.

Randalph remembered being surprised on his travels through India during his stay in Nepal a few years previously that almost none of the locals swam in the sea. This time round he was again wondering why, on the beautiful sandy beaches of the lush coast along the Bay, instead of jumping in for a swim in the wonderfully warm waters, people stood around in their clothes, paddling only as deep as their ankles.

To Randalph, this was completely alien. His idea of what people did, or should do, included swimming where there was sea, especially if the water was warm. He recalled how capable and at home the Vietnamese were in sea water, easily diving to ten metres below the surface to pick up shells from the seabed or catch rays and even small sharks with only a knife. Why were the Indians so shy of water, he wondered?

According to government figures that he found published in a document back in Calcutta, less than 0.5% of the population, or about 3.5 million out of India's population at the time of 700 million, knew how to swim adequately.

This would mean that in a crowd of 200, maybe one person would know how to swim, but not well enough to attempt a rescue if things went wrong. With no one in a crowd knowing how to swim even a short distance, it was no surprise that there were numerous public drownings in India just a few metres from the shore. Randalph couldn't understand it. Why could people swim in Vietnam and all over Europe, but not in India? What was wrong with them?

After two not-so-pleasant weeks by the sea, Randalph and Annette headed back to Calcutta. Their new passports had been issued and they had received cash. Not wanting to go straight back to Switzerland, they decided to fly home via Nepal. This would be Randalph's third visit to the Himalayan kingdom on top of the world of which he had told Annette so much.

The two risked a last visit to the village to bid farewell to the kids, Gopal and Prasad, deposited the motorbike with Peter, said goodbye to him and his wife and headed to the airport for their flight to Kathmandu. They were going to miss the innocent faces of the kids, now already witness to the ignorance and brutality of the big, bad world.

Four decades later, Randalph was relieved to learn that after the challenging period during his time there, the organisation flourished and is now home to around a hundred girls and two hundred boys aged between four and eighteen years of age from leprosy colonies in Calcutta, whose anglicised name was changed in 2001 to Kolkata to match Bengali pronunciation. Over the years, the organization that Peter founded has provided love, care and a brighter future to more than seven thousand children who have been affected by leprosy in some way, leaving the healthy and peaceful environment of the residential school with the education and self-confidence necessary to be productive members of society.

If his path ever passes through West Bengal again, Randalph would love to drop in to pay them a visit.

CHAPTER 18

Nepal revisited

It was June and very hot when they touched down in the land of the green-eyed yellow idol to the north of Kathmandu. The monsoon was threatening but had not yet arrived. Randalph's plan was to spend a few days in the capital, then take the local bus towards Pokhara and get off at the starting point of the Thorong La Pass trek and head up into the Annapurna mountains.

Having spent a year and a half walking from village to village in the Himalayan foothills only a few years previously, where he had been exposed to moderately high altitudes on several occasions when he camped out in the Annapurna Sanctuary or attempted to climb Hiunchuli, Randalph should have known that even though it was summer and warm, protective clothing was essential to crossing the Thorong La Pass. Those who recall the earlier chapters of this memoir will not be surprised that he completely ignored the danger, convincing himself and Annette that he didn't have enough money for the gear and that he knew what he was doing. With only a few changes of clothing, and nothing to keep them warm higher on the trek, Randalph led Annette through the foothill villages and up towards the pass. As before, the scenery was breathtaking, and Randalph was totally exhilarated to be back in the land where he had felt so happy and carefree.

In the few years since his time there, however, things had changed and the Nepal of peacefulness, smiles and warm welcomes had become a land of growing insecurity and fear. Whereas before, Randalph had felt totally safe to sleep outside on someone's veranda, today the talk on the trail was of robbers out to steal from the tourists. Given that the locals living in the bottoms of the valleys where the trekking routes passed were getting rich from tourism and prices were rising, and those living high up on the slopes were losing purchasing power, the thieving was totally understandable.

The imbalance between rich and poor was what motivated the robberies. While it was easy to understand on an intellectual plane why they were occurring, the threat of being robbed reignited Randalph's recent trauma from India, leaving him suspicious and cautious about where to sleep at nights, as well as wary of people on the trail who looked as if they could be thieves.

Many of the trekkers the couple bumped into along the trail told stories of wallets being stollen, cameras disappearing, whole rucksacks being taken, and in one isolated case trekkers even being shot in their tents for their possessions. While this was not the Nepal he had promised to show Annette, it was the one they were now committed to exploring, and the path led upwards.

As on previous treks, covering the foothills was easy for Randalph. He was fit, enthusiastic, and quick on his feet. On this trek, however, the danger of exposure to the cold was very real due to the acute lack of warm clothing they had taken with them. At one point, close to the pass and already at 5,000 metres altitude, while spending a night in a grimy Tibetan guest house trying to get warm under a grubby coarse, thick grey blanket made from yak wool, he even wore underpants on his head to keep his ears from freezing.

The real difficulties set in the next morning, when he again suffered from altitude sickness. It was the same scenario as when he had attempted a high-altitude climb with Crocodile Cale three years previously. With insufficient time on his hands, Randalph had climbed too quickly and become lightheaded. When he woke up after the night in the biting cold, he was in no shape to continue the trek. At only one day's walk from the pass, he had to give up. He would never see the gigantic Damodar Himal and the legendary Manang village or Muktinath on the other side.

Randalph was pissed off with himself and had to admit he had bungled it. So as not to completely spoil the experience, and to avoid the anticlimax of walking down the same path they had come up on, he chose an alternative route, turning west as soon as they reached the first village. After a night there, they would trek cross-country from village to village, flanking the high foothills on the underside of Machapuchari – the fishtail mountain – heading towards the top end of Pokhara.

Although not as spectacular as crossing the pass would

have been, this route had the flavour of the real rural Nepal Randalph had grown to love, where the only foreigners who pass through are those working in one of the country's many development projects.

For Randalph, it was like coming home. He loved the lifestyle in these mountain villages cut off from the rest of the world by distance, timelessness and the practice of the simple life. Many times in later years he romanticised about what his life would have been like if he had settled there and said goodbye to the 'civilised' world. Next life, thought Randalph, as they set off on the last day's walk back to Pokhara, and the noise and clamour of the developing world.

CHAPTER 19

Wedding bells

To fly back to Switzerland, Randalph had again chosen Aeroflot, which was still the cheapest airline at the time, flying from Delhi via Moscow to Zurich. In their row on the window seat was a French-speaking Canadian traveller in orange-coloured hippy clothes and long mousey-brown hair who introduced himself as Olivier. Randalph was delighted to have the opportunity to show off his modest ability to converse in French. Olivier was a strict vegan, which the couple found out to their amusement when the stockily built Russian stewardess, who looked like a champion wrestler, began handing out meals. Before the meal service had begun, Randalph had politely asked her if it was possible to have meals without meat, as the three were vegetarians. Madame the Head Stewardess understood and agreed with an obedient nod of the head. When the meals came, the dishes included eggs and cheese, which vegetarians eat, and for which Randalph thanked her. Olivier, however, ate neither and handed the platter back to her saying that he didn't eat animal products and asking if he could have a vegan meal.

Madame, who possibly thought he was taking the piss, looked him in the eye, stood upright, pointed a menacing finger at him and told him in no uncertain terms that "these two," – pointing to Randalph and Annette – "are vegetarians – they eat eggs and cheese – you will also eat eggs and cheese," and handed the plate straight back to him. As every cloud has a silver lining, the couple enjoyed an extra helping of food from their neighbour, who, as a protest, had decided not to eat anything.

Some three hours into the approximately 2700-mile (4400-km) flight, Madame the Head Stewardess appeared with her flock of lesser stewardesses following her through the cabin, all instructing the passengers to close their window blinds. Why, wondered Randalph? What were they not going to be allowed to see?

The answer came as the plane began to lose height rapidly and Madame ordered everyone to fasten their seatbelts as they were about to land. Where could they be, he thought. Northern Uzbekistan? Western Kazakhstan? Somewhere near the Caspian Sea? As the plane landed and Randalph tried peeking out of the window, he was swiftly reprimanded by one of Madame's flock, who was sitting facing the passengers at the bulkhead only a few rows forward of Randalph's row and gesticulating at him to keep the window blind down.

Wherever it was, the plane only stayed on the ground for the few minutes needed to open the front door and let in three officers in decorated uniforms who sat themselves down in the front of the cabin in a row obviously kept empty for them. This was the cold war. They were flying over Soviet Union territory. You didn't ask questions.

As soon as the young couple got back to Switzerland, they set about organising their wedding. To announce the event to their family and friends, a classmate of Randalph's from university with an artistic touch had designed a card for them with bagpipes and an alpine horn. Apart from this little artistic extravaganza, the wedding was to be a simple affair with only the closest family present. The ceremony was to be held in the records office of the lovely old medieval town of Saint-Ursanne, upstream along the valley of the river Doubs from Randalph's wife-to-be's family's village.

The setting was magical, in the heart of this ancient city nestled on the banks of the river and encircled with massive outcrops of rock, where authentically preserved five-hundred-year-old facades, cobble stones, and the magnificent collegiate church and cloister – parts of which date back to the 10th century – could easily trick the visitor into believing they had landed back in the Middle Ages.

Randalph had previously travelled twice to this little-known part of Switzerland in the heart of its Canton of Jura and had been struck by the endless forests of tall beech trees, the many wildflower-rich pastures, an incredibly dense network of clearly-signposted paths criss-crossing easily-accessible tree-topped hills, picturesque 'authentic' villages with white facades and red roofs dotting the landscape, and a low-key lifestyle, decades behind the hustle and bustle of the country's busy cities. Unbeknown to him at the time, the following year this was where he would settle and later raise a family.

After signing the marriage documents, exchanging rings they had purchased in Calcutta, enjoying a family meal altogether in a local restaurant and a first night as a wedded couple, the next morning the phone rang. It was the Red Cross in London. Would Randalph be available for an urgent deployment to Angola?

Bad timing, thought Randalph, who was still feeling a little guilty about having dragged Anne into their misadventure in India. He nevertheless replied with a clear 'Yes' when he saw her nodding consent, but only under the condition that his wife could travel with him. The people at the Red Cross said they would see what they could do.

Two hours later the phone rang again. Affirmative, Randalph and his wife could fly out together – she would also have a job to do there. "When?" asked Randalph, hoping they would say in about a week or so. "Tomorrow," came the reply. "How about the day after tomorrow?" suggested Randalph, to which the organisation agreed, signalling to the young couple to pack their bags and get ready.

CHAPTER 20

Too close for comfort

Instead of beginning in London like his previous mission with the Red Cross, the pre-mission briefing for Angola was directly at the Agency's Head Office in Geneva, where Randalph had been briefed two years previously for his

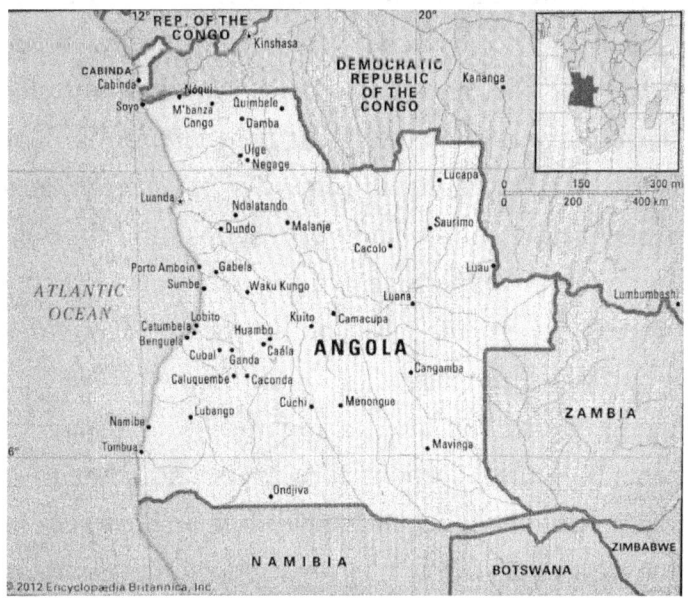

Map of Angola. Photo downloaded from Encyclopaedia Brittanica

assignment to Lebanon. The couple would be flying out with a team of half a dozen others via Paris to Luanda, and then on a domestic flight to Huambo on Angola's high plateau.

The team flying out was made up of logistics people, an accountant, two paramedics, Randalph and his newly wedded wife of three days. The hotel they all stayed at was on the Rue du Mont Blanc on Geneva's Rive Droite, less than a minute's walk from the city's railway station, and around half an hour's walk from where the UN agencies and the many other international organisations present in Geneva had their offices.

The contrast between Geneva's Rue du Mont Blanc and the lush greenery and rural charm of the Jura countryside where Randalph had been married only a few days previously startled him. Stepping out of the hotel onto the noisy street only a short walk from the lakeside, Randalph was struck by the artificiality of the urban environment, where the few trees and flower beds dotted around the city centre were dwarfed by the display of material opulence in all directions. Randalph was reminded of his bewilderment upon seeing so many jewellery shops and horlogeries offering so many expensive articles while on his first brief stop-over in the city of Calvin on his way to Malaysia, three and a half years previously.

After spending five months in rural India, where people are naturally curious about foreigners and want to know everything about them, and now after a short stay in the Canton of Jura, up in the north-west corner of Switzerland, where people greet each other upon eye contact on the street, strangers included, the cold distance of the Geneva city dwellers disturbed Randalph. He had felt it during the previous summer and autumn when he was learning French and remembered how isolated the people seemed from each other in their rat-race display of material wealth.

Randalph's rat race was only with his alarm clock and was about getting to the airport on time the next morning to catch their plane for Paris, which was scheduled to depart at 8 am. To arrive early enough to get comfortably through passports and customs, the team set off in two taxis at 5 am. Back then, in 1984, travel between Switzerland and the rest of Europe was still subject to strict immigration procedures and customs checks, and bags were often searched for exportation or importation of goods in excess of the tolerated limits, in particular for cigarettes, alcohol and meat.

An hour after taking off from Geneva, when they arrived in Paris CDG, the customs people seemed to be on red alert, and were going through almost everyone's bags. Somehow in the fluster of unpacking and repacking their baggage, checking papers, and hoping they had brought everything with them, Randalph and Annette had succeeded in leaving their passports on a chair at their gate, boarding the plane to Luanda without them.

As inspiration often comes in a flash, the realisation that they didn't have their passports with them hit the couple simultaneously like a bolt of lightning, just as their plane had joined the queue of other planes lining up for take-off. By then, the passengers and stewardesses had all fastened their seatbelts in preparation for their imminent departure.

As soon as they realised what had happened, Randalph unbuckled his seat belt, stood up, and called out to the stewardess, who came quickly down the aisle to see what was up. "We've left our passports at the gate", he said, to which Annette added "Nos passeports sont à la porte d'embarquement. On ne peut pas partir sans". She was right. While flying to another European destination without a passport could be sorted out in one way or another, landing in Angola in the midst of civil war without one might be tricky.

The pilot obviously understood the dilemma reported to him by the stewardess, who had dashed off to the cockpit as soon as she had grasped what was happening and manoeuvred the plane out of the queue and back to the gate. Randalph and Annette were then allowed to disembark, pick up their forgotten passports, which had remained on the same spot where they had left them, then climb back on board without needing to go again through formalities.

For years to come, they talked about the feeling of relief they had experienced when they found their passports. To a superstitious person, the mission had got off to a bad start. Sometimes, as Randalph and Annette were soon to learn, superstitions can predict the future with uncanny accuracy.

When they arrived in Huambo – known as Nova Lisboa under the Portuguese until Angola's independence in 1975 – it was early July, skies were blue and temperatures were pleasant up on the Angolan central highlands. Situated at an altitude of 1,721 meters (5,646 feet), Huambo, the third-most populous city in the country, after the capital

Luanda and Lubango in the south, had a population at that time of some 217,000, which has grown to an estimated 750,000 at the time of writing in 2024.

After independence from Portugal in 1975, the bloody Angolan Civil War – which was a power struggle between two former anti-colonial guerrilla movements, the communist People's Movement for the Liberation of Angola (MPLA) and the anti-communist National Union for the Total Independence of Angola (UNITA), and lasted from independence until the death of rebel UNITA leader Jonas Savimbi in 2002 – had halted the country's and Huambo's development, destroying most of its infrastructure.

Upon independence in November 1975, Savimbi declared Huambo to be the capital of the Democratic People's Republic of Angola, making it UNITA's rival to the MPLA's People's Republic of Angola. However, the MPLA took the city back on 8 February 1976 with the help of Cuban troops, though most of the surrounding areas remained under UNITA control. Much later, in 1993, at the height of the civil war, Huambo became the site of the brutal 55-Day War between the rebel forces of UNITA led by Arlindo Pena and the MPLA-led Angolan government. At the end of the war, on 6 March 1993, UNITA emerged victorious, but most of Huambo was destroyed and its civilians either massacred en-masse or fleeing.

By the time the civil war was eventually over, 800,000 people had been killed, 4 million displaced, and nearly 70,000 Angolans became amputees as a result of land mines.

By mid-1976 the Cuban expeditionary force had

established its most important structures in the Province of Huambo in the areas of São Pedro, Lufefena, and Cruzeiro, and strong garrisons in most of the other municipal capitals and main towns, but UNITA had the control of nearly all of the territory in between.

At around that time, displaced people started concentrating in towns, seeking physical protection and humanitarian assistance. In this context, one of the first humanitarian agencies to arrive in the Province of Huambo was the International Committee of the Red Cross (ICRC) in 1979.

In 1984, the conflict escalated dramatically, and so did displacement into towns. A major relief operation was launched in the capitals of the Central Plateau and in a good number of the municipalities still accessible by plane. By then most of the roads were controlled by UNITA and heavily mined. This, briefly, was the context in which Randalph and his newly wedded wife Annette would be spending their honeymoon.

Once he had returned from his mission to Angola, Randalph occasionally recalled the one and only anecdote that had made him laugh on his honeymoon there, amidst the fear, turmoil and insecurity of that country at war. It was a way of pushing aside the horrors he had witnessed.

As he was settling into life in Huambo and could walk around a little, all the while remaining close to their quarters, Randalph noticed a car with two steering wheels approaching. He couldn't believe his eyes and burst out laughing. What the hell was this, he thought, at first believing it was a car stolen from a fairground. As it passed, he saw an 'L' plate pasted to the car's boot. One steering wheel was for the learner and the other for the teacher. Not a bad idea after all, he thought, wiping away the tears.

Upon their arrival in Huambo, the couple were quartered in a delegation building shared by a few administrative and paramedical staff and half a dozen pilots of the airborne relief operation, who rotated every six weeks. Randalph's job was to ensure that supplies and tools necessary for rehabilitating wells and securing spring catchments were flown to designated sites inside municipalities where displaced people had gathered. There, he was to secure water sources and sanitation facilities. Because the roads were heavily mined, the municipalities could only be reached by plane, which meant flying every day to drop-off points across the province, much of which was controlled by UNITA.

In theory, this entailed organising the delivery of cement bags and basic tools to Huambo airport, where his aid agency shared the runway with the Cuban Air Force. The job included helping to load the cement and tools into one of the relief operation's Pilatus PC-6 Porter Short Takeoff and Landing (STOL) aircraft, then flying with the tools and supplies to the designated sites. Once on site, the job continued with unloading the cement and tools, spending the day there training volunteers from the displaced population how to carry out the rehabilitation or construction works, organising and overseeing the workforce, then returning to Huambo on the evening flight.

In reality, Randalph was often more than exasperated at the late or non-delivery of the cement bags, the difficulty of procuring even the most basic tools like shovels, the lack of coordination with the drop-off sites, and the in-house squabbling about who had priority to use which planes.

When Randalph flew out with his supplies, the six passenger seats had to be stripped out to make space for the cement bags and tools, then in the evening, once they had returned to base, the aircraft had to be cleaned. On these flights, where Randalph had the fun of sitting up front in the co-pilot's seat, the pilots were not always happy about the extra work of cleaning.

With a payload of 1200 kg (2645 lbs), the PC-6s could take off within a distance of 200 m (656 ft) and stop within 130 m (426 ft) when landing. In areas with hills and trees bordering the runways, they needed 440 m (1443 ft) to clear an obstacle of 15 m (49 ft) at take-off and 315 m (1033 ft) to clear the same obstacle on landing. Along with the weight of the pilot and co-pilot, the payload was approximately equivalent to 20 bags of cement. During periods when construction or rehabilitation of the water-points was going on, 20 bags would only last a few days and several flights would need to be made to keep up with the needs on site, inevitably resulting in disputes about aircraft allocation priorities.

Could the solution to the disputes be to overload the planes? The runway in Huambo was long enough to land a Boeing 707 and air traffic regulations were not strictly adhered to in the airspace above the plateau, where the Cuban military was in control and only few commercial planes flew in and out. If the PC-6s could be loaded beyond their payload limit, thought Randalph, and if the airstrip at destination was also long enough for landing, the number of supply flights could theoretically be reduced.

The pilots were all for the idea and carried out take-off test runs with 22, 24, 26, 28, and finally 30 bags of cement, which added another 500 kg (1102 lbs) to the aircraft's weight. While the planes could easily take off on Huambo's long runway with the extra weight, the challenges were the reduced climb rate due to the extra load, and the additional distance needed for landing on the grass or dirt strips in the outlying municipalities.

During the first three months of his assignment in Huambo, Randalph frequently flew five days a week to the municipalities with a planeload of aid workers and once a week with his bags of cement. At busy construction periods he would make two supply-flight runs per week with a planeload of cement. Since he was in the air six days a week, he became familiar with the terrain below. This gave him the privilege on many flights of sitting in the co-pilot's seat, from where he could guide new pilots visually along the flight path and take notes of any ground movements along the way. On the supply flights, where Randalph was the only passenger, depending on who the pilot was, he was sometimes allowed to take the joystick and fly the plane for part of the route himself. Randalph was in his element and took to his part-time role as navigator and apprentice pilot like a duck to water.

The flights, however, were not always smooth, and on several occasions came close to ending in disaster. The first hiccup happened on a delayed flight out, when the Huambo runway was not available for civilian movements and he took off late in the day. Instead of dropping Randalph and the cement bags off in the early morning and picking him up again in the evening, the mission was shortened to dropping off the cement bags only and then flying straight back to base.

The problem was that cloud had built up over the hills surrounding Huambo, reducing long-distance visibility and forcing the pilot to zigzag his way between the giant cumulonimbus formations. The further they flew towards their drop-off destination, the denser the cloud became.

To fly below the cloud base was dangerous, as much of the territory was controlled by UNITA, who had anti-aircraft guns, and to fly above it meant taking the risk of losing visual contact with the ground. While being able to see the ground was a necessity, as the airstrips were not equipped with navigation beacons, the risk of being fired at was very real, and so they stayed high, hoping to find holes in the clouds above or close to their drop-off point in which to descend through.

In that part of the world close to the equator, cloud can build up quickly and storms can develop within a very short period of time. As the minutes ticked by, the sky closed up and the clouds became bigger and darker. If they were to drop their load off, they would need to take the first opportunity to dive out of the clouds to see where they were. While hesitation can be dangerous up there in the sky, so can impetuosity.

The opportunity to drop down below the clouds came when the pilot spotted a narrow opening between two billowing cloud formations. Flying at a speed of around

110 knots (200 km/h), he had to react quickly so as not to miss the gap and dived steeply to the left, gaining air speed rapidly as they descended. They had begun their dive at 16,000 ft (5,000 m), which was some 10,500 ft (3,200 m) above the terrain and out of range of light gunfire from the ground, clearing the cloud base at an altitude of around 10,000 ft (3,050 m), which was only some 4,500 ft (1,370 m) above the ground and dangerously within range of anti-aircraft artillery.

At exactly the same instant, they both locked their eyesight onto anti-aircraft fire coming from the ground directly towards them. They froze. Could it be that they had chosen a UNITA fortification for their dive? How could they get the message to them that they were friendlies, thought Randalph in a flash of terror?

There was no time to even think about it. The pilot pulled back hard on the stick, at the same time swerving to the right and pushing the throttle hard forward. Although the aircraft handled sluggishly due to the extra weight of the cement, it was nevertheless flying fast enough to climb quickly into the clouds and disappear from ground sightings in a matter of seconds. It had been a close call, but they were not yet out of danger.

Having regained their cruising altitude high in the clouds, which by then had more or less completely closed the sky, the pilot signalled to Randalph that they would have to abandon the trip and return to base. As he was speaking, he turned the plane around 180° towards Huambo. The cloud which had built up on the hills had by then spread all over the high plateau, covering the airspace all the way towards Huambo. All around, the sky was black and eerily foreboding, like a deep pond in a dense jungle where crocodiles might lurk.

The pilot contacted Huambo to tell them of their dilemma. The tower reported bad weather conditions and approaching storm, warning them to land as soon as possible. In those early days of GPS, with only limited coverage in that region, the Porter's electronic navigation was limited to radio contact with Huambo tower and the plane's altimeter, compass and weather radar, none of which would allow them to spiral safely down above Huambo. They needed help. Seeing no way out of their predicament, the pilot again contacted Huambo tower, informing them that they were in a critical situation. The tower's response informed them that the only way down would be with the assistance of the Cuban Air Force.

A few minutes later, the tower called back to say that the Cubans had launched a MIG 23, which would guide them down. They were saved. Before escorting them to safety, however, the Cuban pilot, whoever he was, was going to have some fun and games with the two stranded Westerners.

When he made his appearance, out of the blue, it was in an almost vertical climb no more than 20 m (65 ft) in front of the Porter with the jet's afterburners on. The deafening din sounded like a bomb going off and the turbulence that followed tossed the little plane around like a feather in the wind. Holy shit, thought Randalph, what the fuck is he playing at? But the game wasn't over yet. All the way back to Huambo, the MIG would appear out of nowhere and either fly close past them at high speed waving at them with its wings or slow down in front of them to give another blast with its afterburners. Randalph's pilot swore loudly in Swiss German. Turning to Randalph he said: "Means fuck him in English".

Eventually, the MIG guided them down through the clouds above Huambo and disappeared for good with a final wave. Thinking the party was over, Randalph and the pilot sighed with relief, nervously joking about the day's adventure. From the Cuban side, however, there was still more to come. Once on the ground, they were ordered to taxi over to the military side of the airport, where they were confronted by a Cuban officer who ordered them out of the plane, demanding them to hand over any cameras or other photographic equipment. The Cubans had warned Randalph's agency that any photography of their installations and infrastructure in Huambo or from the air in the surrounding hills and countryside would result in severe consequences. Randalph had been briefed that photography was strictly prohibited on missions, under penalty of arrest and imprisonment, and could jeopardise the agency's relief operation.

The officer was accompanied by half a dozen military personnel who began their inspection by instructing Randalph and the pilot to unload the cement bags, then continued to check every nook and cranny of the aircraft. They found nothing. There was nothing to find. Two hours later, Randalph and the pilot were invited to load the cement bags back on to the plane, start up, and taxi over to their side of the airport. For once, Randalph had obeyed the rules of the day and as in his missions to Malaysia,

Lebanon and Sudan had not brought a camera with him to Angola.

The second incident happened just after take-off as Randalph's plane, this time flown by another pilot, was spiralling upwards over Huambo with a full load of cement. Without warning, from behind the propellor where a cloud of black smoke was suddenly billowing, blinding their forward vision, flames leapt out on either side of the fuselage and a red buzzer on the instrument panel burst into life. The engine had caught fire.

Luckily, the aircraft had already gained enough height above the ground for the pilot to turn, tilt the nose downwards, and dive to make an emergency landing on the runway. The tower, who had seen the fire as the plane came down, had already alerted a fire engine, which came hurtling along the runway towards them as they pulled to a halt and was able to douse the flames and put out the fire before it spread to the rest of the aircraft.

Before the fire engine had arrived, the two had jumped from the plane and run as fast as they could out of reach of a possible explosion. What had happened, only an autopsy of the engine would reveal, but some already hinted that it was because Randalph was on board. This was his second incident.

The third incident happened on an early-morning flight with a full planeload of passengers as they were approaching an airstrip to deposit a team of aid workers, along with Randalph who would be staying the day to oversee work going on there. As there was a permanent risk of mines being placed on the airstrips during the night, the first flight in the morning overflew the landing strip to alert the people on the ground of their arrival. The ground crew on site then drove the length of the strip and back twice in a truck full of sand to make sure there were no mines. In full view of the plane's passengers and pilot, who were circling some 3,000 ft above the strip, the truck hit a mine and exploded, scattering its burning carcass over the full width of the strip. Everyone on the plane was numbed, some screamed, others held their breath. If they had landed without the truck checking for mines, they would all be dead. The truck driver had given his life to protect them.

As well as these incidents, every day the weather was becoming warmer and increasingly stormy as the season rolled into the southern hemisphere's summer. To avoid cloud build-up and the ever more uncomfortable bumpy rides back, flights out to the municipalities to drop off the workers left Huambo at the crack of dawn, returning to pick them up no later than 3 pm.

One ill-fated day, the plane had dropped most of the team off at one spot and flown Randalph to another. The meteorological conditions were so bad that day that by the time the plane had picked up the other members in the afternoon it was too risky to fly to Randalph's location and the pilot returned to base, leaving him in the village alone. At Randalph's briefing, he had been told that in the event of not being picked up to fly back, anyone left behind should look for a protected spot inside an empty building, lie low, make no sound, avoid contact with anybody, and cover him or herself with as much camouflage as they could find without drawing attention to themselves.

In the dead of night, Randalph discovered why. Having barricaded himself under an upturned bed beneath a windowsill in an abandoned house, too nervous to attempt to sleep, he heard the distant sound of gunfire. As the shooting drew nearer, he could hear people shouting and running around. It sounded like anything between half a dozen and a dozen automatic rifles were approaching. Whoever was attacking the village was also armed with grenade launchers, firing rocket-propelled grenades at buildings not far from where he was crouched.

Randalph clung to his breath as if it were a wild animal struggling to escape his grip. The shouting turned to screaming, as the population ran for their lives. From where he was lying, he could hear the assailants but didn't understand what they were saying. It sounded like they were searching the buildings around. Remembering his briefing, Randalph had chosen a semi-destroyed building to hide in, reducing the chances of it being searched by the invaders.

By Randalph's watch, the attack lasted about an hour, then died down to gunfire fading into the distance. Randalph was petrified and still didn't dare to move an inch. It was only when dawn finally came that he ventured a glance outside above the windowsill. The township was empty, desolate and deadly silent. Some rafters were smouldering on the roof of a nearby burned-down house. A few bodies lay on the ground, motionless, surrounded by traces of the blood that had drained from them. Only the presence of some stray dogs reassured him that there was still some life left.

As the sun climbed higher in the sky, he reckoned his only chance of getting out alive was to get to the airstrip and wait for a plane. He would hide there behind some bushes and run out onto the strip if he heard the sound of one approaching. Towards the end of the morning a plane finally did appear in the sky. It had dropped off the passengers as on the day before and had come looking to see if there was any sign of Randalph.

When Randalph heard the plane, he ran out on to the runway waving his arms in the air, all the while terrified to look over his shoulder or behind him. The pilot spotted him and flew low over the ground, pointing to a spot at the far end of the strip where he would pick him up. He then made another flypast and landed with his brakes full on, reducing the landing distance to a bare minimum. Once on the ground, he turned the plane on its axis to taxi back along the tracks its wheels had made on landing, opened the door to let Randalph jump in, again turned on its axis and took off into the morning breeze in less than a third of the length of the strip.

To get Randalph out, thereby saving his life, the pilot had run the very real risk of detonating mines on the strip. It was like being in a movie, but without the music, props and special effects. This was for real. From then on, every time Randalph watched an aviation movie where some heroic pilot saves the day he remembered this moment, forever reliving the feeling of relief and gratitude.

The fifth incident was the scariest. That day, with Randalph up front navigating, the plane was flying him and six other aid workers out to the field. It was early in the day, the sky was crystal clear, and the passengers were still drowsy and not sufficiently awake yet for lively conversation.

The flight would be a short one, flying on a WNW heading to drop everyone off for the day at Kuito.

Suddenly, Randalph yelled out, clutched his knee, looking down at his hand, which was covered in blood. The radios had gone dead. For a split second he thought there had been a short circuit, which had somehow spiked his knee. But the sudden right-to-left movement of the plane along its axis and the pilot wrestling with the rudder and trim forebode a more serious problem.

Randalph looked over his shoulders and caught the eyes of the passengers, who were in shock and pointing at a dozen or so holes in the fuselage. Their plane had been shot at and hit. Over his right shoulder he could just see the edge of the starboard horizontal stabilizer which had been partially damaged. Hanz, the pilot, looked at him and shouted above the noise of the engine that the rudder and tail had been hit. "We have to land," he said, pointing to the ground ahead.

With the rudder, elevators and trim tabs not responding, the Porter's manoeuvrability was limited to banking to the left or right using its flaps. Randalph and the pilot scanned the horizon nervously and settled for a flat-looking piece of grazing land on the rim of a village. With no obstacles and only the weight of the passengers on board, they would need less than 200 m (656 ft) to stop once they touched down. The danger was that they couldn't fly over the ground first to check it out and would need to land on one approach. Looking anxiously at Randalph, Hanz, pointing downwards, said he hoped the wheels hadn't been hit. He then shouted at everyone to strap in tight, put their heads down and cover their faces with their forearms.

The touchdown was bumpy but controlled. Once out of the plane, feet on the ground, and nervously inspecting the ditched aircraft, the shaking passengers reported over thirty bullet holes. The shots had missed the propellor, the engine and the fuel tanks, landing mostly in the tail, with a dozen in the fuselage and some in the wings. Miraculously, except for Randalph's knee, which had been grazed by a bullet, no one else had been hit.

Hanz had found where the bullet that took out the radio had hit and within a couple of hours was able to bypass the damaged part and send a mayday call to Huambo tower. Meanwhile, it looked like the entire village had gathered round them to see what had happened. Kids were running around shouting "bang bang" and pointing their arms in the form of guns to the sky. The adults were silent, looking on grimly.

Within an hour of Hanz's mayday call, another Porter had landed in the same field to evacuate everyone from the scene. What happened to the damaged plane after the incident nobody knew. All the team heard was that two inspectors from the aircraft hire company had arrived in Huambo and flown out directly to the plane in a helicopter.

After this latest disaster, anyone who previously was wary of flying with Randalph now categorically refused to. One pilot even denied him a seat on his plane. This time word was out that poor Randalph was seriously jinxed. As destiny would have it, however, it looked like young Randalph had a guardian angel who was doing overtime to look after him and had arranged for him to change jobs. Two weeks previously, the crew of a Lockheed C-130 Hercules that had arrived in Huambo to execute a parachute-drop operation to get supplies to the outlying municipalities and transport aircraft fuel to the larger rural airstrips was looking for an extra hand on board to help with the drops.

Randalph had already met the crew of the Hercules at the airport bar a few times. They were a rowdy bunch of Vietnam War veteran pilots who had bought the C-130 to continue their flying careers as humanitarian mercenaries. Nick, the captain, was an outspoken, short-tempered, rough, sturdy Irishman that nobody messed with. The co-pilot was an elegant Englishman who boasted of living in a villa on the Italian Riviera, and the engineer was another Englishman called Jack with a cor blimey London accent that none of the non-Brits could understand. All three drank themselves into oblivion every evening at the bar, cracking jokes and telling stories. Remarkably, at 5 am each morning, no matter how much they had drunk the night before, the three were stone-cold sober for the pre-flight check for their mission that day. They were a tough team with resilience and stamina that none of Randalph's agency colleagues or the Porter pilots could match.

Most of the delegates and humanitarian workers didn't like them. They were loud, boisterous, and didn't give a shit about any of the agency's internal rules and culture. Their job was flying. Even the civilian guy at the tower flown in specially from Switzerland to oversee operations stayed out of their way and let them do things their way. In addition to their bold attitude, they had an aggressive sense of humour and enjoyed having a laugh at the expense of the passengers.

On one particular flight, Randalph also fell prey to their

wicked wit. Once they had reached their cruising altitude at 20,000 ft (6,096 m), Captain Irish called to engineer Cor Blimey to ask what the problem was with the engines. While he was talking to him the two outside turbo props began running down and quickly stopped altogether. "No idea", replied Cor Blimey, adding "Did you fill us up with fuel this morning?" Irish looked over to the copilot, who shrugged his shoulders with a "Not me". Both looked round to Cor Blimey, who piped up with "I thought one of you two had filled it". By then the other two engines had also wound down, their deep-throated mechanical purring replaced by the whistling sound of the wind. "Pair of useless bastards, cried out Irish. "This time we're really fucked. Get out the parachutes".

Randalph had never jumped out of a plane and had never wanted to. In fact, along with swimming with sharks or crocodiles it was the last thing he would dream of doing. When Cor Blimey appeared from the hold in the back with an armful of parachutes, the blood drained out of him. "You put it on like this. Strap tight around the waist. Shoulder straps to the toggles on the waist band. When you jump, count to five and pull this," pointing to the release handle. "You three [Randalph and the two other passengers] go first and we'll follow".

Was he kidding? The only way to get Randalph to jump would have been to sedate him and throw him out. The plane was gliding like a giant bird in the sky scanning for prey from on high. Cor Blimey motioned to Randalph and the other two to step onto the stairs leading down to the door below the cockpit, telling them that when it opened, they should jump at three-second intervals. Was this really happening? Randalph was petrified.

Just when Cor Blimey turned to go back to the cockpit and activate the door lock the first-jump paratroopers could hear the sound of the engines starting up again. "It's all right boys", he called out, "We've connected the reserve tanks". He roared with laughter. The other two in the cockpit followed suit as the lovely old Hercules climbed gently upwards again to take its place as king of the sky.

On another trip, the Hercules was transporting a 15,000-litre (3,300 gallon) tank full of aircraft fuel. Randalph had watched as it was pushed up the loading ramp on the runway by a powerful digger. Expecting that there would be some fun and games en route, he prepared himself psychologically for the worst, but not for what was about to unfold.

While cruising along peacefully high in the sky and listening to music over the radio, Irish suddenly started sniffing and looking around him. "Do you smell anything?" he asked Italian Riviera. "Could that be fuel I'm smelling?" "You're right Nick", Riviera replied, "there is a smell of fuel." Randalph could smell nothing, and neither apparently could the two other passengers, who were looking at each other questioningly. "Jack," he motioned to Cor Blimey, "Could you have a look?"

Jack, the engineer, then approached the two passengers and Randalph, who were sitting on the passenger bench at the rear of the cockpit, and asked if anyone had a lighter. He explained that he was going out back into the hold to check if the fuel tank was leaking. "With a lighter?" asked the passenger next to Randalph, a delegate with a strong French accent. "D'you know a better way to find petrol leaks?" asked Cor Blimey. Nick Irish then turned round saying "Take mine, but don't empty it. I'll need it tonight for me smokes". As he handed it to Jack, the French-speaking delegate sprang out of his seat and grabbed Jack by the arm, telling him to give him the lighter. They argued back and forth until the crew couldn't hold straight faces any longer and burst out laughing, joking about how scared the passengers looked.

When they weren't joking or getting drunk at the bar at night, the C-130 crew were deadly serious. They did their job meticulously and bravely, never flinching in the face of menacing storms or the threat of anti-aircraft fire from the ground. Once Randalph had been accepted as part of their little team for the air-drop operation, they taught him how to secure the hold for take-off, how to attach and prime the parachutes, and how to release the cargo to be air-dropped. Randalph was more than happy to feel their friendship and felt safe under their wings.

Once they got to know each other well, the three also shared with Randalph what they thought about the rest of the delegation, especially about those who didn't like them, like the air traffic controller, who they told what to do, when to do it, and who was boss there. If you didn't like them, tough luck, they didn't give a damn and wouldn't give an inch. They did things their way. They were the cowboys of the big blue sky.

To add to their unpopularity among the delegates, the three veterans had become good friends with the Cubans and could pass through the dividing fence in the evening and have drinks with the Cuban air crews in their mess, in blatant defiance of the very strict rules not to mix with the Cuban military. On a few occasions they took young Randalph with them to the Cuban side, and he watched with bewilderment as the Cubans took group photos of the three posing beside their MIGs. What would the agency say if they knew about this, he wondered?

One evening when everyone had got plastered on shots of Cuban rum, the Cubans persuaded Randalph to put on a flying suit, then propped him up in Cuban flying colours for a group photo with a bunch of MIG pilots and ground crew. Oh my God, he thought, if anybody sees this he'd be hung, drawn and quartered.

Twenty years later, on Randalph's one and only visit to Cuba at a coincidental meeting that only fate could have orchestrated, he was shown that same photo. He had embarked at La Havana on Christmas Eve in 2012 to celebrate ten years of self-employment and rented a mountain bike with the intention of riding solo around the west of the island. After two nights in the capital, he had reached the town of Vinales, where he decided to spend a few days in the lush-green surroundings of the tobacco-plant landscape. To blend in with the locals and not to be labelled as just another gringo, he was wearing khaki-coloured shorts and T-shirt and a Cuban military cap he had bought at a stall in La Havana.

At Vinales town square, Randalph was approached by a guy with a drooping moustache with almost the same curved line as the droop in his cap who introduced himself as Juan. Juan was curious to know where he came from and what he was doing in Cuba. Randalph was sure he was a government tail sent to check on him, as he had the physical appearance of the archetypal South American revolutionary. Even if he was it didn't matter, as for the time being they were chatting in a friendly way about their lives, the countries they had been in, and the deplorable American embargo. Both were surprised to learn that they had been in Angola at the same time, especially Juan, who was so happy to be able to talk with someone who could relate to his experience there which, Juan explained, was rare among Cubans.

That night, back at the house he was staying at, Randalph told the owner of the house about the meeting with a local guy who had served in Angola at the same time that Randalph had been there. The owner, Alejandro, looked questioningly at Randalph and asked if the guy's name was Juan, which Randalph confirmed. Alejandro then beamed with delight, telling Randalph proudly that he had been Juan's commanding officer at the Huambo base. Another of those coincidences that only fate knows how to organise, thought Randalph.

Alejandro then looked at Randalph enquiringly, hesitated, then opened the bottom drawer of a heavy mahogany sideboard next to the door in the living room. He took out a folder and rummaged through it for some minutes, then produced a photo as a magician would produce a rabbit from a hat, scrutinizing it closely. Pointing at a tall young guy in the photo with a beard, asked "eres tu?" (Is that you?) Randalph couldn't believe it. It was indeed him. "Madre mía!" (Oh my god) exclaimed Alejandro. "Es posible?" (Is this possible?) he continued with disbelief in his eyes.

News travels fast, even in a country where most people don't possess a phone, and when Randalph later stepped out onto the street in front of the house for a walk around in the evening air, instead of avoiding him as they had been instructed to avoid gringos, local people and neighbours were approaching him and calling him 'compañero', many with an added salute and a smile. "Hola compañero!", called out just about everyone he crossed on his walk, with some adding "Viva Cuba, viva la revolución!" Angola had left its mark on many more people than just Randalph.

Much as Randalph was enjoying the C-130 trips, he was still part of the delegation and had to abide by its prerogatives. One of these was the lengthy debriefing meetings that the head of delegation insisted on having every evening once everyone was back from the field. The entire team was required to sit in a big circle and report individually on their progress or observations during the day. By then most people were exhausted and thinking only of the evening meal. What a waste of time, thought Randalph.

Twenty years later, when Randalph had become a consultant, experienced internationally in training the executives, managers and employees of some of Europe's biggest multinational organisations in the arts of efficient time management, effective communication and how to conduct results-focused operational meetings, he looked back at how pathetically inadequate the humanitarian world had been in management skills. It was as if they shunned anything coming from what they considered to be the big bad corporate world.

Another pain in the ass for Randalph was a certain retired Sergeant Major U.F., who Randalph referred to as Private Smuf, a jumped-up, self-important, good-at-nothing administrator hired by his agency to look after logistics. Randalph reflected in hindsight that in the commercial world Private Smuf, whose only practised skill was his exceptional ability to create organisational chaos, would long since have been fired, sent home and possibly even investigated.

Smuf, who strutted around in a pair of shorts and the red mountaineering socks and climbing boots the Swiss wear on their weekends in the hills – not exactly appropriate for Angola, only a few hundred miles from the equator – had taken it upon himself to stick his nose into everything operational, including the pre-flight visual checking of the aircraft fleet in the early morning.

The problem was not only that he had no idea what he was doing but that he more often than not got in the way of the pilots, who were solely responsible for carrying out the checks. In spite of the pilots repeatedly telling him to step down, Smuf insisted on pulling out cables, removing chocks and even trying to get involved in refuelling.

Smuf got up Randalph's nose to such an extent that at one of the evening debriefing jamborees when it came to his turn to speak out Randalph stood up, pointed his finger at him, and accused him of endangering the lives of the teams by tampering with the aircraft. He then asked for a show of hands for him to be removed. Of the thirty or so exhausted aid workers in the circle, only one refused to put up his hand, arguing that since Smuf had been a sergeant major in the military, we civilians did not have the power to remove him. The 'neinsager' had also been an officer in the same army. Randalph blew his top, accused him of cowardice, total social irresponsibility, criminal negligence and complicity to manslaughter, then told them both to go and fuck themselves, saying to everyone present in the room that they should look for another 'water guy' because he had had enough and was leaving.

In any case, Randalph was coming close to the end of his contract and a week less would make no difference. As if the gods had concurred to confirm Randalph's departure, two days later, when he was supposed to join the C-130 crew for what would be his last air-drop flight, he turned up late at the runway, missing the flight by a few minutes. As he stood there and watched the majestic old Hercules climb into the glimmering red morning sky, getting smaller and smaller as it headed towards the horizon, Randalph felt sad and alone. The crew had become his family, and he wasn't sure if he would see them again.

Randalph was shaken abruptly out of his melancholy by the streak of a missile fired out of the bush only a few miles from the airport and headed straight for the plane. Fully awake by now, he looked on with bated breath, praying for the missile to miss, hoping the crew had seen it and would bale out. They hadn't, and the missile didn't miss. The intense white flash and the delayed sound of an explosion told Randalph in the language of certain death that his little flying family was no more.

Randolph stood there shattered, devastated, in total desperation. His protectors and friends were dead. Was there something he could have done to save them? What if he had caught the plane, would that have changed anything? Would he also have been killed, had they waited for him? Was it his fault? Had anyone else witnessed the strike? Would people suspect him of something?

Randalph was in shock. He felt numb all over, as if he had been injected with a general anaesthetic. Was this a divine beacon lit to signal to him that the time had come to leave and go home? He had no answers. It certainly felt like the end of the road and looked like the game was definitely over.

Two days later, Randalph caught a flight in Luanda, heading via Paris to Geneva and the end of his five-year career in humanitarian aid.

Randolph's debriefing in Geneva left him with a sour taste in his gut. He had voiced his disappointment regarding the management and his anger regarding Smuf. To make his point, he had penned a scathing report that he asked his debriefers to pass on to higher authorities, which of course they never did. Anticipating this, he had made a copy which he sent to a UN commission, requesting an inquiry into the Huambo operation, with a particular spotlight on management and logistics. There was no reply.

Some weeks later, to his immense surprise, another UN organisation contacted him to ask if he was interested in a job in war-torn Somalia, offering Randalph a management position in charge of infrastructure rehabilitation and new construction for displaced people. He was flattered, but refused. Deep down, he knew it was time for him to step down from the humanitarian bandwagon. Angola had been one narrow escape too many.

With that, consoling himself that he had at least achieved his student-days goal of moving south and leaving his homeland far behind and forever, in the early months of 1985 he and Annette settled in Switzerland's Canton of Jura, where cows roam freely in the fields, forests are cared for and thrive, rivers sparkle with unpolluted water, trains and buses run on time, honey is made locally, people smile and say hello to strangers, citizens have democratic rights, thugs don't pick fights with you, streets are safe, roads are not mined, and friends are not blown into a thousand pieces by missiles.

Young Randalph, who by then was 27, had a lot to digest, but a whole life ahead to digest it in. And in any case, thought he as he looked over his shoulder at the bumpy years gone by: Que sera sera…

Le Clos du Doubs, Canton of Jura, Switzerland, where young Randalph settled in early 1985, remaining in the country until called again for humanitarian emergencies in 2015 to Greece, Jordan, Syria, Iraq, Lebanon and finally Bangladesh, before retiring in 2022 to plant an orchard and look after a flock of sheep on a Greek island in the middle of the big blue Mediterranean Sea, far from the wars and turmoil of the world. Stay tuned for Nine Lives II…

www.ingramcontent.com/pod-product-compliance
Lightning Source LLC
Chambersburg PA
CBHW070456120526
44590CB00013B/658